ROUTLEDGE LIBRARY EDITIONS:
HISTORY OF EDUCATION

THE CONCEPT OF POPULAR EDUCATION

THE CONCEPT OF POPULAR EDUCATION

A study of ideas and social movements in the early nineteenth century

By

HAROLD SILVER

Volume 35

Routledge
Taylor & Francis Group

LONDON AND NEW YORK

First published in 1965
Second edition published 1977

This edition first published in 2007 by
Routledge
2 Park Square, Milton Park, Abingdon, Oxon, OX14 4RN

Simultaneously published in the USA and Canada
by Routledge
711 Third Avenue, New York, NY 10017

Routledge is an imprint of the Taylor & Francis Group, an informa business

Transferred to Digital Printing 2007

First issued in paperback 2013

© 1965, 1977 Harold Silver

British Library Cataloguing in Publication Data
A catalogue record for this book is available from the British
Library

Library of Congress Cataloging in Publication Data
A catalog record for this book has been requested

ISBN13: 978-0-415-41978-9 (Set)
ISBN13: 978-0-415-43285-6 (Volume 35 hbk)
ISBN13: 978-0-415-86068-0 (Volume 35 pbk)

Publisher's Note
The publisher has gone to great lengths to ensure the quality
of this reprint but points out that some imperfections in the
original copies may be apparent.

The Concept of Popular Education

*a study of ideas and social movements
in the early nineteenth century*

———

HAROLD SILVER

LONDON

METHUEN & CO LTD

ROWMAN AND LITTLEFIELD

TOTOWA, NEW JERSEY

First published in 1965
This edition published 1977 by
Methuen & Co Ltd
11 New Fetter Lane
London EC4P 4EE
ISBN 0 416 70740 8
and
Rowman and Littlefield
81 Adams Drive
Totowa New Jersey 07511
ISBN 0 8476 6016 8

Printed in Great Britain by Whitstable Litho

CONTENTS

ACKNOWLEDGMENTS

I owe a major debt in the compilation of this material to the staff of the Goldsmiths' Library, University of London. I should also like to express particular thanks to the Librarian of the Co-operative Union, Manchester, for permission to use the MSS collection of Owen correspondence and for help with copying material. I am indebted to the Newcastle City Reference Library for help with the collection of Newcastle Literary and Philosophical Society records, the Manchester Literary and Philosophical Society for help with transcribing material, the Portico Library, Manchester, for permission to use their facilities, and the Meltham and Meltham Mills Co-operative Society for permission to consult their trading ledgers and other material. I have had invaluable and consistent help from the libraries of Hull University and of its Institute of Education. I am grateful to Verlag Herbert Lang & Cie, Bern, Switzerland, for permission to print the translation from Kurt Guggisberg's *Philipp Emanuel von Fellenberg* (in Appendix C). Responsibility for this translation and from Russian texts quoted is my own.

I am deeply indebted to Mr J. Lawson for his help and encouragement over a long period of time.

I owe a debt to Mr W. E. Lawn, Education Secretary of the Huddersfield Branch of the Co-operative Retail Services Ltd., for help in locating material, and to the late Academician V. P. Volgin and the Soviet Academy of Sciences for bibliographical and other material in Russian. Professor F. J. C. Harrison read an early draft of this manuscript and pointed out a number of errors. I would also like to thank Professor W. H. G. Armytage for his encouragement and Professor D. V. Glass who, as editor of this series, made some extremely helpful suggestions at various stages on the way to the finished product.

John Saville's enthusiastic advocacy of the cause of social history helped me to define terms of reference within which to work, and to keep going through a vast and (to me) unfamiliar territory. To one book which appeared while I was engaged on this task, Brian Simon's *Studies in the History of Education*, I owe a more general debt than is apparent from the scant acknowledgment I make to it in the text.

ACKNOWLEDGMENTS

Edward Thompson's *The Making of the English Working Class* appeared after this was written; had it appeared earlier my own would have been a better book.

Finally, to Pam, Claire and Vicki, for their understanding and endurance, I owe the biggest debt of all.

Chelsea College of Science and Technology, 1965   HS

ABBREVIATIONS

Bibliography	*A Bibliography of Robert Owen, the Socialist 1771–1858*, The National Library of Wales, Second Edition, Revised and Enlarged, 1925.
Co-operative Congresses	*Co-operative Congresses, Reports and Papers, 1831–2*, Proceedings of the first three Congresses and other papers, bound in one volume, Goldsmiths' Library, University of London.
CUL	A collection of MSS letters in the Co-operative Union Library, Manchester.
GL	Goldsmiths' Library, University of London.
Life	*The Life of Robert Owen by Himself*, London, 1857, edition of 1920, with an Introduction by M. Beer.
Life, Vol. IA	*A Supplementary Appendix to the first Volume of the Life of Robert Owen. Containing a Series of Reports, Addresses, Memorials, and other Documents, referred to in that Volume. 1803–1820. Volume I.A.*, London, 1858.
Newspaper Cuttings	*A collection of newspaper cuttings relating to Owenite Co-operation*, from the library of William Pare, in the Goldsmith's Library, University of London.
A New View	Robert Owen, *A New View of Society and other Writings*. Introduction by G. D. H. Cole. Everyman's Library, edition of 1949.
N.M.W.	*The New Moral World.*
An Outline	Robert Dale Owen, *An Outline of the System of Education at New Lanark*, Glasgow, 1824.
Pare MS 578	A collection of MSS, newspaper cuttings, etc., in the library of the Family Welfare Association, Goldsmiths' Library, University of London.
Podmore, *Robert Owen*	Frank Podmore, *Robert Owen. A Biography*, London, 1906, one-volume edition of 1923.

PREFACE

Since the late 1950s the history of education in Britain has been more widely interpreted in relation to other areas of historical change. Some of the most important published and thesis literature has been concerned with the interrelationships of political, social and educational ideas, movements and institutions. The history of education in medieval, Tudor, Stuart or industrial Britain has been thrust firmly towards a concern with its interdependence with state and church, scientific inquiry and political protest and reform, the changing profiles of social class and population, urban and regional development, the altered statuses and composition of social groups and professions, changing forms of communication, work and leisure, ideas and ideologies. Important historical discussions have taken place around the relationships between education and social class in pre-industrial England, education and industrialisation, education and the balance of church and state. New or more prominent areas of interest have developed, such as those of the historical connections between education and literacy, the concept of childhood, and the labour movement. Some aspects of the 'formal' institutions of education have at the same time received increased attention—including the history of the curriculum, technical education, adult education, the universities, teacher unionism, educational administration, the inspectorate, and many more. The main change in the shape of the history of education, however, has been its increasing breadth of interests.

When the work for *The Concept of Popular Education* was being done, at the end of the 1950s and in the early 1960s, not only were many of these avenues still relatively unexplored, but also much work of critical importance in adjacent fields, and relevant to the period with which the book is concerned, had still to appear. Thompson's *The Making of the English Working Class*[1] and Foster's *Class Struggle and the Industrial Revolution*,[2] had not been published, and none of the related discussion about the growth of a labour or working-class consciousness and identity

---

[1] E. P. Thompson, *The Making of the English Working Class*, London, 1963. Although published in 1963, this appeared after the work on *The Concept of Popular Education* had been completed.
[2] John Foster, *Class Struggle and the Industrial Revolution*, London 1974.

had yet taken place. The intellectual and social history of nineteenth-century Britain had not yet had its approaches and instruments refined by works as outstanding in their fields as Kitson Clark's *Churchmen and the Condition of England 1832–1885*,[1] Musson and Robinson's *Science and Technology in the Industrial Revolution*,[2] and the many important contributions arising from the research on family reconstruction. The quantitative approaches which were to have a particularly important effect on American social history were barely discussed in Britain until the 1970s. The field of labour history did not have its own academic association until 1960, the History of Education Society was not created until 1967, and the journal *Social History* was not launched until 1976. On the particular areas covered by this book there was little in existence that was helpful—Simon's *Studies in the History of Education 1780–1870*[3] being an important exception. Such relevant published work as Laqueur's *Religion and Responsibility*[4] was not to appear until the second half of the 1970s, and such theses as that of Turner[5] with somewhat different analyses than my own of Robert Owen and the infant school were still several years ahead. The work that perhaps helped more than anything to establish the guidelines for my own research had been published nearly half a century before—Dobbs's *Education and Social Movements 1700–1850*.[6]

It is clear from the title of my own book that I was interested in the conjoint fields of the history of ideas and the history of social movements and I could not begin to treat of the one without a major concern with the other. As Owen Chadwick has underlined: 'without the intellectual enquiry the social enquiry is fated to crash; as fated as was the intellectual enquiry when historians asked no questions about the nature of the society in which ideas were propagated or repudiated'.[7] While Thompson was exploring the growth of forms of popular and working-class consciousness, action and organisation, my own narrower theme

[1] G. Kitson Clark, *Churchmen and the Condition of England 1832–1885*, London, 1973.
[2] A. E. Musson and Eric Robinson, *Science and Technology in the Industrial Revolution*, Manchester, 1969.
[3] Brian Simon, *Studies in the History of Education 1780–1870*, London, 1960.
[4] Thomas Walter Laqueur, *Religion and Respectability: Sunday Schools and Working Class Culture 1780–1850*, New Haven, 1976.
[5] D. A. Turner, 'The Educational Influence of Robert Owen with particular Reference to the Development of Infant Schools in England 1819–1839', London, M.Phil. thesis, 1969.
[6] A. E. Dobbs, *Education and Social Movements 1700–1850*, London, 1919.
[7] Owen Chadwick, *The Secularization of the European Mind in the Nineteenth Century*, Cambridge, 1975, p. 14.

was the process by which popular movements helped to establish education as part of the available range of social objectives and activities between the 1790s and the 1830s. *The Concept of Popular Education* looked at people and movements as agencies in the translation—through education—of Enlightenment ideals into practical action. It saw education as a point of tension between conflicting groups and classes, and 'it' was as complex as the social movements and realities in which it was fought over and acted upon.

It seemed to me then, as now, that the inescapable figure in understanding that complex transformation is Robert Owen. Whatever reservations may be expressed as a result of later research on Owen and Owenism, and whatever other participants claim attention, it still has to be emphasised that the Owenites in general and Owen in particular did most in the period up to the late 1830s to see social ideals and educational ideas through to action. In one sense Owen was the last eighteenth-century Enlightenment figure (whether, as I still believe, the ancestry lay through French rationalism and its English radical interpretation in the 1790s, or whether—as J. F. C. Harrison has suggested[1]—it lay through the Scottish Enlightenment). In another sense, with regard to understanding the need for and possibilities of social action, Owen was the first nineteenth-century hero. Both seem to me correct. My research had begun with Owen. I am sure that if it had begun with social movements and education in general it would still have ended by focusing on Owen. However wide their implications, the title and the sub-title of this book still remain mainly a tribute to Robert Owen.[2]

The twin aims of *The Concept of Popular Education* were to explore the role of education in establishing a popular or working-class consciousness, and to confront some questions of educational historiography. The first of these aims has been pursued and enhanced with various emphases and conclusions by other historians—for example, by Thompson and Foster in relation to social class, by Hollis in the field

[1] J. F. C. Harrison, *Robert Owen and the Owenites in Britain and America: The Quest for the New Moral World*, London, 1969, pp. 83–6; *Utopianism and Education: Robert Owen and the Owenites*, New York, 1968, pp. 12–13.

[2] For elaborations of the views on Owen and education expressed in this book see also Harold Silver, introduction to *Robert Owen on Education*, Cambridge, 1969; 'Robert Owen as Educationalist', in *Robert Owen and his Relevance to our Times*, Co-operative College Papers, No. 14, 1971; 'Owen's Reputation as an Educationalist', in Sidney Pollard and John Salt (eds.), *Robert Owen: Prophet of the Poor*, London, 1971; *English Education and the Radicals 1780–1850*, London, 1975, Ch. 4.

of radical publications and politics,[1] by Yeo in that of Owenite culture[2] and by Laqueur in relation to working-class community and the Sunday school. The second aim, which was more complex and more important than I understood at the time, has not been a popular theme in the writing and discussion of educational history in Britain. Disputes have tended to be about the interpretation of data, of events, of motives, with little or no interest in related questions of historical methodology.[3] This has not been true in the past two decades in the United States, nor of some other historical fields in Britain—for example labour history and the history of population and the family. Historians of education have not generally been moved in the 1960s and 1970s to define their interests, worry about their philosophies, expose their methods and objectives, consider their relationships with other branches of history and the social sciences, or see their exercise as problematical. There are exceptions, but it is broadly true that neither their 'field' nor their 'approach' has occasioned much sustained discussion. Developments in related fields of inquiry therefore assume all the more importance.

This is particularly true of the 'popular' or working-class experience discussed in this book. What was the 'working class'? How common was 'its' experience? At what pace and in what conditions did its 'consciousness', its sense of 'identity', grow? The literature of this debate is now considerable, and most of it was provoked by the publication of Thompson's *Making of the English Working Class*.[4] John Foster has more recently attempted to sharpen Thompson's definitions by analysing the transition from 'labour' to 'working-class' consciousness in the period of early industrial capitalism in three towns, with the main emphasis on Oldham.[5] Thompson's work has stimulated criticism and counter-

[1] Patricia Hollis, *The Pauper Press: A Study in Working Class Radicalism of the 1830s*, London, 1970, especially Ch. 1.

[2] Eileen Yeo, 'Robert Owen and Radical Culture', in Pollard and Salt, *Robert Owen: Prophet of the poor*.

[3] For a more extended discussion of this theme see Harold Silver, 'Aspects of Neglect: The Strange Case of Victorian Popular Education', *Oxford Review of Education*, Vol. 3, No. 1, 1977; *Nothing but the Present, or Nothing but the Past?*, London, 1977.

[4] For an introduction to this discussion and some reprinted material see Open University, *Popular Politics 1750–1870* (Arts: A Fourth Level Course, Great Britain 1750–1950, Sources and Historiography, Block II), 1974. For a defence of Thompson see F. K. Donnelly, 'Ideology and early English Working-Class History: Edward Thompson and his Critics', *Social History*, No. 2, 1976.

[5] Foster, *Class Struggle and the Industrial Revolution*, especially Chs. 3 and 4. For a discussion of this book see A. E. Musson, 'Class Struggle and the Labour Aristocracy, 1830–60', *Social History*, No. 3, 1976, and Foster's reply in the same issue.

criticism, outstandingly over the concept of 'class' itself, and the notion of unifying experience that it implies. In the field of class relationships, and the role of institutions in establishing or perpetuating them, Laqueur has offered a view of the Sunday school as an integral part of the working-class community. He suggests in doing so that Thompson's 'social control' model is defective because it oversimplifies the role of such institutions as instruments of bourgeois hegemony. It seems to me possible to accept a substantial part of Laqueur's view of the Sunday school as a corrective to Thompson's (and my own) analysis of it, without damaging Thompson's overall analysis. Laqueur's discussion of the cultural meanings of the Sunday school does not bear the weight of the wider discussion of class relationships that he attempts to place upon it.

My view is still that in the period 1780 to 1840 the effect of early industrialisation in Britain was increasingly the perception of common, shared experience, and the formulation of common ideals, on the part of the labouring population. The point at which it is most appropriate to talk about a 'working class' is not for discussion here. The working class was, in Thompson's terminology, 'made' in this period, including by its own responses and initiatives. Foster's view is that a class consciousness did not effectively exist until the 1830s and 1840s, but what is important here is that throughout the period from the 1780s, to use one of Foster's descriptions, the radicals 'guided mass understanding from one level to another'.[1] The analysis has to be conducted in terms of understanding and opinion and consciousness at many levels, including, as others have approached it, in terms of culture, institutions, and political experience and dynamic. Within the complexities of these formulations it still seems to me true that education was integral to the 'making' process, so long as education is interpreted in the broad framework I tried to construct in *The Concept of Popular Education*—education not only by institutions, not as a receiving process, but by the making of ideals, by conflict, by impact.

The early history of the working class in the wake of Thompson is crucial to the historiography of education in this period, and the challenge to relate education and working-class experience has been taken up most directly by Laqueur in his *Religion and Respectibility*, a book which more than any other modifies the argument of my own. Laqueur's theme is that the Sunday schools were not solely or not even

[1] *Ibid.*, p. 109.

discussions of the nature (or utility) of the concept of social control, as developed by Johnson and Marcham,[1] as well as by Thompson and Laqueur. What all of this work represents is an attempt not just to identify and juxtapose the elements in the history of popular education, but to interpret them in their relationships with one another and within the dynamics of social conflict, social adaptation, social change. They point towards a more sensitive understanding of social relationships, of the interconnection between ideas and experience, of the interweaving of what have too often in the past been seen as separate phenomena or traditions.

The essential argument of *The Concept of Popular Education* nevertheless seems to me to remain intact—the place of education in the centre of ideological and political debate, its growing importance to popular movements as a lever of social change and as an ideal—'Knowledge was dignity. Knowledge was power'.[2] We need to know a great deal more about the changing interpretations and use of that ideal, about popular experience of schools and educational activities of all kinds in the late eighteenth and early nineteenth centuries, and about the range of educational and cultural impacts of popular movements themselves. More research is needed at local level of the kind that Salt conducted for Sheffield,[3] and more systematic use needs to be made of press, autobiographical and manuscript sources for the early decades of the kind that Burnett drew together mainly for a later period in *Useful Toil*.[4] Perhaps the outstanding contribution of Laqueur's work is its indication that in the history of education, and for the early period of industrialisation in Britain, it is possible to exploit a considerable range of sources hitherto used unsystematically or not at all. He has shown that in the social history of education an effort of imagination can be sustained by usable source materials.

The research of the past two decades, and our awareness of the inadequacies of our knowledge, do not seem to me to move education from its central position in the social and political consciousness of the

---

[1] Richard Johnson, 'Educational Policy and Social Control in early Victorian England', *Past and Present*, No. 49, 1970; A. J. Marcham, 'The Revised Code of Education 1862', London, Ph.D. thesis, 1976, particularly Ch. 3, 'Educational policy as social control'.

[2] Hollis, *The Pauper Press*, p. 23.

[3] John Salt, 'Isaac Ironside 1808–1870: The Motivation of a Radical Educationist', *British Journal of Educational Studies*, Vol. XIX, 1971.

[4] John Burnett (ed.), *Useful Toil: Autobiographies of Working People from the 1820s to the 1920s*, London, 1974.

predominantly a product of middle-class ideology and philanthropy, but were widely rooted in working-class experience and initiative. From their early foundation and increasingly in the first half of the nineteenth century the Sunday schools were, in his view, a 'working-class institution', the focus of an independent working-class culture, enmeshed at many levels in the life of the communities that produced them, and not an instrument of middle-class control. Laqueur's extremely valuable analysis disturbs the too easy pattern of class relationships and experience assumed in earlier descriptions of education in the first half of the nineteenth century. It does not, however, seriously undermine the previous picture of middle-class educational ideologies in the last decades of the eighteenth century—and one of the weaknesses of Laqueur's analysis is that it does not take sufficient account of the rapidly shifting shapes and emphases from decade to decade in the late eighteenth and early nineteenth centuries. Nor does it help directly towards an understanding of other educational institutions in the first half of the nineteenth century—monitorial schools, pauper schools, dame schools or factory education. Since research in these areas is still at a minimal level, however, Laquer's discussion of the Sunday school —more than anything else in recent years—has alerted us to the need for careful scrutiny of our assumptions in these other fields.

The educational debates and activities of the period between 1780 and 1840 therefore need to be approached with caution. There are some aspects of working-class and community experience about which we now know more but from which it is difficult to generalise. About the realities of all working-class educational experience we still know far too little, although the nature of ideological debates and impacts in this period has been more seriously explored.

At other points also more recent interpretations impinge on some of the assumptions and arguments of this book. This is true, for example, of Harrison's work on Owen and Owenism, Turner's on the infant school, and the re-examination of the mechanics' institutes by Royle and Inkster.[1] Attempts to approach educational developments with some of the instruments of social theory have also raised questions which extend the argument of this book. This applies primarily to

[1] Edward Royle, 'Mechanics' Institutes and the Working Classes, 1840–1860', *Historical Journal*, Vol. XIV, 1971; Ian Inkster, 'The Social Context of an Educational Movement: A Revisionist Approach to the English Mechanics' Institutes, 1820–1850', *Oxford Review of Education*, Vol. 2, No. 3, 1976.

period discussed in this book. Popular education, as a changing concept, a changing ideal, a changing range of experiences, remains crucially important to an understanding of English society in this period.

Chelsea College, June 1977   *HS*

INTRODUCTION

THE HISTORY of ideas has meaning only when it is concerned with the processes by which ideas come to be held, oust other ideas, become a force in the social world. The history of an idea begins with the search for the kind of people who held it, an assessment of the point at which it became socially significant, and of the nature of its social significance. The story of the fate of an idea is the story of the social machinery and movements that promote, develop and implement it, or distort trim, contain and destroy it.

The concept of popular education, in its British environment, appears as a range of attitudes, of sub-concepts, at one historical moment, and is demonstrably something else at another. Changes become visible in what is being asked for and what is being offered, in the evaluation of what is attainable and of what cannot be avoided. The history of such a concept, therefore, is in essence a history of the social forces which made various transmutations of it common currency.

Indeed, in its historical context, it is difficult to use the expression 'popular education' at all, though it is a familiar and useful part of our vocabulary today. In the late eighteenth century and the first two or three decades of the nineteenth century—the period with which we are concerned in this study—it hardly existed. The most familiar phrase in this area of thought was, at the beginning of the period, the 'education of the poor', an eighteenth century label that continued to abound in books, pamphlets and articles[1] well into the nineteenth, reflecting accurately enough the charitable view of the commodity. Lancaster's monitorial schemes were being referred to in 1810–1 as being 'for the Education of the Children of the Labouring Classes of the People', 'for the Education of the Poor', 'for the Education of Poor Children', and 'for the Infant Poor'.[2] Only with a wider philosophy of education does 'the education of the people' establish itself, and 'popular education' is a late settler.[3] 'National education' is what a Mary Wollstonecraft

[1] E.g., Sir Thomas Barnard, *Of the Education of the Poor* (1809), and 'On the Importance of promoting the General Education of the Poor', *The Philanthropist* (1811).

[2] *The Edinburgh Review* (November 1810 and November 1811).

[3] E.g., Brougham's *Practical Observations upon the Education of the People* (1825), and Hamilton, *The Institutions of Popular Education* (1845).

or a Robert Owen would tend to use, though in this case the phrase was reserved for a grandiose ideal, a vision of mass education far broader than that of the educators of 'the poor' or 'the people'. Andrew Bell's monitorial Society, it should be remembered, included in its title the word National, but it was the Society that was 'National'; the education it offered was for 'the Poor'. None of these expressions, then, used alone, indicates both the range of intentions in the provision of limited forms of education, and the vision of those who made fuller ideals more accessible.

We are, in fact, dealing with the period in which recognisably modern connotations gathered around such expressions as 'popular' and 'the people', but only in the latter part of the period did they acquire a stable identity. In 1812, when the venerable parliamentary reform campaigner, Major John Cartwright, asserted that 'The People are not represented in Parliament,'[1] he was still using eighteenth century currency. What he, and all the middle-class reform movements of the late eighteenth and early nineteenth centuries, were urging was that 'political liberty being a common right, Representation co-extensive with direct Taxation ought, with all practicable equality, to be fairly and honestly distributed throughout the community'.[2] 'The people', 'the community', were those who, outside the ranks of the aristocracy, and therefore outside the realities of political representation and power, *owned property*. Six years later, William Hazlitt, than whom no-one in early nineteenth century England had a greater sensitivity to the significance of ideas and social developments, was asking the question 'What is the People?' The discussion here, however, is in terms of the enslaved and degraded, and with them Hazlitt's sense of identification was total:

'Shall we never serve out our apprenticeship to liberty? Must our indentures to slavery bind us for life?'

Anyone, he protests, 'above the rank of an idiot is supposed capable of exercising the highest functions of royal state. Yet these are the persons who talk of the people as a swinish multitude. . . .'[3] If governments

[1] John Cartwright, *Six Letters to the Marquis of Tavistock, on a Reform of the Commons House of Parliament*, London, 1812, p. vii.
[2] *Institution and Early Proceedings of the Union for Parliamentary Reform*, London, 1812, p. 3.
[3] William Hazlitt, 'What is the People?' (1818), *Political Essays*, London, 1819, pp. 324–7.

'are determined that the people shall have no redress . . . but violent and desperate ones, they may thank themselves for the obvious consequences'.[1] 'People' and 'liberty' have very different connotations from those in Major Cartwright's usage. The use of such terms (and there are, of course, other uses, with derogatory overtones) is clearly changing considerably across this centre-page of the period under discussion. The expression changes because the centre of gravity of men's interest and attention does. 'Popular education' is used in this study, therefore, as an after-the-event shorthand to cover a range of thinking about the education of the poor and deprived, from the most limited and condescending charitable approach to the labouring classes, to the most ambitious plans for national education.

The institutional story of popular education in the nineteenth century is a kind of military history. It consists of skirmishes and battles, orders of the day and battle-cries, campaigns and counter-campaigns, and, more often than victories or defeats—weary armistices and cease-fires. This story of attempts to provide popular education in the early nineteenth century has become an accepted component of educational and social history. It tells of monitorial schools, Bell and Lancaster; of abortive bills and parliamentary investigations, Whitbread and Brougham; of the prides and conflicts of Church and Dissent; of the beginnings of public spending and inspecting; of the long manoeuvrings up to 1870, and after. But, important though this is, it is not all, or enough. There are, as has been suggested here, other questions to be asked. What, for example, were the motives behind the diversification of charity education at the end of the eighteenth century? Why was popular education resisted? Why supported? How did attitudes die, and in what circumstances and through what media, new thinking about education make its appearance? Who wanted to be educated?

It is from the starting-point of questions such as these that this book looks at developments in attitudes to the education of the people between, essentially, the 1790's and the late 1830's. It begins with the assumptions and practice of the late eighteenth century and examines the rise to prominence of alternative views of society and human nature, and their relevance to the growth of popular movements. By the 1830's the pattern of social and political thought and alignments had been entirely recast, and the analysis of the range of opinion at this point of

[1] *Ibid.*, p. 333.

time seeks to show, in terms of attitudes to education, what had been the dynamic of ideological and social change in roughly the half-century beginning with the French Revolution.

A central figure in this study is Robert Owen. Owen's metamorphosis from cotton baron to pioneer of co-operation, trade unionism and socialism has been immensely documented and discussed. He is present here as key witness, propagandist, organiser and stimulant, and as catalyst in vast changes of attitudes. Owen and Owenism are crucial to the discussion, in that they offered a basis from which to challenge prevailing practices in such forms of 'popular' charity education as existed, and the confidence of an alternative view of society in which to believe.

Although much of the background of educational thought and practice at the end of the eighteenth century is sketched in, much is omitted. There is no discussion, for example, of dame schools, because they did not constitute a movement; they had neither uniformity nor ideology. Although the spectrum of late eighteenth and early nineteenth century educational thought is traced, the story of Bills, Acts, parliamentary debates and committees is not. The target is the diffuse and difficult story of education for, and action by, 'the people'.

CHAPTER I

Some Eighteenth Century Attitudes

(i) The almost expiring controversy

'AT THIS time of day', wrote Mrs Catharine Cappe, in the first annual report on a charity school for girls founded in York in 1785, 'it will hardly be urged as an objection, that they are taught to read.'[1] Four years later, however, Hannah More described the reaction to her attempt to found a village Sunday school. She had been to see 'the chief despot of the village', who 'begged I would not think of bringing any religion into the country; it was the worst thing in the world for the poor, for it made them lazy and useless'.[2] After the French Revolution, the Sunday schools became a special target for opposition to popular education, to such an extent that Pitt seriously considered introducing a Bill for the suppression of Sunday schools.[3]

Catharine Cappe, described as 'not only a good writer, but a woman of ingenuity and judgement',[4] in hoping that 'at this time of day, it will hardly be urged as an objection, that they are taught to read', was clearly indulging in wishful thinking, and had, of course, misjudged the 'time of day'. There had been protracted resistance to education for the poor in the eighteenth century, seen largely in the controversies that surrounded the institution of charity schools, but she and others were hoping that the battle had now been won for a form of education whose defence had always been that it formed 'a Fence against Schismaticks and Heretics, in general; against Arians, Socinians, Deists, Free-Thinkers, and Atheists',[5] and that it contributed towards 'the reformation of a class of persons, whom, taken as a body, we have long been accustomed to regard with suspicion'.[6]

---

[1] Catharine Cappe, *An Account of Two Charity Schools for the Education of Girls*, York, 1800, p. 97.
[2] *The Letters of Hannah More*, Selected with an Introduction by R. B. Johnson, London, 1925, p. 163.
[3] See Guy Kendall, *Robert Raikes, A Critical Study*, London, 1939, pp. 120–1.
[4] In *The Philanthropist*, Vol. V, No. XVII, 1815, pp. 1–2.
[5] W. Hendley, *A Defence of the Charity-Schools*, London, 1725, p. 2.
[6] Cappe, *An Account of Two Charity Schools*, p. iv.

Throughout the later eighteenth and early nineteenth centuries, the protagonists in the struggle for and against education ranged themselves on an apparently wide spectrum of positions. Some, like Hannah More's 'chief despot of the village', resisted education (and religion) for the poor in any shape whatsoever. Others, like Hannah More herself, were in favour of an extremely limited form of education, largely out of fear of the consequences of ignorance. The spectrum of attitudes then extends, as we shall see, from these positions, through attempts to promote effective, nation-wide voluntary systems of education, to demands for the widest possible education as a right.

The important preliminary point to be established is that the battle for any step, major or minor, in education, was never won once and for all. People went on, like Catharine Cappe, assuming that there would be no objection, and they went on being wrong.

In 1806, for example, Joseph Lancaster, in his account of and appeal for *Improvements in Education* through monitorial schools explained his system, but scarcely defended it. One feels, reading his account, that Lancaster considered defence unnecessary. The aim of his Borough Road school was straightforward—not to promote the religious education of any particular sect, but 'to instruct Youth in useful Learning, in the leading and uncontroverted Principles of Christianity, and to train them in the practice of moral habits, conducive to their future welfare, as virtuous men and useful members of society'.[1] This principle, he clearly assumed, was defence enough, and though he will have expected to meet religious scruples about any educational system advocated by a Quaker (and virtually apologised for being such), he obviously felt that the economic advantages of the monitorial system, and the royal and other patronage he had obtained, would preserve him from any major attack. Yet, in the controversy that began to surround him in the same year, Lancaster had to defend himself not only against the charge of deism, but against opposition to the inclusion of writing and arithmetic, in addition to Bible reading, in the education of the poor.[2]

In 1809, Sir Thomas Bernard, in a panegyric on Dr Bell's version of the monitorial system, argued that the 'most corrupt' state of christianity sought to 'keep the great mass of the people in ignorance', whereas the

[1] Joseph Lancaster, *Improvements in Education as it respects the Industrious Classes of the Community*, London, 1806, p. 25.

[2] See Joseph Lancaster, *An Appeal for Justice, in the Cause of Ten Thousand Poor Children ... being a Reply to the Visitation Charge of Charles Daubeny*, 1806, Third Edition, London, 1807.

2

'most pure' was concerned with 'freely and benevolently offering instruction to all'. 'Happily', he added, 'the dark period of slavery and superstition is now past.'[1] If slavery and superstition were of the past, however, Bernard did not argue as though they were: he proceeded, in stating his preference for the monitorial over the charity school, to counter 'objections, which have been sometimes (however unjustly) urged against any instruction of the poor, even as day scholars. It unfits them for a cottage life, and cottage fare . . . It raises their view above the condition in which they were born . . .'[2] Although, as time went by, a series of factors, social, religious, industrial and moral, combined to enable minor educational gains to proceed less challenged, usually because a fresh would-be gain of more substantial dimensions had appeared to attract the challenge, educational plans of every description continued to meet with attack from forces of 'slavery and superstition'.

In 1818, *The Edinburgh Review*, discussing a speech of Henry Brougham's in the House of Commons, commented:

'Nobody can have forgotten the murmurs and dissonant clamours with which the first proposal for communicating the blessings of Education to the great body of the people was lately received. Already, however, that disgraceful opposition is extinct . . .'[3]

Some three years later, however, we find the same journal discussing High Church opposition to the British and Foreign School Society and Brougham's education bill:

'Mr Lloyd (the author of such an attack) really is an advocate of Ignorance, by its proper name . . . we question whether, in any age, a more plain defence of ignorance was ever *openly* made.'[4]

Again, in 1825, when Brougham published his *Practical Observations*[5] in support of Mechanics' Institutes and adult education, *Blackwood's Edinburgh Magazine* commented:

'We cannot be ignorant, that if in our endeavours to educate the

[1] Sir Thomas Bernard, *Of the Education of the Poor*, London, 1809, p. 3.
[2] *Ibid.*, pp. 14–15.
[3] Vol. XXX, No. LX, September 1818, p. 486.
[4] Vol. XXXIV, No. LXX, July 1821, p. 513.
[5] Henry Brougham, *Practical Observations upon the Education of the People*, London, 1825.

3

working orders we injure their industry and morals, and give them tastes and habits discordant with their situations in life, we do both them and the empire very grievous disservice . . . however desirable the "education of the people" may be, it is a thing which, by mismanagement, might be rendered destructive to the nation . . .'[1]

The form of the attack may have altered slightly, the concessions may appear somewhat more liberal than they did a quarter of a century earlier, but the vision of popular education, without powerful safeguards, as being 'destructive to the nation' is not very different from the basis of the attacks on Sunday Schools in the 1790's or on Lancaster in 1806. It is ironical, in considering the attacks on Brougham's 1825 pamphlet, that Brougham had written in its conclusion that he thought it unnecessary to combat

'objections to the diffusion of science among the working classes, arising from considerations of a political nature. Happily the time is past and gone when bigots could persuade mankind that the lights of philosophy were to be extinguished as dangerous to religion.'[2]

At the end of 1825 *The Edinburgh Review* still had to find it 'strange, and not a little melancholy, to observe the alarm which, after all the powers of reason have been exhausted upon the subject, still arises in a very respectable portion of the community, not quite periodically, but at intervals, respecting the progress of the people in improvement',[3] and in 1826 it was still engaged in what it called 'the almost expiring controversy between the dark-loving school and the educators'.[4] Brougham in 1825 and *The Edinburgh Review* in 1826 were only relatively less wrong than Catharine Cappe had been forty years earlier. 'No victory of liberation', we have been reminded, 'is ever final.'[5]

(ii) A place in the social world

The place where medieval ideas of a rigidly-moulded social order can most clearly be seen to have persisted into the modern world is in education. Educational advances are related to, even if they do not

---

[1] Vol. XVII, No. C, May 1825, p. 535.
[2] Brougham, *Practical Observations*, p. 31.
[3] Vol. XLIII, No. LXXXV, November, 1825, p. 242.
[4] Vol. XLV, No. LXXXIX, December 1826, p. 194.
[5] David Riesman, *Constraint and Variety in American Education*, New York, 1956 (Anchor Books edition, 1958, p. 119).

necessarily cause, disturbances in traditional social patterns, and a determination to preserve the existing order involves in some shape or form, resistance to such advances. Erich Fromm has drawn a picture of the medieval individual, unfree yet secure in his possession of 'a distinct unchangeable, and unquestionable place in the social world from the moment of birth.' Being 'rooted in a structuralized whole,' his life 'had a meaning which left no place, and no need, for doubt. A person was identical with his role in society; he was a peasant, an artisan, a knight, and not *an individual* who *happened* to have this or that occupation'.[1] Increased 'individuation', with the breakdown of the medieval order, led both to disturbances of security and wider ambitions and horizons, to different extents in different social groups. New hierarchies and rulers, in and from the seventeenth century continued, however, to ensure that the ambitions and horizons of the mass of the people were held in check, and that the modified social order was not fundamentally challenged. The medieval 'natural order' had been exploded, but in the new pattern the mass of the people were to retain, whatever tensions and contradictions this might involve, the same position in the social world. Increasingly, however, the ideas of an inevitable order which had been an integral part of the medieval world, had to be defended and re-defended.

In the eighteenth century, Leslie Stephen tells us, 'there were . . . no troublesome people with philanthropic or political or religious nostrums, proposing to turn the world upside down and introduce an impromptu millennium'.[2] This is true as a broad generalisation, though there was no absence of fear that the pattern of society might yet be subjected to major upheavals. Conscience and philanthropy might stop short of nostrums, but, it was feared, even their restricted operation might, in their consequences, if not turn the world upside down, at least cause it some perturbation.

A typical mid-century restatement of the inevitability of the status quo can be found in a popular treatise called *Self-Knowledge*, published in 1745 by John Mason, a presbyterian minister.[3] What Mason meant by 'self-knowledge' is not what psychology in the twentieth or even phrenology in the nineteenth century might interpret it to mean. Mason

[1] Erich Fromm, *The Fear of Freedom*, London, 1942, edition of 1960, p. 34.
[2] Leslie Stephen, *English Literature and Society in the Eighteenth Century*, London, 1904, p. 97.
[3] John Mason, *Self-Knowledge. A Treatise, showing the Nature and Benefit of that Importance Science, and the way to attain it*, London, 1745. The book went through six editions before 1763.

5

was not advocating self-knowledge in order to discover, rectify or improve:

> 'A man that knows himself, will deliberately consider and attend to the particular Rank and Station in which Providence hath placed him; and what is the Duty and Decorum of that Station.'[1]

The 'self-knowledge' of the nineteenth century phrenologist, for example, in the pattern of post-French-rationalist nostrums, involved knowing in order to direct behaviour to a given end, a leverage of personal and social improvement. This element, significant also in the analysis of Owenite and other radical and working class movements, was not present to any degree, it is important to remember, in Mason's thesis. To 'consider and attend to' one's rank, in his view, a man had but to accept and fulfil the implications of an unalterable status, 'it is always self-ignorance that leads a Man to act out of Character'. 'Is it a mean and low Station of Life thou art in?' he asks. 'Know then, that Providence calls thee to the Exercise of Industry, Contentment, Submission, Patience, Hope, and humble Dependence on Him, and a respectful Deference to thy Superiors.'[2] The first care, on the other hand, of those called on by providence to 'act in a more publick character' and be of 'more extensive Benefit to the World' must be to set an example, to be 'an Encouragement to the Practice of Universal Virtue . . . to shine in those Virtues especially which best adorn they Station; as, Benevolence, Charity, Wisdom, Moderation, Firmness . . .'[3]

Just as self-knowledge shows us and confirms us in our station, it must necessarily also help us to avoid the pitfalls involved in trying to follow the example set by our superiors. A man's knowledge of his station in life will show him 'whom to imitate, and wherein'. The danger lies in trying to imitate the conduct of 'those who have a very different Part assigned them from ours'. As no man can excel in everything, 'we must consider what Part is allotted us to act, in the Station in which Providence hath placed us, and to keep to that be it what it will, and seek to excel in that only'.[4] People were no longer identical with their role in society, or not convincedly so; Mason was, in fact, urging that an effort to strengthen them in their identity was required. He had nothing to say about education, because his precept to attend to one's particular and unchangeable station was education enough.

[1] *Ibid.*, 10th edition, 1778, p. 55. [2] *Ibid.*, pp. 56–7.
[3] *Ibid.*, p. 57. [4] *Ibid.*, pp. 57–8.

The implications of Mason's view were pressed explicitly in the eighteenth century by, in the Chartist William Lovett's words, 'the hawks and owls of society', those who 'were seeking to perpetuate that state of mental darkness most favourable to the securing of their prey'.[1] It is not only Bernard de Mandeville attacking the Charity Schools in the 1720's[2] but Soame Jenyns in the 1750's[3] and Mr Davies Giddy in the 1800's, who fought bitterly against any educational provision as being detrimental to the interests of society. Jenyns, expressing a view resisted by Samuel Johnson, described ignorance as the 'opiate' of the poor, 'a cordial administered by the gracious hand of providence'.[4] Mr Davies Giddy's frequently-quoted speech in a Commons debate in 1807 followed similar lines:

> 'Giving education to the labouring classes of the poor ... would be prejudicial to their morals and happiness; it would teach them to despise their lot in life, instead of making them good servants in agriculture and other laborious employments. Instead of teaching them subordination, it would render them fractious and refractory.'[5]

The only difference between Giddy's thesis and those of writers like Mandeville and Jenyns before him is that Giddy felt strengthened in his view by the evidence of the French Revolution and its influence in Britain. Mandeville had maintained, in his *Essay on Charity and Charity-Schools* in 1723, after describing the passion for charity schools as a 'Distraction the Nation has labour'd under for some time',[6] that without vast numbers of people to do the drudgery 'no great Nation can be happy'. To make the poor, and society, happy, 'it is requisite that great numbers of them should be Ignorant as well as Poor'. The welfare and happiness 'of every State and Kingdom, require that the Knowledge of the Working Poor should be confin'd within the Verge of their Occupa-

---

[1] *The Life and Struggles of William Lovett*, London, 1876, p. 134.

[2] In *The Fable of the Bees: or, Private Vices, Publick Benefite*, to the second edition of which (London, 1723) Mandeville appended an *Essay on Charity and Charity-Schools*.

[3] In *Free Enquiry into the Nature and Origin of Evil*, London, 1757.

[4] Quoted in Basil Willey, *The Eighteenth Century Background*, London, 1940, p. 50. Willey also quotes Johnson's protest. See also James Boswell, *Life of Johnson*, O.U.P. edition, 1927, Vol. I, p. 465, for further evidence of Johnson's more enlightened views on education ('. . . you must not neglect doing a thing immediately good, from fear of remote evil . . .').

[5] Quoted in J. L. and Barbara Hammond, *The Town Labourer*, London, 1917 (Guild Books revised edition, 1949, Vol. I, p. 66).

[6] *The Fable of the Bees*, second edition, p. 303.

tions'.[1] Mandeville was concerned to reaffirm a principle which would perpetuate the existing situation. Giddy was already aware of vast changes subsuming his whole world.

The assumptions of writers like John Mason in the eighteenth century about pre-ordained social status were the framework within which any educational practice had to evolve. Those who provided charity schools, for example, did not at any point challenge the *assumptions* about station, they merely drew different *conclusions* as to how the continuity of a stable, hierarchical society could best be ensured. Ultimately, in the situation of the early nineteenth century, it was not the massive resistance to education as such that proved important, but the attempt to come to terms with education as a necessary form of defence.

(iii) Delaying the voyage

In the 1860's, Professor W. B. Hodgson, in a brilliantly argued paper on some fallacious views on education, explained that there were people

'who, as I once heard Archbishop Whateley say, embark in the ship of knowledge in order to delay the voyage, being quite willing to appear as promoters of education if they can but gain the power to limit it within what they consider to be safe bounds'.[2]

Hodgson described the dilemma of 'social opinion' in the nineteenth century:

'The inconveniences of total darkness were more and more recognized, and the advantage of, at least, a sort of twilight state of mind was more and more perceived; but it may well be questioned whether the noonday blaze of knowledge was not more dreaded by the educational patrons of the lower classes than even the midnight blackness of total ignorance . . .'[3]

This dilemma of the 'educational patrons of the lower classes' became, of course, most acute as the French Revolution went its way and as the working class began to emerge in Britain as an independently operating force in politics.

[1] *Ibid.*, pp. 327–8.
[2] W. B. Hodgson, *Exaggerated Estimates of Reading and Writing as Means of Education. A Paper read at the . . . Social Science Association, on 24th September,* 1867 (second edition, Reading, 1875, p. 6).
[3] *Ibid.*, p. 3.

The primary purpose of efforts to provide a carefully defined and restricted education for the poor was, in Catharine Cappe's words, to effect a 'reformation of a class of persons, whom, taken as a body, we have long been accustomed to regard with suspicion'. Those responsible for both the thinking and the practice involved in this 'rescue' work, to use a familiar phrase of the period,[1] did not differ from John Mason in his analysis of the duties involved in one's pre-ordained station. Sarah Trimmer, for example, one of the most active influences in late eighteenth century education, wrote in her *Oeconomy of Charity*, over forty years after Mason's *Self-Knowledge*:

> 'It is obvious to common sense that a want of concord among the various orders of people must be prejudicial to a nation at large; for, in appointing different ranks among mankind, our all-wise and beneficent CREATOR undoubtedly intended the good of the whole . . . he . . . has ordained to each peculiar duties . . .'[2]

The duties she outlined for those in 'superior stations' were justice, humanity, condescension and charity, and for the poor—honesty, diligence, humility and gratitude. The spirit and the letter of Sarah Trimmer's basis analysis were unrecognisable from Mason's.

We have seen that in his *Defence of the Charity-Schools* in 1725 Hendley spoke of them as a 'Fence against Schismaticks and Heretics' (and also, and principally, against Popery), and it was, naturally, in terms of religion that the major defence of education was made. A modicum of education, some felt, encouraging a modicum of religious faith, would not only provide a barrier against Jesuits, Heretics and the like, it would militate against the dangers involved in the neglect of religious and moral precepts. John Wesley, in a discussion of the purpose of both education and religion, outlined it as lying in 'humility, gentleness, patience, long-suffering, contentedness *in every condition*'.[3] However special to the Methodist position virtues such as patience and long-suffering might have been, Wesley was at this point stating a widely-held view of the education of the people in the precepts of Christianity. 'I am well aware,' wrote a pamphleteer in 1803, 'that there are many men in this country . . . who view with decided aversion, the

---

[1] For an analysis of the 'rescue motive' in education see A. E. Dobbs, *Education and Social Movements 1700–1850*, London, 1919 (Chapters I, II and IV).

[2] Sarah Trimmer, *The Oeconomy of Charity*, London, 1787, p. 3.

[3] John Wesley, *A Thought on the Manner of Educating Children*, in *Works*, Vol. XIII, 1841, p. 448 (my italics).

plan of extending the benefit of Education to the lowest orders of the community . . .' Such a liberal mode of treatment in early life, some would argue, would have a tendency 'to detach them from the discharge of the low, menial, but necessary offices of laborious life'. No one, he suggested, however, would dispute the advantage of providing 'such a portion of Education as would serve to impress upon the minds of children universally, but more particularly of those of the lower ranks, a sense of moral and religious duty'. They would then grow up to 'become more dutiful sons, more faithful servants, and more exemplary parents . . .'[1] Rescuing the poor for religion and a concomitant stable society was a, if not the, key facet of the entire educational operation.

The Rev. Andrew Bell, in a comprehensive summary of the purposes of his monitorial education, which, though a nineteenth century phenomenon, was ordered upon principles identical with the eighteenth century ones under discussion, talked of the reformation he wished to effect among the children of the lower classes, 'by a moral and religious education, and by habits of useful industry, adapted to their condition and rank in life, to the demands of the army and navy, to the exigencies of the community, and to the state of agriculture, the handicrafts and arts'.[2] A visitor to Joseph Lancaster's monitorial school in the Borough Road enthusiastically applauded the way in which a thousand children collected from the streets were reduced 'to the most perfect order, and training to habits of subordination and usefulness, and learning the great truths of the gospel from the Bible . . .'[3] The restricted training in 'subordination' to be provided by the religious education advocated throughout the eighteenth and early nineteenth centuries was intended to achieve its object by inculcating the right form of predisposition to accept authority—'it materially secures the moral conduct of the children, both in and out of school'.[4]

The problem of pauperism was, of course, closely bound up with that of maintaining social order, and 'moral conduct' became a salient social

---

[1] George Harrison, *Education respectfully proposed and recommended as the surest Means within the Power of Government to diminish the Frequency of Crimes*, London, 1803, pp. 9–10.

[2] Rev. Dr Andrew Bell, *The Madras School, or Elements of Tuition*, London, 1808, pp. 9–10.

[3] *Life of William Allen, with Selections from his Correspondence*, London, 1846, Vol. I, p. 94. Allen, like Lancaster, was a Quaker. As one of Owen's partners at New Lanark, his religious scruples were later to be disturbed by aspects of Owen's educational work.

[4] Bell, *The Madras System*, p. 36.

problem primarily as a result of pauperism. The problem of moral conduct, in its simplest terms, therefore, cannot be separated from the wider issues of social stabilisation; we find the advocates of minimal forms of education in this period arguing the 'rescue' principle with reference to specific forms of moral misconduct.

'It has always been reckoned Wisdom and Policy in a Nation to have as few Beggars, and idle Strollers about their Streets as possible. And how is this so effectually prevented as by these (Charity) Schools . . .?' asked Hendley in 1725.[1] Education, it was argued, would train the children of the poor in habits of industry and thrift, and by reducing the number of 'beggars and idle strollers' would combat the immorality associated with the idle life of the streets. Prostitution was, of course, one of the targets against which the work of the charity schools, and the exertions of Sarah Trimmer and Hannah More were directed. Joseph Lancaster summarised the philanthropic attitude to prostitution:

'. . . *forty thousand impures* drag on a miserable existence, in the metropolis of this nation; and, if there is any feeling and benevolence yet left unexhausted, let something be devised to lighten this intolerable load of human misery . . . let the national eye be directed to the education and employment of females, as a means to obviate the evil in future'.[2]

In such attempts to protect society against the dangers inherent in profligacy, in Lancaster's concern to alleviate the *consequences* of profligacy, and the crime with which it was so closely bound up, we see a motive which was urgent and central to the whole idea of philanthropy in the eighteenth century. The protection of property was, until the 1790's, largely a question of protection against the criminal, against the effects of a pauperised, increasingly urban population. Only after the French Revolution did education have to be discussed significantly in the context of the *political* protection of property. There can be little doubt that without the existence of a series of social problems caused or intensified by pauperism, the eighteenth century debate around the desirability of education would scarcely have taken place. Education as an antidote to crime was to remain, of course, a central feature of nineteenth century educational discussion.

The interwound motives behind the advocacy of a limited education

[1] *A Defence of the Charity-Schools*, p. 4.
[2] *Improvements in Education*, pp. 116–7.

in the eighteenth century can be seen extremely clearly in the servant problem. Bernard de Mandeville had in 1723 firmly argued the case for ignorance as the appropriate state for the servant:

'When Obsequiousness and Mean Services are required, we shall always observe that they are never so chearfully nor so heartily perform'd as from Inferiours to Superiours; I mean Inferiours not only in Riches and Quality, but likewise in Knowledge and Understanding. A Servant can have no unfeign'd Respect for his Master, as soon as he has Sense enough to find out that he serves a Fool.'[1]

Hendley's *Defence of the Charity-Schools* emphasised that the girls 'are taught to knit their Stockings and Gloves, and to mark, sew, mend their cloaths, spin, or any other work used in the Places where they live, to fit them for Services and Apprenticeships'.[2] Fitting poor girls for domestic service, as well as various craft employments, with a proper moral attitude to the service they undertook was a persistent theme in eighteenth century educational writing, as the obverse to the theme of anti-idleness, anti-crime and anti-prostitution. Sarah Trimmer, writing in 1787, summed up the situation with crystal clarity:

'It is a general complaint that domestic servants are not attached to their masters and mistresses, but act towards them from selfish and mercenary motives . . . This may justly be imputed to their being sent into the world without a proper sense of the duties of their station . . . Do we wish our daughters to have modest, discreet, trustly maid-servants?—let us unanimously resolve to give a helping hand towards inducing good principles into the minds of poor girls. Do we desire they should be served with affectionate esteem?—let us take them to Sunday-schools, where, by a thousand little attentions which they will be happy to shew, they may engage the gratitude of those whom they will probably hereafter have occasion to employ.'[3]

Aware of the strong resistance to making even such limited gestures, she emphasised that she had no intention of proposing anything 'that may have a tendency to destroy the subordination of ranks which is requisite in all civilized societies', and she was prepared, therefore, to dispense even with the practice she had already advocated, of 'ladies in elevated

[1] *The Fable of the Bees*, 1723 edition, p. 330.
[2] Pp. 15–16.
[3] *The Oeconomy of Charity*, pp. 27–8.

12

stations' visiting 'the lowly cottager', as being a practice which 'the present custom of the world represents . . . as an act of two great condescension'. The training of maid-servants in the spirit of modesty and subordination was, as Sarah Trimmer indicated, a contribution towards the greater social good of preserving the overall 'subordination of ranks'.[1]

Catharine Cappe's Spinning School in York faced the same objection, that if the children of the poor were better taught and educated 'they will become so aspiring, that we shall have no lower servants'. 'Should we be worse served', asked the school's first annual report, 'if our domestics were sober, industrious, honest, and obedient, the ends at which this Institution aims'.[2] The objectives that educationists like Sarah Trimmer and Catharine Cappe set themselves included, therefore, acts of both rescuing *from* and rescuing *for*. The nineteenth century saw a continuing change in emphasis to the 'rescuing-for' motive, a change which we can begin to see in the domestic servant situation, and which was to become of vital importance in the industrial one. Society began to need not only an adequate supply of maid-servants, but a supply of industrial workers. When steam power made it possible to site factories and mills in the growing towns in the latter part of the eighteenth century, and with the need to train ex-cottager paupers in attitudes towards collectivised industrial work, education began to be seen as an essential part of the process of transition. A writer in 1803 made the far-sighted point that education, even if restricted to the Scriptures and our 'pious and moral authors', might 'induce the health and personal comforts of the poor, and that manly character, which . . . are intimately connected with individual exertions for obtaining an independent maintenance; exertions of no small political importance in our manufactories'.[3] In arguing that industry needed diligent workers,[4] Harrison had adopted the self-interest motive of Adam Smith and French rationalism. The interests of the worker in his 'individual exertions' were identical with those of the manufactories.

---

[1] *Ibid.*, p. 60.

[2] Cappe, *An Account of Two Charity Schools*, p. 97.

[3] Harrison, *Education respectfully proposed . . . as the surest Means to diminish the Frequency of Crimes*, p. 10.

[4] It also needed literate, skilled craftsmen, but this question had not yet assumed large-scale proportions. It is more relevant to the discussion of, for example, the Society for the Diffusion of Useful Knowledge and the Mechanics' Institutes. See Chapter V (iii) below.

Adam Smith had, in fact, a quarter of a century earlier, put forward a theory of education in line with his analysis of a growing division of labour, a theory which pin-pointed very clearly the nature of the transition which education was being asked to cope with. Adam Smith 'could not agree that an ignorant slave was more useful to his master's happiness or could increase a prince's dignity more than an educated, free man',[1] and in *The Wealth of Nations* he showed the advantage a nation, as well as a master, would derive from extended popular education, however slight, in reading, writing and accounting, plus 'parts of geometry and mechanics'.[2] He started, in his educational thinking, from the contention that in the process of the division of labour 'the employment of the far greater part of those who live by labour, that is, of the great body of the people, comes to be confined to a few very simple operations; frequently to one or two'. The simplicity of the repeated operations required neither understanding nor the use of 'invention', and the worker 'naturally loses, therefore, the habit of such exertion, and generally becomes as stupid and ignorant as it is possible for a human creature to become'.[3] This brutalisation, Smith contended, made a man incapable of rational judgment in matters affecting his private life and the interests of his country. Although Smith did not at this point argue directly, as George Harrison did in 1803, that education would benefit industry as well as the individual and the society as a whole, it is clear that he assumed an identity of all sets of interests:

> '. . . if, instead of a little smattering in Latin, which the children of the common people are sometimes taught there (in charity schools) and which can scarce ever be of any use to them, they were instructed in the elementary parts of geometry and mechanics; the literary education of this rank of people would, perhaps, be as complete as can be. There is scarce a common trade, which does not afford some opportunities of applying to it the principles of geometry and mechanics . . .'[4]

Adam Smith drew the educational deductions from the major point of change he had detected, and the analysis he made both of the problem and the kind of educational provision which would be advantageous to

[1] Ian Cumming, *Helvétius, His Life and Place in the History of Educational Thought*, London, 1955, p. 141.

[2] Adam Smith, *An Inquiry into the Nature and Causes of the Wealth of Nations*, London, 1776 (World's Classics edition, 1904, Vol. II, p. 421).

[3] *Ibid.*, p. 417.　　　　　　　　　　[4] *Ibid.*, p. 421.

the industrial system was to be borne out and taken up in the industrial and educational discussions of the 1820's and 1830's. The eighteenth century charitable schools of industry were to some extent fulfilling an industrial purpose, but their aims were tuned to the handicraft, non-industrial situation. Theirs was still a 'rescue from' purpose, in a situation where there was no important social organism dependent on them as a supply of labour (excepting the maid-servant 'industry').

We have already seen that the Rev. Andrew Bell's purposes for a moral and religious education included 'habits of useful industry adapted to their condition and rank in life, to the demands of the army and navy . . .'[1] Adam Smith had pointed out over thirty years earlier that one of the results of the division of labour and the brutalisation of the worker was that the uniformity of his stationary life naturally corrupts the courage of his mind, and makes him regard with abhorrence the irregular, uncertain, and adventurous life of a soldier'.[2] In advocating an expansion of the system of education, Adam Smith therefore also had other motives and models in mind, stressing the fact that it was by encouraging military and gymnastic exercises,

> 'and even by imposing upon the whole body of the people the necessity of learning those exercises, that the Greek and Roman republics maintained the martial spirit of their respective citizens'.[3]

What we have now seen is that resistance to education as such was, in William Lovett's words, the act of those 'hawks and owls of society' who 'were seeking to perpetuate that state of mental darkness most favourable to the securing of their prey', and also that advocacy of a restricted form of education, to quote Lovett further, was the work of another portion, who, 'with more cunning, were for admitting a sufficient amount of mental glimmer to cause the multitude to walk quietly and contentedly in the paths they in their wisdom had prescribed for them'.[4] There were, of course, advocates of education with more fully liberal and humanitarian motives, but before examining this section of the spectrum of eighteenth century educational thinking, it will be useful to see briefly to what extent the kind of attitudes and purposes we have been examining were reflected in the movements which aimed to provide education.

[1] See p. 26 above.
[2] *Wealth of Nations*, 1904 edition, Vol. II, p. 417.
[3] *Ibid.*, p. 422.   [4] *The Life and Struggles of William Lovett*, p. 134.

15

(iv) *Make me dutiful*

Of eighteenth century movements to provide some form of education for the poor, the charity school movement really concerns us least, because, though embodying very clearly many of the attitudes we have been discussing, its influence in the period with which we are concerned at the close of the eighteenth century was already considerably on the wane. The first charity school was founded in 1688.[1] As a movement, fostered by the Society for Promoting Christian Knowledge, and with the aim of educating the poor in the principles of the Established Church, it gained rapid momentum from the last decade of the seventeenth century. From its peak-point at mid-century providing an education for some 30,000 children, the movement went through a period of 'disappointment, lowered ideals, and partial failure',[2] and as a major force in British education it was supplanted by the National monitorial school movement.

The importance of the charity schools lay in the fact that they attempted to provide full-time education for the children of the poor, not only in the principles of the Church, but in disciplines and skills which would enable the children to continue to behave according to those principles in later life. Most of the schools, therefore, in addition to religion, grounded the children in the three R's and normally in skills which would fit them for some local employment or service. One of the two York schools described by Catharine Cappe was a spinning school, the other (Grey Coats) was virtually a servant training centre.

Charity school children wore the soberest of school uniforms in order to make them aware of their station as recipients of charity. Dr Isaac Watts explained that 'the clothes which are bestowed upon them once in a year or two are of the coarsest kind, and of the plainest form, and thus they are sufficiently distinguished from children of the better rank, and they ought to be so distinguished'.[3] In a story published by the Society for Promoting Christian Knowledge, Sarah Trimmer illustrated what she thought the proper attitude of the charity school child to its uniform should be. Thomas, son of the widowed Mrs Simpkins, has been admitted by the Squire to the village charity school:

---

[1] See Hendley, *A Defence of the Charity-Schools*, p. 1.

[2] Charles Birchenough, *History of Elementary Education in England and Wales from 1800 to the Present Day*, 3rd edition, 1938, p. 13.

[3] Quoted in M. G. Jones, *The Charity School Movement*, Cambridge, 1938, p. 75.

'At length the wished for day arrived; a whole suit of apparel was sent home for him: and Thomas, with a joyful heart, put on the coat of grey, the band and cap, and other articles which composed the uniform of the school; and though there was a badge on the sleeve of the coat, his pride was not hurt at it, as that of many foolish boys has been, for he considered it as a mark which distinguished him as one whom God favoured with clothes, and the means of instruction, which many a poor, naked, ignorant wretch could not obtain.'[1]

The children were constantly reminded of their status in life, now and ever after. In the view of Edmund Gibson, Bishop of London, in 1724, 'fine singing, like fine writing and fine needlework, had no place . . . in schools designed to make good Christians and good servants . . . Singing did not become a recognised subject of the elementary school curriculum.'[2] Sarah Trimmer, again, emphasised the need for this constant awareness of status. Tom Simpkins, newly dressed in his charity school uniform, is lectured to on his arrival at school by the master:

'The design of the charity schools is to give the children of poor people such a degree of knowledge, as may enable them to learn from the Holy Scriptures their duty to God and man. For this happy advantage they are indebted to the benevolence of persons in higher stations; and they ought to be very grateful for it . . .'

He advises Tom to 'pray for blessings on those who founded this school, and on your benefactor Squire Villars in particular, who gave you admittance into it'. He then reads to Tom the *Rules to be observed in this School*, the final one of which is that: 'Every boy must take a bow at coming in and going out of the school; and is advised to behave with humility and respect to persons in superior stations at all times.'[3]

Clara Reeve, the 'Gothic' novelist, in 1792 published a survey of *Plans of Education* in which she made a brutal interpretation of the idea of a charitable school of industry, and called for the mass provision of such schools. Her startling frankness was not typical, but what she asked for was not in essence very different from what the schools did in fact provide. She began by describing how 'in all cities and great towns, there are numbers of poor children walking about half naked, hungry

[1] Sarah Trimmer, *The Servant's Friend*, London, 1787, edition of 1826, p. 11.
[2] Jones, *The Charity School Movement*, p. 81.
[3] Trimmer, *The Servant's Friend*, pp. 13–14.

and wretched, without any visible means of support . . . Human nature here is degraded to its lowest state, even below slavery . . .'[1] This was certainly the point of social reality at which any eighteenth century charity school (or nineteenth century ragged school, for example) can be said to have begun. She went on to advocate that committees should be established in the localities to gather such children together, purchase an old house and found a school of industry. The children should be clothed in 'the most ordinary materials' and wear wooden shoes, 'not such as the peasants wear in France, but such as I have seen made for the prisoners in the lately erected gaol for the county of Suffolk'. The children should be brought up 'to hard labour and qualified to get an honest livelihood'. Clogs apart, this was a picture of charity schools as they were. 'As the youths grew up,' she continued, 'and they had strength sufficient, they might assist as porters at wharfs and quays, or help sawyers and fellers of timber and other works. In harvest time, they should be let to work in the fields, at small prices . . .'[2] This was merely an extension of the kinds of trades industrial schools actually did prepare their children for. But her change of emphasis should be noted —the trades she quotes here are ones for which the training of a school specialising in spinning or basket-weaving is not necessary. Criticism had been levelled against the charity schools throughout the eighteenth century (Hendley defended them against it as early as 1725) to the effect that their children, with their accomplishments, tended to replace those of, for example, tradesmen, in certain occupations.[3] Clara Reeve's stress appears to have taken this kind of criticism into account. For the future porters, sawyers and fellers of timber she planned, therefore, an appropriate prototype school of industry in great detail, following the policy that:

'these paupers are not to be taught to write or read; being rescued from extreme poverty, they are to be hewers of wood and drawers of water, and to be thankful for their deliverance; but they are to be taught their duties to God, their neighbours, and themselves; and to attend the service of the church regularly, and to use private devotions every morning and evening; and to know that no undertaking can succeed without the blessing of Heaven'.[4]

[1] Clara Reeve, *Plans of Education; with Remarks on the Systems of other Writers*, London, 1792, pp. 84–5.
[2] *Ibid.*, pp. 85–6.   [3] See Jones, *The Charity School Movement*, p. 86.
[4] *Plans of Education*, p. 87.

Charity schools did, in fact, teach their children to read in order better to appreciate these duties and Clara Reeve's ideal charity school of industry can be taken as close to the reality of such schools, merely stripped of their last vestige of literary content and any trace of a generous philanthropic purpose.

(v) A dinner of herbs with quiet

The Sunday school movement began with Robert Raikes in Gloucester in 1780. The 'rescue motive' lay as firmly behind this movement as it had done behind the charity schools, and in confining its attention to rescuing the children on the one day a week, the movement set itself more limited and perhaps more explicit aims. There was no question, for example, of a vocational or industrial training. The purpose was much more directly and simply the inculcation of piety through an ability to read the Bible.

The importance of the Sunday school movement from our point of view lies in two facts—firstly, that in its period of major development it had to contend with a new factor in social attitudes towards education—the impact of the French Revolution, and secondly, that the spread and prestige of the movement became closely identified with the thinking of and example set by the Evangelical Movement.

Whatever new features we find in these schools, there were orthodox motives behind them. It was realised that 'something out of the common way is necessary to induce many parents to send their children; and many children would be averse to going if they were not assured of exemption from that kind of discipline practised in weekly schools',[1] but their purpose remained firmly within the eighteenth century pattern. Sarah Trimmer, in her justification of Sunday schools, made it clear that the work of the master and the mistress in the school was not enough: Sunday schools, she believed, 'unless visited by persons of superior rank in life to the masters and mistresses, seldom answer the proposed ends'.[2] In this view of the crucial role of the 'persons of superior rank' we see the typically eighteenth century conception of the school's purpose, with any educational considerations completely overweighed by explicit social ones.

The unorthodoxy of method which characterised the work of the Methodist movement and to a lesser degree the Evangelical movement

[1] Trimmer, *The Oeconomy of* Charity, p. 15.
[2] *Ibid.*, p. 15.

in no way detracted from their essential social orthodoxy of *purpose* (though certainly not of *result*, in the case of Methodism). Methodist organisation and spirit (particularly the form of church government and the class meeting) undoubtedly made a distinct contribution to the democratisation of social processes,[1] but the intentions behind Methodist activity were very close to the 'limiting' ideology we have already examined. John Wesley described the overall purpose of the Methodist school at Kingswood, for example, as being to ensure that those who were educated there should be brought up 'at the utmost distance, as from vice in general, so in particular from idleness and effeminacy',[2] and he spelled out elsewhere, as we have seen, the essential virtues which religion should foster as 'humility, gentleness, patience, long-suffering, contentedness in every condition'.[3]

Methodism in the eighteenth century was interested, as a movement, not so much in the spread of education as such, as in the educational effect of the movement itself, through, for example, the class meeting and reading circle, through 'training simple people all the time in the art of community self-government'.[4] The Evangelicals, on the other hand, as a religious movement based on more aristocratic traditions, were in no way anxious to promote such a degree of popular involvement in the process of attaining their ends. They were, therefore, interested in education, and in Sunday schools in particular, as a form of *disseminating*, from above, knowledge and piety. It is no accident that the most far-reaching and representative act of the Evangelical movement in the sphere of popular education was the introduction of the cheap tract. Cobbett, in 1830, attacking Henry Brougham and the Society for the Diffusion of Useful Knowledge, traced the origin of that movement:

[1] See H. F. Mathews, *Methodism and the Education of the People 1791–1851*, London, 1949, pp. 78–83, and Hammond, *The Town Labourer*, Guild Books edition, 1949, Chapter XIII.

[2] *A Short Account of the School in Kingswood, near Bristol* (1768), in *Works*, Vol. XIII, 4th edition, 1841, p. 270.

[3] See p. 25 above. Hazlitt was particularly vicious on this aspect of Methodism: '. . . a most pitiful sect . . . a collection of religious invalids . . . they are not comfortable here and they seek for the life to come' ('On the Causes of Methodism', *Complete Works*, London, 1930, Vol. iv, pp. 58–9).

[4] S. C. Carpenter, *Church and People, 1789–1889*, London, 1933, p. 11. The Methodists did, of course, found Sunday schools as part of this process, though 'the Wesleyan Methodists dropped (writing), no doubts from a fear of the uses to which working men might put their skill' (Hammond, *The Town Labourer*, Vol. II, p. 107).

'This *educating* work, this *feeding with tracts*, began, about forty years ago, under the guidance of that prime old prelate in petticoats, that choice tool of the boroughmongers, HANNAH MORE...'[1]

and the equation of 'educating work' with 'feeding with tracts' is an accurate statement of the Evangelical educational outlook. The Sunday school also suited this outlook admirably as an instrument. Asa Briggs describes the Evangelical viewpoint as one of anxiety 'not to abolish the distinction between rich and poor or to shatter the traditionalist theory of orders, ranks and degrees, but rather to justify both by introducing into the world a new leaven of righteousness',[2] and certainly in an age of revolution the Evangelical image of popular education was closely associated with the preservation of 'orders, ranks and degrees'.

With her deep commitment to the Church of England, which, 'on the most important survey of all similar institutions which have been known in the Christian world, will be found the most admirable for its purpose',[3] Hannah More based her educational thinking on a strict puritanical view of the essential corruption of human nature. 'Is it not a fundamental error', she asked, 'to consider children as innocent beings, whose little weaknesses may perhaps want some correction, rather than as beings who bring into the world a corrupt nature and evil dispositions, which it should be the great end of education to rectify?'[4] Out of her commitment to such a view of human nature, and by the catalysis of William Wilberforce, to whom, and to whose views, she was completely devoted,[5] the most famous of the efforts to found Sunday schools came to be made. The immediate stimulus behind the Mores' schools came from Wilberforce in 1789 when, on a visit to the More sisters, he 'was appalled by the distress and ignorance of the inhabitants' of the Cheddar

[1] G. D. H. and Margaret Cole (eds.), *The Opinions of William Cobbett*, 1944, p. 293.

[2] Asa Briggs, *The Age of Improvement*, London, 1959, p. 71. See also Jacques Pons, *L'Education en Angleterre entre 1750 et 1800*, Paris, 1919: 'L'éducation populaire telle que l'envisageaient Mrs Trimmer, Hannah More et beaucoup d'autres, n'était qu'un moyen de faire accepter au peuple agité par les idées révolutionnaires ambiantes sa sugétion séculaire au roi et à l'Eglise' (p. 62).

[3] Hannah More, *Hints Towards Forming the Character of a Young Princess*, London, 1805, p. 301.

[4] Hannah More, *Strictures on the Modern System of Female Education*, London, 1799, Vol. I, p. 64.

[5] 'Mrs H. More was with me last night; she is so exalted by your book (*Practical Christianity*) that she almost forgets humility is one of the Christian requisites' (Letter to Wilberforce from Maria, Duchess of Gloucester, April 14, 1797, in *Private Papers of William Wilberforce*, London, 1897, p. 107).

21

district.[1] Hannah and Martha went out among the miners and glass-glowers and their families, Martha producing a Dantean description of the glassblowers:

'voluptuous beyond belief . . . the great furnaces roaring—the sweating, eating, drinking of these half-dressed, black-looking beings, gave it a most infernal and horrible appearance . . . we proceeded to enter the very glass-houses, amidst black Cyclopean figures, and flaming, horrible, fires. However, we were again agreeably surprised as well as affected, for every one of these dismal looking beings laid down their tools, and . . . speaking in the civilest terms, calling all the great boys out of their black holes, and using really persuasive language to them to induce them to listen to us and do what we wished'.[2]

On the basis of such visits among the poor, and to clergymen and 'village despots', Sunday schools were established in the district, with the financial support of Wilberforce and Henry Thornton. The most comprehensive summary of the school work is to be found in a letter from Hannah in 1801:

'When I settled in this country thirteen years ago, I found the poor in many of the villages sunk in a deplorable state of ignorance and vice. There were, I think, no Sunday schools in the whole district, except one in my own parish . . . and another in the adjoining parish of Churchill. This drew me to the more neglected villages, whose distance made it very laborious. Not one school there did I ever attempt to establish without the hearty concurrence of the clergyman of the parish. My plan of instruction is extremely simple and limited. They learn, on week-days, such coarse works as may fit them for servants. I allow of no writing for the poor . . .'[3]

Work in the Sunday schools was based on *The Church Catechism* 'framed and half a dozen hung up in the room', on two tracts called *Questions for the Mendip Schools*, and on 'Spelling Books, Psalter, Common Prayer, Testament, Bible. The little ones repeat "Watts's Hymns". The Collect

[1] J. C. Colquhoun, *William Wilberforce and his Friends and Times*, London, 1867, p. 117.
[2] Quoted in Mary Alden Hopkins, *Hannah More and her Circle*, New York, 1947, pp. 182–3.
[3] *The Letters of Hannah More*, p. 183.

is learned every Sunday. They generally learn the Sermon on the Mount, with many other chapters and psalms.'[1]

The kind of attitudes which Hannah More and her collaborators tried to inculcate among the poor, can be seen most clearly from the *Sunday School Tracts*, begun in 1792, of which she was the prime organiser.

The History of Charles Crawford[2], for example, tells the tale of the charity school boy, whose father fractured his skull and was carried to the infirmary almost dying. 'How thankful we should be', the story comments, 'that such places are open for the relief of the poor!'[3] Charles proves to be a very good boy, possessing 'one rare quality . . . namely—that his master's interest was always uppermost in his mind'.[4] Some envious people, the story points out, 'would sneer at his being brought up in a charity-school; but he was thankful that he had such a good opportunity'.[5] Even more interesting, in that it conveys not only the precept, but the rationale, of the Sunday school movement, is No. 20 in the same series, *The Plough-Boy's Lesson*. It begins with an account of a Sunday school, where, before the children left for home, the curate or 'some other discrete person' always gave the children a 'short exhortation'. On the evening in question, Mr Goodman spoke to them. He had observed that:

'many promising young people, almost as soon as they have left this school, have become restless at home, and have manifested a desire to leave our village, and go to service in *London*, or some of our great towns . . . Perhaps some of you may soon have the same restless disposition, and what is equally bad, your parents, who ought to know better, may wish to turn you suddenly into fine gentlemen and ladies, by sending you to London; because, as they think, you have *gotten good learning*. In this way has the ability to read been abused by idle boys and girls, and their thoughtless parents. Learning is now so common, that there will always be people enough out of employ in London, and other places, with greater knowledge than you will ever attain. It is *now* disgraceful *not* to be able to read. The learning we are able to communicate is only intended to enable you to read the scriptures, and to see, that it is the will of God, that you should be contented with your stations, and therein "abide with God".'[6]

[1] *Ibid.*, p. 184.
[2] *Sunday School Tracts*, January 1806, monthly tract No. 1.
[3] *Ibid.*, p. 3.   [4] *Ibid.*, p. 6.
[5] *Ibid.*, p. 9.   [6] P. 2.

This last sentence is a frank statement of the intention of the Sunday school, as it would be of any other eighteenth century English steps in the field of popular education. Hannah More and Sarah Trimmer were, in fact, perturbed by the later monitorial school development because it took education a stage beyond their provisions. Wilberforce held views fully in line with the hierarchical society postulated in this kind of Sunday School Tract.[1]

In retrospect, therefore, the attacks made on the Sunday schools from the mid-1790's, as being training centres of sedition, seem some kind of elaborate joke. What we witness from about 1793 is a recrudescence of outright opposition to popular education as such, under the impact of developments in France and the treason trials in Britain. The dispute was one between two wings of the movement to preserve the status quo, and the Sunday school movement, despite the hysteria and setbacks of the 1790's and early 1800's, continued to act as a bulwark of the 'rescue' wing of conformity. An account of the Bath Sunday School Union in 1814, for example, reported a total attendance of 2,418 at the schools in Bath and district, where, 'in addition to a common education' (which appears to have consisted solely of reading the Bible and religious tracts) 'these youth are favoured with a *religious* one: they are taught their duty . . .'[2] Hannah More's letters show in detail the nature of the attacks against her schools, as hotbeds of Methodism and subversion.[3] The More sisters, the schools, the schoolmasters, all came under sustained attack from local and national sources, leading to schools being closed. Hannah had tried to restrict schooling to the reading of the Bible, and had added writing and arithmetic for the local farmers' sons only, so as to give them 'such knowledge as should qualify them for churchwardens, constables, jurymen, etc.' Even 'these sinister designs', as Hannah put it, 'were quashed!'[4]

Sunday schools elsewhere, at different times and for different reasons, set similar bounds for their education. In 1786, in Manchester, 'a rule was adopted 6th September by the joint committee of Sunday schools

---

[1] 'At Peterloo, he (Wilberforce) was sorry for the victims, but he supported the Six Acts. He approved of various schemes for relief work and education, but did not press them so as to embarrass the Government' (Carpenter, *Church and People*, p. 45).

[2] *The Philanthropist*, Vol. IV, No. XIV, 1814, pp. 188–9.

[3] See *The Letters of Hannah More*, pp. 176–7, and Hopkins, *Hannah More and her Circle*, Chapter XX.

[4] Letter to Wilberforce, 1823, in *The Letters of Hannah More*, p. 201.

that writing should not henceforward be taught in the schoolroom'.[1]

The attack mounted on the Sunday schools on a national scale followed the general pattern of anxiety about revolution in Britain. Attacks on Paine went side by side with attacks on the notion of popular education; resistance to reform involved resistance to education which might make the poor aware of the possibility of reform. The Bishop of Rochester proclaimed in 1800:

'... the Jacobins of this country are I very much fear making a tool of Methodism ... schools of Jacobinical rebellion and Jacobinical politics ... schools of atheism and disloyalty abound in this country; schools in the shape and disguise of Charity Schools and Sunday Schools, in which the minds of the children of the very lowest order are enlightened—that is to say taught to despise religion and the laws and all subordination'.[2]

One has only to set this kind of attack against, for example, Hannah More's own attacks on Jacobinical principles,[3] to realise how narrow was the spectrum of thought about social developments, including education, that we have so far seen.

As late as 1811 a trial took place at Portsmouth instituted on information brought by the Chaplain of Portsmouth Dock-yard Church, against one John Maybee, 'for running Sunday School ... under colour and pretence of exercising religious worship, in other manner than according to the Liturgy of the Church of England, did unlawfully teach ...'[4] The

[1] W. E. A. Axon, *The Annals of Manchester*, London, 1886, p. 114. Axon adds: 'The bigotry and cruelty of such a regulation at a time when the means of education were so scanty needs no comment.' Even half a century later, at the laying of the foundation stone of the Manchester Hall of Science, one of the speakers, emphasising his long experience as a Sunday school teacher, stated that such schools were so much 'under the influence of pseudo religious men, who have such pretensions to *piety* (!) that they cannot allow the children of the poor to write on the Sunday ... Wesleyan Methodists, it is well known, have strenuously opposed its introduction.' (Temple of Free Enquiry. *A Report of the Proceedings consequent on laying the Foundation Stone of the Manchester Hall of Science, with an address by Robert Owen*, Leeds, 1839, p. 29.)

[2] Quoted in Kendall, *Robert Raikes*, p. 122.

[3] For example in her *Remarks on the Speech of M. Dupont*, London, 1793, and *Strictures on Female Education*, London, 1799, with its call to oppose 'the most tremendous confederacies against religion, and order, and governments, which the world ever saw' (Vol. I, p. 5).

[4] *The Philanthropist*, Vol. I, 1811, p. 388 (a reprint of the report which was published in *The Times* on August 7, 1811). *The Philanthropist* was edited, from 1811–19, by William Allen.

only real evidence against Maybee (who was acquitted) was, according to the report, 'a ranting tone of voice'. The point, however, is the nature of the defence that was advanced by Maybee's counsel:

> 'It was not easy to conceive in what manner instructing men in their duties could prompt them to neglect those duties . . . The admiralbe mechanism of society, together with that subordination of ranks which is essential to its subsistence, was surely not an elaborate imposture, which the exercise of reason would detect and expose. Nothing in reality rendered legitimate government so insecure as extreme ignorance in the people. It was that which yielded them an easy prey for seduction . . . These were not the times in which it was safe for a nation to repose in the lap of ignorance.'[1]

Even allowing for the exigencies of the courtroom, the social assumptions from which this defence was argued are indistinguishable from those of the most inveterate opponents of education.

In Hannah More's poem *The Riot; or, Half a Loaf is Better than no Bread*, Tom, hungry, proposes 'a bit of a riot', but is resisted by Jack (who in the end is victor in the argument):

> *'On those days spent in riot, no bread you brought home;*
> *Had you spent them in labour, you must have had some . . .*
> *A dinner of herbs, says the wise man, with quiet,*
> *Is better than beef amid discord and riot . . .*
> *So I'll work the whole day, and on Sundays I'll seek*
> *At the church how to bear all the wants of the week.*
> *The gentlefolks too will afford us supplies,*
> *They'll subscribe—and they'll give up their puddings and pies.'[2]*

Although the gentlefolks finally preferred Peterloo to giving up their puddings and pies, the doctrine of herbs with quiet was that of the whole range of educational patrons with whom we have been concerned.

(vi) Ally of religion . . . instrument of delusion

A final necessary case study in eighteenth century educational movements must be the monitorial school. The schools of Joseph Lancaster and Andrew Bell appeared at the very end of the century and had their

---

[1] *The Philanthropist*, Vol. I, 1811, p. 390.
[2] *The Poetical Works of Hannah More*, London, 1843, pp. 472–4.

major expansion in the early part of the nineteenth century, within the traditions we have been examining in the eighteenth.

Apart from all considerations of scale of operation (including the fact that the two rival movements were in the 1830's to become the first recipients of government grants for educational purposes) the outstanding feature of the monitorial movement, differentiating it from anything that had come before, was that, in setting children (monitors) to teach other children, with a single teacher in charge, it of necessity elaborated a body of thought about educational practice. Previous movements had put forward implicit or explicit social justifications and asserted ultimate purposes. The monitorial movement advanced, and carried out, an educational theory, justified in terms of efficiency and economics, as well as defending certain social positions or combating certain social dangers. Limited and self-limiting like all eighteenth century education, this new form of mass charity education was to be defended from new standpoints.

There is neither place nor deed here to consider detailed differences in method or purpose between Joseph Lancaster and the British schools on the one hand, and Dr Andrew Bell and his National schools on the other. The contested claims to having 'invented' the monitorial machinery are not our concern; the only facts that we need to note are firstly, that Joseph Lancaster, a Quaker, 'began his career as an educationist in the year 1798, at the age of eighteen, when he opened a school for ninety children, in the house of his father, and taught many of them free of all expense',[1] and that by 1808, under royal and other patronage, the Royal Lancasterian Society (subsequently the British and Foreign School Society) was spreading a wide network of undenominational monitorial schools; and secondly, that on his return from Madras in 1797, the Rev. Dr Andrew Bell published *An Experiment in Education*, an account of his monitorial experiment there, and by the end of 1811 the National Society for promoting the Education of the Poor in the Principles of the Established Church had come into existence, to foster the spread of a network of monitorial schools dedicated to a more exclusive religious principle.

'Every populous village, unprovided with a National School, must be regarded as a stronghold abandoned to the occupation of the enemy', proclaimed the Bishop of London in 1814,[2] and though there were, of course, differences in method between the two movements it was

---

[1] *The Westminster Review*, Vol. XLVI, No. 1, October, 1846, p. 220.
[2] Quoted in A. Irvine, *Reflections on the Education of the Poor*. London, 1815, p. 4.

essentially in this sort of terms that the warfare between the Church and nonconformist educational movements was conducted.

Given the need for a wholesale expansion of popular education, if the rescue operation was to be conducted adequately, it was argued, the monitorial system, with its huge numbers of pupils and minimal staff was the most efficient and economical way of achieving the aim. Lancaster was sure that the expansion of his school from 350 to nearly 800 children in six weeks, and the successful establishment of a school for some 200 girls, educated on the same plan, proved his system to be 'adequate to the instruction of a thousand children, or more, in one institution; *and without any adult assistant teachers*'. This economical plan had been carried out at a much less expense than any of my friends ever expected me to reduce to practice'.[1] Sir Thomas Bernard, who thought the details of Bell's methods superior, argued the economic case in 1809 on the basis that it cost 12–18 guineas a year to maintain and instruct a boy in a charity school, whereas the cost of educating a boy at one of Dr Bell's schools was 4–10 shillings a year. 1,500 guineas spent on the board and tuition of a hundred children in a charity school 'would have provided for the *education of* FOUR THOUSAND FIVE HUNDRED day scholars'.[2] Both Lancaster and Bernard insisted that they had no objection to charity schools, which should continue to fulfil the functions ascribed to them by their founders, but they argued that only the monitorial system could reach out to the bulk of the poor. An enthusiastic writer in *The Philanthropist* in 1811 (probably James Mill) described 'the economical plan of Lancaster' as being 'well calculated to answer every purpose, and may fairly be considered as the most important discovery of the kind ever made.'[3]

The economic arguments, of course, were accompanied by clearly-defined social advantages. Andrew Irvine outlined some of those to be derived from education on the National model: it inculcated 'useful and excellent habits', increased cleanliness, enabled mothers to go out to work (and hence provided more domestic comforts), ensured greater religious observance, indirectly reformed the adult poor through observing changes in their children), formed a new 'bond of union' in the family, and 'unites the lower orders in a Parish to each other, and attaches them to their superiors'.[4] These, by and large, had been merits

[1] *Improvements in Education*, 1806, pp. 8–9.
[2] *Of the Education of the Poor*, pp. 17–18.   [3] Vol. I, No. 1, p. 81.
[4] *Reflections on the Education of the Poor*, pp. 26–33.

invoked for previous systems, expressed this time perhaps more humanely (though no less benevolent-philanthropically) and in a different, growingly industrial context. That behind such purposes of reform and rescue traditional eighteenth century limiting factors were at work, both Lancaster and Bell were, in fact, at pains to admit.

Bell went furthest in his self-imposed limitations. He made it clear that:

'It is not proposed that the children of the poor be educated in an expensive manner, or all of them to be taught to write and to cipher. Utopian schemes, for the universal diffusion of general knowledge, would soon realize the fable of the belly and the other members of the body, and confound that distinction of ranks and classes of society, on which the general welfare hinges . . . there is a risque of elevating, by an indiscriminate education, the minds of those doomed to the drudgery of daily labour, above their condition, and thereby rendering them discontented and unhappy in their lot'.[1]

The Edinburgh Review, commenting indignantly on this passage, lamented 'to find Dr Bell among the followers of Mandeville' and sounding 'the same foolish alarm about the dangers of knowledge to society'. Although Bell, it agreed, was 'friendly to a certain portion of education, nay, has been one of the most useful promoters of the new system', when he boggled 'at the *excess*', and drew 'lines of distinction between reading, which is innocent, and writing and arithmetic, which are pernicious, he exposes himself to a charge of inconsistency, perhaps, not to be paralleled in the history of feebleness and bigotry'.[2] Sir Thomas Bernard sadly came to Bell's defence, by pointing out that Lancaster had expressed the same reservations. Dr Bell's principles had received much attention, and:

'. . . he whom millions of the poor in future ages will bless as their Benefactor and Instructor, has been called the "Foe to general education, the disciple of Mandeville, and the friend of ignorance." Mr Lancaster's has not attracted the same kind of notice . . . he only asks "that every child should be able to read his Bible".'[3]

[1] *The Madras School*, p. 292.
[2] Vol. XVII, No. XXXIII, November 1810, p. 63. The review was by Brougham (see John Clive, *Scotch Reviewers: The Edinburgh Review, 1802–1815*, London, 1957, p. 139).
[3] Sir Thomas Bernard, *The Barrington School, being an Illustration of the Principles, Practice, and Effects, of the New System of Instruction*, London, 1812, p. 7 (note).

We must remember, however, that the bulk of Lancaster's *Improvements in Education* was taken up precisely with indicating methods of writing and cyphering. In practice, he had no hesitation about the wider curriculum. Although with greater reluctance and timidity, Bell also admitted in practice what he half-feared in principle, and *The Madras System*, in spite of its reservations, also contained a scheme for teaching writing and arithmetic.

In the entirely new situation after the French Revolution and the growth of an urban working class and articulate radical discontent, reservations about how far to go in education have to be seen in a new context.

Andrew Irvine's *Reflections on the Education of the Poor* in 1815 is particularly interesting in this connection. 'The Poor,' he argued familiarly, 'are destined to labour: and to this supreme and beneficial arrangement of Providence, they must of necessity submit.'[1] Together with this continued sense of a permanently structured society, however, there was now special pleading. Something had to be done, but as action would be dangerous it must rest in the hands of the Church. He quoted, as we have seen, the Bishop of London's conviction that every village without a National School 'must be regarded as a stronghold abandoned to the occupation of the enemy', and described the monitorial system as an engine which, 'so powerful as the ally of religion and virtue, may become an irresistible instrument of delusion, in the hands of infidelity or fanaticism'.[2] The dilemma of the defender of the status quo was no longer the same as in the mid-eighteenth century. To do nothing, Irvine maintained, was to abandon the field to an already well-organised enemy, one who, for all his protestations, by the sheer fact of being a schismatic, lent himself to the work of social disruption. 'Nothing is so hostile to good government', he affirmed, 'as ignorance in the governed, who thus become an easy prey to seduction, and instruments of mischief in the hands of unprincipled and designing men'.[3] This from the 1790's became a common theme, and Irvine was aware that increasingly these 'unprincipled and designing men' had a local habitation and a name. 'Suspicion', says one commentator on Britain' in the 1790's, 'had the widest range, and attacked even to geological speculations and to Lancaster's new methods of teaching.'[4] There were two important

---

[1] *Reflections on the Education of the Poor*, p. 14.
[2] *Ibid.*, pp. 3–4.   [3] *Ibid.*, p. 19.
[4] P. A. Brown, *The French Revolution in English History*, London, 1918, edition of 1923, p. 168.

consequences of this situation for the nineteenth century. A first, short-run consequence, lay in the heightened tension involved in the decision as to what to teach, to whom, and to what degree. The second, long-run consequence, was that this tension became increasingly involved with the question of *who* was going to take the decisions; a great deal of the battle over education *among the providers* was fought more and more bitterly around questions of Establishment versus Nonconformity, and State versus Voluntary provision.

How great was the tension involved in decisions of this kind can be seen from the form and direction of the early attacks on the monitorial system. Joseph Lancaster registered his acknowledgment in *Improvements in Education* to the work of Sarah Trimmer,[1] and included among the list of reading lessons *Trimmer's Introduction to the Knowledge of Nature and the Use of the Scriptures*. This did not prevent her, neverthe-less, from stigmatising Lancaster's schools 'as training schools for the army of the approaching revolution.'[2] Lancaster, in defending himself principally against Archdeacon Daubeny, and the charge of 'deism under the imposing guise of philanthropy',[3] counter-attacked also against Sarah Trimmer, who, he explained visited his institution 'two years ago for about a quarter of an hour'. He had formerly 'used *one* of her books in the school, but foreseeing that I should be exposed to controversy, whether I would or not, I laid it aside and took up a better ... That book is the Bible'.[4] Sir Thomas Bernard, in 1812, was extremely conscious of resistance to the extension of education and was at great pains to dispel fears. About the time of the establishment of the Society for bettering the Condition of the Poor (founded in 1796 by Bernard and others, including William Wilberforce), he explained, 'the horrors of the French Revolution had renewed the prejudices against any *general* system of Education ... There are, however, still some pious

[1] *Improvements in Education*, 4th edition, p. 158.
[2] Elie Halévy, *England in 1815*, 1913 (revised edition, London, 1949, p. 531). *The Edinburgh Review* defended Lancaster with great zest: 'Mr Lancaster has made it (school) quite pleasant and interesting to them (the boys) by giving to it the air of military arrangement; not foreseeing, as Mrs Trimmer foresees, that in times of public dangers, this plan furnishes the disaffected with the immediate means of raising an army; for what have they to do but to send for all the children educated by Mr Lancaster, from the different corners of the kingdom into which they are dispersed,—to beg it as a particular favour to them to fall into the same order as they adopted in the spelling class twenty-five years ago ...' (Vol. IX, No. XVII, October 1806, pp. 182–3).
[3] Daubeny's phrase, quoted by Lancaster in *An Appeal for Justice*, p. 13.
[4] *Ibid.*, p. 35.

31

and conscientious persons adverse to the extension of instruction to the poor, beyond reading merely: and one of the labours of the Society has been, to remove these prejudices.'[1] Three years later we find Andrew Irvine making the same point, pleading with those who were afraid that education was being carried too far to consider with attention the moderate views and objects of the National Society'.[2] Hannah More remained hostile towards the monitorial schools, though publicly remaining silent. 'I have exerted my feeble voice', she wrote in 1821, 'to prevail on my few parliamentary friends to steer the middle way between the Scylla of brutal ignorance and the Charybdis of a literary education.' To her friends she expressed her opposition to the affectation of teaching poor children anything but the modicum required for a reading of 'the Scriptures, and such books as are preparatory to, and connected with them'.[3] In many schools, she had heard, writing and accounts were taught on Sundays. 'This', she maintained, 'is a regular apprenticeship to sin. He who is taught arithmetic on a Sunday when a boy, will when a man, open his shop on a Sunday.' 'All this', in her judgment, 'has a revolutionary as well as irreligious tendency.'[4] Her own, and others', criticism was not confined, of course, to the *Sunday* teaching of arithmetic.

The monitorial movement itself, however, had no doubts about the social necessity of what it was seeking to achieve. Its concern was and remained to train the children of the poor in a range of desirable attitudes to society. The main concern of the British system was not 'success in any, or in all of the branches of learning . . . Respect for the teacher, and implicit obedience to his commands, are principles which should be assiduously cultivated.'[5] The organisation and methods, as well as the purpose, of the monitorial schools were aimed at training character, here equated with obedience. The system of training in implicit obedience was in reality so closely bound up with success in learning (through the elaborate system of rewards and punishments) that the two were scarcely separable. Sir Thomas Bernard saw this very clearly when he described the object of the monitorial system as being one of 'division of labour':

'"DIVIDE AND GOVERN" is as correct a motto for a school, as for

---

[1] *The Barrington School*, pp. 6–7.
[2] *Reflections on the Education of the Poor*, p. 13.
[3] *The Letters of Hannah More*, pp. 199–200.   [4] *Ibid.*, p. 202.
[5] *Manual of the System of Primary Instruction pursued in the Model Schools of the British and Foreign School Society*, London, 1834, p. 8.

a cabinet. It is the division of labour which facilitates the execution of every thing arduous and desirable.'[1]

The selection of the children who were to become monitors[2] was both an academic and a social selection, and the punishment for not knowing a lesson could range from the academic punishment of repetition until a lesson was learnt,[3] to the extremely social punishments elaborated by Lancaster in particular.

We are used to accounts of punishments of fairly barbarous types through the nineteenth century. Of this period early in the century, William Lovett, for example, recollected his schooldays at Newlyn, near Penzance (about 1807–8). He was sent to the only school in the town, where there were two masters. The first 'was a severe one, and the second was somewhat worse. Custises on the palm of the hand and very severe canings were punishments for not recollecting our tasks, and on one occasion I saw him hang up a boy by the two thumbs with his toes just touching the ground for playing truant.'[4] John Reilly Beard, remembering his schooldays (at a Grammar School this time) in Portsmouth, described an 'ingenious device' for inflicting punishment:

'From the roof of the high schoolroom there was suspended a huge basket, which could be let down or raised by tackling . . . Few boys were there who had not been made to take their stand therein, after which it was elevated between the roof and the floor, where the unfortunate wight remained suspended for hours—sometimes an entire day.'[5]

Against this background of the normality of punishment ranging from severe to sadistic, Lancaster's elaborately worked-out code of punishment, including this last one, is an interesting phenomenon. Much of Lancaster's *Improvements in Education* today still reads as the product of a fairly humane and at points generous attitude. He describes,

[1] *The Barrington School*, p. 52.
[2] 'The proportion of boys who teach, either in reading, writing, or arithmetic, is one to ten' (Lancaster, *Improvements in Education*, 4th edition, p. 37).
[3] 'In Dr Bell's schools, if *three mistakes*, however trivial, are made in the course of the hearing of a lesson, the class is ordered back again to learn and relearn it; and a second lesson is never given them, until they have *all perfectly* learnt the first' (Bernard, *The Barrington School*, p. 36).
[4] *The Life and Struggles of William Lovett*, p. 4.
[5] Quoted in H. McLachlan, *Records of a Family 1800–1933. Pioneers in Education, Social Service and Liberal Religion*, Manchester, 1935, p. 3.

for example, how one boy played truant continually, and his father 'got a log and chain, chained it to his foot, and, in that condition, beating him all the way, followed him to school'.[1] Though in principle opposed to wagering, Lancaster bet the monitor of the boy's class a shilling to an old rusty nail that another class would excel in writing on slate. Both classes concerned contained habitual truants, but both on this occasion were determined not to be excelled. Lancaster lost the wager, 'but if it had been fifty times the value it could not have had a better effect . . . The interest they took in the thing was so great, that they became pleased with school; and, above all, the almost incorrigible boy became reformed.'[2] And yet, together with the humane spirit displayed in this anecdote, Lancaster could also, in describing ways of dealing with offenders at his Borough Road school, detail punishments the more extreme of which included: a wooden log, serving as a pillory, round the neck; fastening the legs with shackles, and making the offender walk round the school-room till tired; tying of the elbows together behind the back; hoisting children to the roof in a basket (so dreaded that resorted to only rarely); yoking of old offenders together by the neck, so that, walking round the school, backwards, they hurt their necks or fall; and keeping the child in school after hours, tied to the desk, so that the teacher does not need to stay also.[3]

Bell's scheme of boys trying each other 'by jury' was certainly a more humane concept, but Bell himself was not prepared to press it as vital to his system,[4] and it is doubtful whether there was a great deal of difference in practice between the disciplinary codes of the average British and National school.

Both of them relied, similarly, on reward as well as punishment, reward in cash or in kind or in prestige: cash to the monitor, kind perhaps in the shape of things confiscated from offenders, and prestige (and power) by being promoted to monitorship or progress to a higher class.

There were, in this period, people who felt that the whole process of

[1] *Improvements*, p. 32.   [2] *Ibid.*, p. 33.
[3] *Ibid.*, pp. 100–6.
[4] 'Another grand objection to the Madras School is its jury . . . Though fitted to inspire youth with a love of justice, respect for the laws, and a deference to the institutions of their country, yet opposite effects have been ascribed to it in theory . . . To relieve my readers from such apprehensions, I assure them that it is no otherwise necessary to the system than as a mild engine of discipline, which they are at perfect liberty to dispense with, if they retain a predilection for a more summary mode of correction' (*The Madras School*, pp. 266–7).

child teaching child was not merely economical and adequate, but educationally the most desirable form of instruction. The first issue of *The Westminster Review*, for example, in 1824, reviewed Jeremy Bentham's proposals to adapt the monitorial system to the needs of middle-class education, and expressed the view that when children teach children they are better taught, 'because from the sympathy they take in each other, they learn every thing communicable by one to the other more easily and perfectly'.[1]

Francis Place, who, for all his association with a variety of radical movements, held astonishingly primitive (or, as Robert Owen described them, 'Whig'[2]) notions about education and human nature, 'with regard to the monitorial system . . . was no wiser than his generation. He conceived of it not as a necessary makeshift in the absence of trained masters and of money to pay them, but as the best method possible.'[3] These were exaggerated claims, but one must remember, as Graham Wallas pointed out (in 1898), that the monitorial system, though discredited, was, at least, 'the first serious attempt to think out any system of class-teaching whatsoever.'[4] This view certainly has some validity, and is an important counter-balance to the sort of hindsight with which many writers have dismissed the monitorial schools.

Thomas Cooper, the Chartist, with a memory in 1879 of schooldays in 1813 that may not have been quite so rosy as the picture he later painted of them, made two important points about the monitorial Free School he attended in Gainsborough where instruction was 'limited to, reading the Scriptures, writing, and the first four rules of arithmetic simple and compound. Our frequent practice in spelling, and the working over and over, of the four introductory rules of arithmetic, formed at least, a good preparation for larger acquirements. I liked the school'.[5] The first point, that the education formed 'a good preparation

[1] Vol. I, No. 1, January 1824, p. 53.

[2] 'He was a conscientious, firm, hard Whig and modern political economist, mistaken in all his political views, except upon education, and of that he had only Whig knowledge' (*Life*, p. 169).

[3] G. Wallas, *The Life of Francis Place 1771–1854*, London, 1898, (edition of 1925, p. 103). In the period (1816–19) when Cobbett and Hunt were counselling the working classes to undertake action independently of the upper classes, 'Place believed that such a separation must of necessity lead to failure. Cobbett, he says, was "too ignorant to see that the common people must ever be imbecile . . . when not encouraged and supported by others who have money and influence" ' (*ibid.*, p. 117).

[4] *Ibid.*, p. 100.

[5] *The Life of Thomas Cooper, written by himself*, London, 1879, p. 13.

for larger acquirements', was clearly of importance to anyone like Cooper, with gifts both anxious to be developed and capable perhaps of surviving any form of development. Although the monitorial system made its rudimentary contribution, however unintentionally, to training a labour 'élite', it would be very easy to exaggerate the number of Thomas Coopers who found their way through the monitorial situation to 'larger acquirements' and it would be dangerous to suggest that the schools thought in terms of preparing children to acquire them.

Cooper's second important point was that he liked the school. In his autobiography Cooper made explicit what many of his fellow working class 'intellectuals' must have felt:

> 'Oh that I had been trained to music—or painting—or law—or medicine—or any profession in which mind is needed; or that I had been regularly educated, so that I might have reached a university.'[1]

It is astonishing that after a lifetime of such frustrated ambitions Cooper should have retained such an affectionate memory of his school. The fact should help us to remember that education sometimes (though not often) achieves more than it intends.

(vii) Une infinité d'événements

What we have been examining so far is the range of those attitudes to education in the late eighteenth century that were in one way or another linked to a form of educational provision. What is missing, of course, from the total spectrum of educational ideas is the most radical position, the largely rationalist, 'enlightened' set of views. The dividing line between this position and some of the views we have already examined is not always very clear, but it is separable from the remainder of eighteenth century thinking in England because it was to all intents and purposes a body of theory without any accompanying embodiment in popular practice. What the educational thinking of radical movements in the early nineteenth century inherited was a detailed philosophy and psychology, with a domestic history reaching back to Locke in particular and a modernised framework elaborated by the French radical philosophers of the eighteenth century; it was an inheritance which had no meaning before the re-energising of political and social thought in Britain in the 1790's, and it found its most important embodiment in the social action of popular movements from the 1820's.

[1] *The Life of Thomas Cooper*, pp. 16–17.

Locke, Rousseau and Godwin might in their different ways and ages have made education a firmly-held ideal for many liberals. It was Robert Owen who made it a mass issue.

The forms of schooling so far discussed did not produce of themselves any widespread enthusiasm for education among the poor.[1] The process of speeding up the awakening to education in the early decades of the nineteenth century must be understood in relation to the overall awakening of the working class to their political and social rights, and we must bear in mind constantly, in examining the radical position on education, that it found its practical expression ultimately not only in the educational work of particular reformers, but in the acceptance of educational aims as part of the stock-in-trade of mass movements. The educational thinking or efforts of men like William Godwin and Robert Owen, are, in fact, of interest primarily in examining the process whereby such educational theory and aims became an integral and vital element in social action. It is this process from idea to action that is our primary concern here.

The eighteenth century rationalist position was not, of course, born, Minerva-like, fully-armed; nor was it uniform and unchanging. Neither 'rationalist' nor 'radical' adequately defines, in fact, the educational position we are considering because of the precise philosophical and political connotations they bear. In educational terms the identification-mark of this position was that, in contrast to that of men like John Mason, it held that change could be effected and controlled in the world of men, that reason was not only the key to all knowledge and under-standing—it was the key to human betterment. Unlike the view of Hannah More that human nature was from origin vile and had to be restrained, it held that human nature was by origin, nothing, and had, as it grew, to be formed and moulded: 'from Locke's picture of the mind at birth as a *tabula rasa* came the view that education and environment make all the difference between men'.[2] The implications of the rationalist view, above all in educational terms, were accepted by men not strictly definable as rationalists, though adopting one of a series of possible liberal or radical viewpoints in opposition to the salient corruptions of society. By the end of the eighteenth century these had crystal-

[1] See Jones, *The Charity School Movement*, p. 149, for a brief discussion of factors making for an increase in interest in education in the eighteenth century, and the 'indifference, and, at times, the hostility of the poor to instruction'.

[2] Alfred Cobban, *In Search of Humanity. The Role of the Enlightenment in Modern History*, London, 1960, p. 118.

lised into two main currents, the revolutionary political creed of equality and justice, and the utilitarian creed of 'the greatest happiness of the greatest number', though these and other positions frequently ran parallel or coincided.[1]

The range of interpretation of particular aspects of the rationalist doctrine was extremely wide, and though the rationalist creed 'came into the nineteenth century as a single system of ideas, to be accepted or rejected as a whole',[2] acceptance of the creed allowed considerable room for redefinition and selection of emphasis. The concept of Nature, for example, as Basil Willey has stressed, 'may be conceived rationally or emotionally . . . Nature and Reason are normally associated in the earlier part of the (eighteenth) century, Nature and Feeling in the latter', yet in the French Revolutionary period, ' "Nature and Reason" continued their partnership long after the cult of sensibility began, and the revolutionary struggle was carried on in the joint name of both'.[3] We therefore find a range of thinkers from Locke and Descartes to Condorcet, Helvétius and Rousseau, Godwin and Owen, differently interpreting and emphasising the roles of reason and emotion, and the concept of nature as being man's primitive, pristine uncorrupted-by-society state, or his sophisticated, controlled and 'rescued' state.[4] In education, however, the ambiguities and confusions of the rationalist position are less pronounced, if one remembers its invariable insistence on the *possibility* and *desirability* of individual and social improvement through social action, an insistence which in political terms belongs to the term 'radical'. It is in the extent of the change considered desirable that the 'radical' view is least homogeneous.[5] We cannot, obviously, attempt to trace the history of this general approach to education, but it is essential to see in a little more detail the rationalist amalgam inherited by the nineteenth century reformers.

[1] For a discussion of the common basis of these two standpoints in the eighteenth century rationalist tradition, see Kingsley Martin, *French Liberal Thought in the Eighteenth Century*, London, 1929 (revised edition of 1962, particularly pp. 6–8).

[2] *Ibid.*, p. 4.

[3] Willey, *The Eighteenth Century Background*, pp. 207–8.

[4] 'Most of the philosophers of the French Revolution combined science with beliefs associated with Rousseau. Helvétius and Condorcet may be regarded as typical in their combination of rationalism and enthusiasm' (Bertrand Russell, *History of Western Philosophy*, London, 1946, edition of 1961, p. 693).

[5] 'Liberal' and 'libertarian' are also, unfortunately, difficult words to use in this context.

The puritanical view of human nature we have seen in Hannah More, led to an interpretation of education as a fight against innate corruption. Since children came into the world with 'a corrupt nature and evil dispositions' the most important quality in an instructor of youth, she proclaimed was '*such a strong impression of the corruption of our nature, as should insure a disposition to counteract it.*'[1] The rationalist position accepted the opposite assumption. It rejected any notion of evil or other innate dispositions, and since the child was not innately corrupt the roots of social malformation and injustice must lie in the structure of society itself, in mistaken social processes. Inequality and injustice are aspects of social and institutional decay. Under the impact of 'those religious puritans for whom the child was a limb of Satan', William Walsh has reminded us, the concept of the innocence of childhood had been thrown aside. Coleridge 'reminded the puritans of his own day that Christ blessed the children not in order to make them innocent but because they already were so'.[2] For Rousseau, in the motto to *Emile*, 'tout est bien, sortant des mains de l'auteur des choses, tout dégénère entre les main de l'homme'. 'And has not kind, impartial Heav'n,' asked Robert Merry, in *his Ode on the Fourteenth of July* in 1791, 'To every rank an *equal feeling* giv'n?'[3] The child's initial legacy, for thinkers from Locke and Hartley to David Hume and Helvétius, Rousseau, Godwin and Owen, was this equality of feeling, upon which the superstructure of assumptions about human and social processes was built. It was from the starting point of his attack on notions of 'original determination', 'original bias', 'innate impressions' or 'innate principles of judgment' that Godwin went on to elaborate his pattern of social and political justice.[4]

All men, therefore, are born equal. They share the same original feelings, and the difference between their abilities to discriminate between sensations and ideas is a result either largely or completely of differences in environment. From such assumptions follow two of the mainsprings of the rationalist position. Firstly, the theory of self-interest, the importance, the supremacy, of reason in choosing between

[1] More, *Strictures on the Modern System of Female Education*, Vol. I, p. 64.
[2] William Walsh, *The Use of the Imagination*, London, 1959, p. 16.
[3] Quoted in Crane Brinton, *The Political Ideas of the English Romanticists*, Oxford, 1926, p. 25.
[4] See *Enquiry concerning Political Justice and its Influence on Morals and Happiness*, 1793, edition edited by F. E. L. Priestley, Toronto, 1946, Book I. Godwin uses all these phrases in Chapter IV.

sensations, in producing an identity of individual and social well-being. Secondly, the importance of adapting social (especially directly educational) forces to ensure that the individual's mental processes are developed and perfected, not retarded and denied.

The rationalist position is concerned, then, with the concept of justice, because it is unjust for society to deprive the individual of his equal right to the fullest development. It is concerned with the concept of truth, because it is only by diffusing an awareness of the true nature of society and man that the unjust structure of society can be rectified. It is concerned with happiness, because happiness lies not in fettering the individual to his artificial status in an artificially organised society, but precisely in releasing him from such fetters and enabling him to participate on a footing of equality in areas of human experience which have been withheld from him.

This is necessarily a sweeping summary of the rationalist view, and it is one which would completely fit any given thinker of the French Enlightenment only with adjustments; it assumes, for example, notions of liberty which many of the French rationalists, Voltaire for instance, would have rejected categorically.[1] It is the view, however, which came in its essentials to be accepted by those British radical thinkers associated with democratic movements, including, and especially, Robert Owen. It is a view, finally, which concerns itself with the relationship between the good society and the good man, and with the remoulding of society in order to secure the development of the perfectible qualities of man. John Thelwall, one of the outstanding of the reformers of the 1790's, making notes for some unpublished lectures on Roman history, wrote:

'First Romans, dissolute refuse of society (banditti, runaway slaves). Chose a good government: virtue the consequence. Institutions and circumstances of society produce virtue or vices. Liberty and good laws make good men.'[2]

---

[1] Harold Laski commented that the philosophers of the French Enlightenment, with some exceptions, 'are not the least democratic; on the contrary, as with Voltaire, they have a genuine fear of the multitude, and some of them, Voltaire included, are not even certain that popular ignorance is not a means to social security . . .' (in F. J. C. Hearnshaw (ed.), *The Social and Political Ideas of Some Great French Thinkers of the Age of Reason*, London, 1930, p. 22). See also pp. 64–5 below for a discussion of Rousseau in this connection.

[2] Quoted from Thelwall's manuscripts by Charles Cestre in *John Thelwall. A Pioneer of Democracy and Social Reform in England during the French Revolution*, London, 1906, p. 57.

The remoulding of institutions in order to produce virtue in this way goes hand in hand with the dissemination of truth. It is an important feature of the rationalist position that it considered truth and reason, once revealed and established, to be unassailable. For example, Thomas Holcroft, the actor, dramatist and reformer implicated in the 1794 treason trials, was described by Hazlitt as 'trusting to the power of reason to make itself heard, and not doubting but that the result would be favourable to freedom and virtue. He believed that truth had a natural superiority over error, if it could only be heard; that if once discovered, it must, being left to itself, soon spread and triumph.'[1]

This was certainly the assumption behind the work of the reform organisations of the 1790's. It was the assumption, for example, behind the language of the London Corresponding Society's address to the French National Convention on September 26, 1792:

> '. . . with certainty we can inform you, Friends and Freemen, that information makes a rapid progress among us. Curiosity has taken possession of the public mind; the conjoint reign of Ignorance and Despotism passes away . . .'[2]

It is important at this point, however, before we examine the way in which the ideas of men like Holcroft and Godwin spread from the 1790's, to have in mind some of the thinkers whose work helped to define the position popular movements came to adopt.

'Locke', said Leslie Stephen, 'represents the very essence of the common sense of the intelligent classes',[3] and John Locke, at the end of the seventeenth century, was anxious to define the means whereby the widest and most sensible dissemination of education among 'the intelligent classes' might be obtained.[4] Locke's significant relation to later, more radical educational thinking does not lie in any advocacy of

---

[1] William Hazlitt (ed.), *Memoirs of the late Thomas Holcroft, Written by Himself, and continued to the Time of his Death, from his Diary, Notes and other Papers*, 1816. Reprinted in *Complete Works of William Hazlitt*, London, 1932, Vol. 3, p. 132.

[2] Quoted in Edward Smith, *The Story of the English Jacobins*, London, 1881, p. 46. See also p. 51.

[3] *English Literature and Society in the Eighteenth Century*, p. 47.

[4] Harold Laski, more specifically than Stephen, discusses the implication for Locke of the rise of the bourgeoisie: 'It had for Locke, so to speak, fought its fight and established its title to share with the gentlemen in the direction of governance; henceforward its problem was to discover the educational means to maintain the equilibrium it had achieved' (*The Rise of European Liberalism*, London, 1936, Unwin Books edition of 1962, p. 62).

41

popular education. Locke, it is true, strongly advocated the establishment of industrial or 'working schools' for pauper children in every parish,[1] a scheme which, according to G. J. Holyoake, would have provided 'much wiser schools than Mr Forster was able to recommend two hundred years later . . . If this scheme had been carried out, the working classes of England would have been the happiest, the wisest, the most self-supporting, and the healthiest population in the world.'[2] The significance of Locke's educational ideology is that, aimed though it was at the rational extension and reformation of education for the purpose of one section of the community, his premises and deductions in the field of educational psychology became readily adaptable in a different situation.

He started from the hypothesis that 'of all the Men we meet with, nine Parts of ten are what they are, good or evil, useful or not, by their Education. 'Tis that which makes the great Difference in Mankind.'[3] Locke did not, however, make such unreserved claims for the potentialities of education as Helvétius, Godwin and Owen, for instance, were later to make from the same hypothesis. Locke, later in the *Thoughts*, redefined his hypothesis:

'We must not hope wholly to change their original Tempers, nor make the Gay, pensive and grave; nor the melancholy sportive, without spoiling them. God has stamp'd certain Characters upon Mens Minds, which, like their Shapes, may perhaps be a little mended, but can hardly be totally alter'd and transform'd into the contrary.'[4]

If men can to any extent, however, be made more or less good or evil, he deduced, 'we have reason to conclude, that great Care is to be had of the forming Children's Minds . . . For when they do well or ill, the Praise and Blame will be laid there.'[5] He considered it necessary to adapt the classical curriculum to more modern needs. But not only the curriculum. Locke laid considerable stress on the need for more humane and therefore more effective methods of teaching. In teaching children

[1] See M. G. Mason, 'John Locke's Proposals on Work-house Schools', *The Durham Research Review*, Vol. VI, No. 13, September 1962, pp. 8–16.
[2] G. J. Holyoake, *Life of Joseph Rayner Stephens*, London, 1881, p. 64.
[3] John Locke, *Some Thoughts concerning Education*, London, 1690, edition of 1752, p. 2.
[4] *Ibid.*, p. 66.
[5] *Ibid.*, p. 34.

to read, write, dance, speak foreign languages, etc., Locke considered blows and force would be unnecessary. The right Way to teach them was 'to give them a Liking and Inclination to what you propose to them to be learn'd, and that will engage their Industry and Application.'[1] The result was an approach to learning which 'might be made a Play and Recreation to Children . . . they might be brought to desire to be taught.'[2] In this Lock was both continuing a strong humane tradition in Renaissance thought and elaborating an approach to teaching techniques inherent in a viewpoint which assumed that men could be led to behave rationally.[3]

Locke's search for 'play' methods, for educational stimuli, was his answer to 'a Fault in the ordinary Method of Education; and that, is the chargeing of Childrens Memories, upon all Occasions, with *Rules* and Precepts, which they often do not understand, and constantly as soon forget as given'.[4] Such views, and Locke's basic position, stressing the educability of man and the supremacy of reason were to be widely re-echoed in the literature of the French Enlightenment.[5] Although Locke's views and the body of rationalist thought generally implied and expressed attitudes towards discipline and teaching techniques, and however much radical thought may have kept alive this kind of thinking in the eighteenth century, the educational practitioners were clearly uninfluenced by it.[6]

---

[1] *Ibid.*, p. 87.   [2] *Ibid.*, p. 222.

[3] See, for example, Montaigne's advice to the tutor on how to approach his scholar: 'It is therefore meet, that he make him first trot-on before him, whereby he may the better judge of his pace . . . Where there profit lieth, there should also be their recreation' (*Of the Institution and Education of Children*, in *The Essays of Montaigne* done into English by John Florio, Tudor Translations edition, London, 1892, Vol. I, pp. 155 and 176). A comparison between the *Thoughts* and Montaigne's essay shows how much Locke, while pushing far back the frontiers of the Renaissance tradition to include modern linguistic and scientific studies, was nevertheless working within it.

[4] *Some Thoughts concerning Education*, p. 63.

[5] See *John Locke, Ses Théories Politiques et leur Influence en Angleterre*, Paris, 1907, p. 230. For an impressive discussion of this ideological tradition, see J. B. Bury, *The Idea of Progress. An Inquiry into its Origin and Growth*, 1932, Dover Books edition, New York, 1955, particularly Chapter VIII.

[6] With the major exception of the Dissenting Academies, a tradition out of which many of Owen's associates in Manchester had come. For a discussion of the contribution of the Academies to the 'modernisation' of grammar school and university education see I. Parker, *Dissenting Academies in England*, London, 1914, passim, and J. W. A. Smith, *The Birth of Modern Education: the Contribution of the Dissenting Academies 1660–1800*, London, 1954 (particularly pp. 265–8).

The French eighteenth century thinker whose influence, though less spectacular than Rousseau's, is most relevant to some of the English ideological and social movements with which we are going to be concerned, was Helvétius. *De l'Esprit* appeared for the first time in 1758[1] and *De l'Homme* posthumously in 1773; by the 1790's the ideas of Helvétius were already, as we shall see, part of a well-established tradition of thought in Britain.

Helvétius was concerned with a broader social canvas than Locke (and than most of his fellow eighteenth century philosophers, including Rousseau). *De l'Esprit*, less concerned with an egalitarian statement about education and society than the later *De l'Homme*, firmly laid down, nevertheless, Helvétius' basic position, his antagonism to the 'darkness of ignorance':

> 'A quel mépris faut-il . . . condamner quiconque veut retenir les peuples dans les ténébres de l'ignorance? L'on n'a point jusqu'à présent assez fortement insisté sur cette vérité . . .'[2]

His broad canvas contained a sympathetic appraisal of the position of the poor, and, explaining popular ignorance, he was without malice against the ignorant:

> 'Peu d'hommes ont le loisir de s'instruire. Le pauvre, par exemple, ne peut ni réfléchir, ni examiner; il ne reçoit la vérité, comme l'erreur que par préjugé: occupé d'un travail journalier, il ne peut s'élever à une certaine sphère d'idées . . .'[3]

He was anxious, in *De l'Esprit*, not to proceed too hastily in upsetting patterns of society ('non qu'on doive renverser en un jour tous les autels de l'erreur: je sais avec quel ménagement on doit avancer une opinion nouvelle . . .'[4]) and in the chapter specifically on education he preferred not to go into detail on the subject of *popular* education, because 'l'on est, à cet égard, trop éloigné de toute idée de réforme, pour que j'entre dans des détails, toujours ennuyeux lorsqu'ils sont inutiles . . .'[5] and such details were irrelevant when even the worst and most easily corrected abuses were nowhere being corrected.

[1] Four years before Rousseau's *Emile*.
[2] *De l'Esprit*, edition published in London, 1776, Vol. I, p. 301.
[3] *Ibid.*, Vol. I, p. 86.
[4] *Ibid.*, Vol. I, p. 301.
[5] *Ibid.*, Vol. II, p. 208.

Helvétius made, however, a straightforward demand for popular education, and a blunt attack on those who, 'jaloux de la domination, veulent abrutir les peuples pour les tyranniser'. He called for a bold hand to break 'le talisman d'imbécilité auquel est attaché la puissance de ces génies mal-faisants'.[1] In breaking this domination, he wished to reveal to the people 'les vrais principes de la morale', and the one principle he immediately affirmed was the one that most clearly made Helvétius central to the social thinking of the next half century and more. He insisted that men sought pleasure, avoided pain, and that the driving force in human affairs was the self-interest that followed:

'. . . insensiblement entraînés vers le bonehur apparent ou réel, la douleur & le plaisir sont les seuls moteurs de l'univers moral, & que le sentiment de l'amour de soi est la seule base sur laquelle on puisse jeter les fondements d'une morale utile'.[2]

Helvétius was here expressing a variant of Locke's doctrine of educability. Locke, as we have seen, postulated, with reservations, that 'of all the men we meet with nine parts of ten are what they are . . . by their education', but he laid great stress on the ability of the individual to repress or direct his desires and follow the dictates of reason. Helvétius, in redefining the power of reason, in insisting on its role as a concomitant of the emotions, also asserted the possibility of perfectibility through the emotions, without making the kind of reservation Locke had to make. Man is much more, in Helvétius, at the mercy of external factors, and therefore the governing of the external environment in order to enable him to pursue personal and social good becomes even more important.

Helévtius set out, in an extremely important passage, to answer, for example, those who insisted that there is a 'grande inégalité d'esprit des hommes' on the grounds that such an inequality can be seen to exist between men who have had the same education. The fact is, Helvétius points out, that men only *appear* to have had the same education. It is not good enough to state that they have been educated in the same place by the same teachers. We must give to the term education a truer, wider

---

[1] *Ibid.*, Vol. I, p. 302. Harold Laski, when he suggests that 'the social problem was, for Helvétius, an intellectual problem felt in a superficial way—the kindly compassion of a *grand seigneur*—he is uneasy about the conditions he confronts...' (*The Rise of European Liberalism*, 1936, Unwin books edition, 1962, p. 141) is underestimating the evidence of Helvétius' very real anger.

[2] *De l'Esprit*, Vol. I, p. 302.

meaning ('une signification plus vraie & plus étendue') and include in it all the factors that contribute to our education:

> 'alors je dis que personne ne reçoit la même éducation; parce que chacun a, si je l'ose dire, pour précepteurs, & la forme du gouvernement sous lequel il vit, & ses amis, & ses maîtresses, & les gens dont il est entouré, & ses lectures, & enfin le hasard, c'est-à-dire une infinité d'événements . . .'[1]

From the role of an 'infinity of events' in shaping our make-up, it is a logical step to an analysis of the power of education in eliminating the inequalities consequent on abandoning men to the tyranny of chance. Having established that 'l'inégalité d'esprit des hommes peut être indifféremment regardée comme l'effet de la nature ou de l'éducation' (a theme he investigated more fully in *De l'Homme*), Helvétius went on to analyse, for example, the sources of our ideas and the operation of our memories, in order to demonstrate his point. Like Locke, he also riduculed out-dated educational principles and advocated a more realistic, modern and 'professional' curriculum. Like Locke, he was, of course, speaking out for an education more relevant to newly-emerging élites and would-be rulers, for whom the traditional gentleman's education was no longer of value. But while advocating that studies should be suited more appropriately to the 'poste qu'on doit vraisemblablement remplir',[2] Helvétius maintained a generous concern for liberal educational principles: he was not in favour of a narrow curriculum adapted purely to the social status of the student:

> 'L'éducation d'un jeune homme doit se prêter aux différents partis qu'il peut prendre: le génie veut être libre. Il est même des connoissances que tout citoyen doit avoir: telle est la connoissance & des principes de la morale & des lois de son pays.'[3]

Helvétius' stress on the all-powerful role of education provided a major impetus to a belief in human perfectibility among radical thinkers

---

[1] *De l'Esprit*, Vol. I, p. 331. H. N. Brailsford hints at the extent to which the 'philosophers of hope' at the end of the eighteenth and beginning of the nineteenth centuries were indebted to Helvétius for this extension of the concept of education. 'Burke,' he explains, 'opposed to all their schemes . . . the unchangeable fact of human nature. They answered (diving into Helvétius) that human nature is itself the produce of "education" or, as we should call it, "environment" ' (*Shelley, Godwin and their Circle*, London, 1914, p. 31).

[2] *Ibid.*, Vol. I, p. 210.

[3] *Ibid.*, Vol. I, pp. 210–11.

in Britain at the end of the eighteenth century, and well into the nineteenth century Helvétius' doctrine of perfectibility through education was at the centre of debate. We find Robert Owen's newspaper *The Crisis* in 1833 quoting without comment a passage from Helvétius, expressing his belief that 'the understanding, the virtue, and genius of man' were 'the product of instruction'.[1] And we find Thomas Carlyle, in 1838, poking (for him) gentle fun at 'Helvétius and his set' for maintaining that: 'an infant of genius is quite the same as any other infant, only that certain surprisingly favourable influences accompany him through life', expanding him, 'while others lie closefolded and continue dunces. Herein, say they, consists the whole difference between an inspired Prophet and a double-barrelled Game-preserver.' Whereupon Carlyle's Professor Teufelsdröckh cries:

> ' "With which opinion . . . I should as soon agree as with this other, that an acorn might, by favourable or unfavourable influences of soil and climate, be nursed into a cabbage, or the cabbage-seed into an oak.
>
> "Nevertheless," continues he, "I too acknowledge the all-but omnipotence of early culture and nurture: hereby we have either a doddered dwarf bush, or a high-towering, wide-shadowing tree; either a sick yellow cabbage, or an edible luxuriant green one . . ." '[2]

The emphasis placed by Helvétius on the far-reaching power of education is to be found also, of course, though to a lesser degree, throughout radical French thought in the later eighteenth century, and finds embodiment in the social programmes of radical thinkers and movements, and formed a salient feature of debate throughout the Revolution. Babeuf, in *Le Tribun du Peuple*, called for 'instruction de tous, égalité, liberté, bonheur pour tous',[3] and attacked a form of education, which, unless it be founded on equality, 'donne aux plus intelligents, aux plus industrieux, un brevet d'accaparement, un titre pour dépouiller impunément ceux qui le sont moins . . . l'éducation est

---

[1] *The Crisis*, Vol. II, No. 17, May 4, 1833.

[2] *Sartor Resartus*, 1836, *Collected Works*, London, 1869, pp. 93–4. James Mill commented that Helvétius believed the majority of men to be 'equally susceptible of mental excellence', and that although only Helvétius was of this opinion, 'Helvétius, alone, is a host' (quoted from Mill's article on education for the *Encyclopaedia Britannica* by Elie Halévy, *The Growth of Philosophic Radicalism*, London, 1928, p. 282).

[3] Quoted in Josette Lépine, *Gracchus Babeuf*, Paris, 1949, p. 174.

une monstruosité lorsqu'elle est inégale . . .'[1] and Morelly's scheme of education in the *Code de la Nature* was designed 'to foster the social sense of the children. All pernicious ideas about property will be eradicated.'[2] Rousseau made a startling restatement, primarily in *Emile* and *Considérations sur le Gouvernement de Pologne* of ideas about education already 'in the air'. Rousseau was not primarily concerned with the problems of mass education: the education of Emile was the education of economically independent man. In his treatise on Poland he insisted that:

> 'Tous étant égaux par la constitution de l'Etat doivent être élevés ensemble & de la même manière, & si l'on ne peut établir une éducation publique tout-à-fait gratuite, il faut du moins la mettre à un prix que *les pauvres* puissent payer . . .'[3]

Rousseau is not, however, including the mass of the people in this 'tous'. The 'éducation publique' which is intended for 'les pauvres' is, in fact, intended for the 'enfants des pauvres gentilshommes qui auroient bien mérité de la patrie.'[4]

Rousseau, arguing in the name of the sovereignty of the people was prophet neither of popular revolution, nor of a concept of democracy that would involve any far-reaching popular enlightenment.[5] None the less, though the stimulus for his specific ideas on education was as exclusivist as those of Locke, his ideology had ultimately revolutionary implications, When he announced that 'tout est bien, sortant des mains de l'auteur des choses, tout dégénère entre les mains de l'homme', Rousseau set his ideas in the forefront of the attack on the institutions which led to such a degeneration. *Emile* may not be a plan for popular education, but by implication, when Rousseau tells us, like Locke and Helvétius, that 'la nature donne au cerveau d'un enfant cette souplesse

---

[1] *Ibid.*, pp. 178–9.

[2] C. H. Driver, 'Morelly and Mably', in Hearnshaw (ed.), *The Social and Political Ideas of some Great French Thinkers of the Age of Reason*, p. 217.

[3] *Considérations sur le Gouvernement de Pologne*, 1771, *Collection Complète des Oeuvres*, Geneva, 1782, Vol. II, pp. 285–6 (my italics).

[4] *Ibid.*, p. 286.

[5] J. B. Bury, discussing the Physiocrats, indicated that 'neither they nor the philosophers nor Rousseau . . . had any just conception of what political liberty means. They contributed much to its realisation, but their own ideas of it were narrow and imperfect. They never challenged the principle of a despotic government, they only contended that the despotism must be enlightened' (*The Idea of Progress*, edition of 1955, p. 176).

qui le rend propre à recevoir toutes sortes d'impressions . . .'[1] we are at the beginning of a whole social philosophy, designed to relate the most desirable impressions and developments in the individual to the most desirable forms of social organisation which can ensure that such developments take place.

John Wesley described Rousseau's *Emile* as 'the most empty, silly, injudicious thing that ever a self-conceited infidel wrote',[2] and Hannah More, attacking novels ('they are . . . daily becoming vehicles of wider mischief . . . employed to diffuse destructive politics, deplorable profligacy, and impudent infidelity'), singled out Rousseau as 'the first popular dispenser of this complicated drug, in which the deleterious infusion was strong, and the effect proportionably fatal'.[3] The attack on Rousseau was in some ways misdirected, because from the point of view of the organised attack on established social institutions, of organised movements in Britain which adopted such objectives as the provision of education, the influence of Helvétius probably had greater ultimate effect. The important fact, however, is that by the 1790's, alongside restrictive educational thinking and practice, another area of opinion had come into existence in Britain under the impact of thinkers like Helvétius and the adoption of their social philosophy in the French revolutionary movement. The ideas of the French radical thinkers had built up a kind of composite vision, a set of assumptions about society, man, character and education, which percolated through to English intellectual circles.

It is impossible here to attempt to trace all the processes whereby such a set of assumptions came to exist among British thinkers, but it is important to realise that the early impact of the radical position on Adam Smith in the 1770's, and therefore on Bentham and the utilitarians subsequently, was a real one. Smith did not have the same level of generous sympathy with the poor that Helvétius did. He was concerned largely with amending the educational system to further the more

---

[1] *Emile ou de l'Education*, 1762, *Collection Complète des Oeuvres de J. J. Rousseau*, Geneva, 1782, Vol. IV, Livre II, p. 165.

[2] *A Thought on the Manner of Educating Children*, 1783, in *Works*, 1841, Vol. XIII, p. 447.

[3] *Strictures on the Modern System of Female Education*, Vol. I, p. 32. She described the total effect of Rousseau's writings as 'a net of such exquisite art and inextricable workmanship, spread to entangle innocence and ensnare inexperience . . . unhappily, the victim does not even struggle in the toils, because part of the delusion consists in imagining that he is set at liberty' (*ibid.*, p. 34).

rational integration of the workers into the developing economic system, but his advocacy started out from the social causation of differences among men. 'The difference in natural talents in different men, is, in reality, much less than we are aware of', he asserted, in more guarded tones than Helvétius, but 'the difference between the most dissimilar characters, between a philosopher and a common street porter, for example, seems to arise not so much from nature, as from habit, custom and education'.[1] This could be described as the beginning of the process of reintroducing Locke to Britain via Helvétius. For a more far-reaching world picture, based on such an analysis, Britain had to wait until the French revolutionary situation and an intensification of domestic social problems had set ideological discussion more thoroughly in motion.

---

[1] *The Wealth of Nations*, World's Classics edition, 1904, Vol. I, p. 18.

CHAPTER II

Principles into Practice

(i) Perennial fountain of science

MODERN concepts of popular education, as of political democracy, leap into historical prominence in Britain in the 1790's. It is our concern here to see how, against the backcloth of the French Revolution, in the situation of growing industrialism, and through the activities of people and of movements concerned with the radical regeneration of British politics and society, some of the rationalist assumptions we have examined came to be disseminated, as a challenge to the established order of 'mental darkness' or 'mental glimmer'.

On October 4, 1793, Robert Owen attended his first meeting of the Manchester Literary and Philosophical Society,[1] and on one occasion, called on to give his comments in a discussion on cotton spinning, 'blushed, and stammered out some few incoherent sentences, and felt quite annoyed at my ignorance and awkwardness being thus exposed'.[2] In December 1793 the house of the Manchester radical, Thomas Walker, was attacked by a King-and-country mob; Tom Paine had been tried (in his absence) the previous year, and 1793–4 was the period of treason trials against booksellers and radicals (including Walker himself). Paine's *Rights of Man* had appeared in 1791–2, Mary Wollstonecraft's *A Vindication of the Rights of Men* in 1790 and her *A Vindication of the Rights of Woman* in 1792. Godwin's *Political Justice* appeared in 1793.

When Owen, therefore, at the age of twenty-two began to attend the meetings of the Manchester Literary and Philosophical Society, it was against a background not only of the expansion of Britain's, and particularly Manchester's, industry and population, but of social and intellectual conflict. Information about how, through the Society and elsewhere, he came to a greater self-confidence than he displayed in the

---

[1] See E. M. Fraser, 'Robert Owen in Manchester, 1787–1800' in the *Memoirs and Proceedings of the Manchester Literary and Philosophical Society*, Vol. LXXXII, 1937–8, p. 37. The Minute Books of the Society, on which Miss Fraser's paper was based, were destroyed in the last war.

[2] *Life*, p. 51.

discussion on cotton spinning, his contact with the world of ideas, and the growth of his conviction that some of the ideas of the Enlightenment we have discussed were not only true but practicable, is unfortunately fragmentary; in trying to piece the story together, however, we will be looking at a case study in the emergence of a whole new social outlook in Britain, in a recasting of the terms in which popular education was discussed.

Owen had arrived in Manchester in the late 1780's,[1] having previously worked as a draper's assistant, in Stamford and London, and highly conscious, as he was to be for many years, of his lack of any advanced education. In his *Life* he describes how, when he first became manager in a large mill in Manchester he had been 'a thoughtful, retiring character, extremely sensitive, and could seldom speak to a stranger without blushing, especially to one of the other sex ... and I was diffident of my own powers, knowing what a very imperfect and deficient education I had received'.[2]

Such schooling as Owen did have was in the small Newtown, in Wales, under, as Owen tells us, 'a Mr Thickness, or some such name'. He started school at the age of four or five, and learned to 'read fluently, write a legible hand, and understand the four first rules of arithmetic', which was considered 'a good education' in schools in these small towns, and in any case 'I have reason to believe ... the extent of Mr Thickness'a qualification for a schoolmaster—because when I had acquired these small rudiments of learning, at the age of seven, he applied to my father for permission that I should become his assistant and usher, as from that time I was called while I remained at school ... about two years longer'.[3] At the age of ten he set off for his first job, in Stamford.

The only record we have of Owen's early reading is in his autobiography. The books he read, he tells us, included '*Robinson Crusoe, Philip Quarle, Pilgrim's Progress, Paradise Lost,* Harvey's *Meditations*

[1] One would deduce from Owen's *Life* that it was 1786 (the date used by Margaret Cole in *Robert Owen of New Lanark*) or 1787 (used by Miss Fraser). W. H. Chaloner puts it at 'about 1788' (*Robert Owen, Peter Drinkwater and the Early Factory System in Manchester, 1788–1800*, Manchester, the John Rylands Library, 1954).

[2] *Life*, p. 38. In 1822, at the crest of his industrial fortunes, when called upon to speak at a meeting, he apologised 'for addressing you, because I feel how very incompetent I am to speak to this Meeting in the manner I wish: the want of an early education renders me unfit for the task ...' (*Proceedings of the First General Meeting of the British and Foreign Philanthropic Society*, London, 1822).

[3] *Life*, pp. 2–3.

among the Tombs, Young's *Night Thoughts*, Richardson's and all other standard novels'.[1] He also read navigators' voyages, some history 'and all the lives I could meet with of the philosophers and great men'. His employer in Stamford, a draper called McGuffog, in whose house he lived, had a 'well-selected library' and he read 'upon the average about five hours a day', though the only author he specifies is Seneca.[2] After three years in Stamford he moved to London, to a firm where the work was so hard that he had time to read only 'in the less busy season'.[3] Deductions about the ideological equipment with which Owen arrived in Manchester are therefore extremely difficult to make. Colonel M. Jullien, 'the philanthropic friend and historian of Peslatozzi',[4] is said to have claimed that with Owen:

> '. . . what first pleaded the cause of nature and of sense was reading the adventures of Robinson Crusoe, contemplating what might be called the manual and practical education of necessity, remote from the institutions of men, which are often maleficent . . .'[5]

Jullien may have heard Owen himself comment on the impact on him of this story of 'economic man'; Owen merely confirms that he had read the novel. We can only speculate, therefore, as to whether Defoe's novel, with its total situation of the absence of any dominant social institutions (or unmanageable natural handicaps), contributed to Owen's receptivity to the rationalist position. We can do nothing but speculate, similarly, despite the attention the reference has subsequently attracted, as to the importance of the mention of Seneca;[6] the only useful clue in the reference is to the fact that Owen was no doubt familiar at this early

[1] *Ibid.*, p. 4.
[2] *Ibid.*, pp. 18–19.
[3] *Ibid.*, p. 27.
[4] R. R. Rusk, *A History of Infant Education*, London, 1951, p. 29.
[5] Quoted from an anomymous, undated newspaper cutting in a copy of Six Lectures by Owen, in the Reference Library at Newcastle-upon-Tyne. 'Julian de Paris' visited New Lanark and became friendly with Owen (see *Life*, pp. 228–9), who presented him to the Co-operative Congress in October 1833 (*The Crisis*, Vol. III, No. 7/8, October 19, 1833).
[6] Joseph McCabe, discussing Owen's theory of character formation, offered the view that Seneca and the Stoic 'charity of the human race' probably had 'much to do with it. They never had a younger convert . . . and one may question if they had ever made a more momentous convert since the death of Rome' (*Robert Owen*, London, 1920, p. 6). For a fictionalised version of this theme, see R. R. Wagner, *Lebensroman eines Menschengläubigen*, Zürich, 1942, p. 34.

stage with habits of abstract thought, and above all with simple humanitarian philosophy.

He was familiar, similarly, with religious controversy. He tells us that when he was probably eight or nine, some friends of the family, gave him Methodist books to read, being 'desirous to convert me to their peculiar faith'. He read these and other religious works 'of all parties' and was surprised, 'first at the opposition between the different sects of Christians, afterwards at the deadly hatred between the Jews, Christians, Mahomedans, Hindoos, Chinese, etc. etc., and between these and what they called Pagans and Infidels'.[1] And so, he tells, at the age of ten he became convinced that there must be something fundamentally wrong in all religions, as they had been taught up to that period'.[2] He went on to abandon the Christian religion and 'all others'.[3]

His first job in Manchester was again with a draper, but before long, on borrowed capital, he was in partnership on a small scale making machinery for spinning cotton and in 1792 he became manager over some five hundred workpeople at the new mill of Peter Drinkwater.[4] Relatively inexperienced and awkward in his social relations, he assiduously devoted himself to learning the complexities of his new and responsible task. He remained at Drinkwater's, acquiring a growing reputation as a spinner of fine cotton, probably until 1794, when, feeling that Drinkwater was not keeping faith with him over an agreement that he should become a partner, he left and entered into a partnership which was to build cotton mills, and then into another partnership—the Chorlton Twist Company, of which he was manager in Manchester from 1796 to 1800.[5] Owen's reputation as a cotton spinner had won him a leading position in the world of industry.

Peter Drinkwater held relatively advanced views on some aspects of factory organisation. In a letter on the subject of sanitary arrangements, for example, he indicated that 'the object of keeping the factory sweet

[1] *Life*, p. 4.
[2] *Ibid.*, p. 5.
[3] *Ibid.*, p. 22. For a Catholic view of Owen's religious difficulties, evoking the ghosts of Knox and Calvin, see Joseph H. Fichte, *Roots of Change*, New York, 1939, p. 90 (Chapter V is about Owen).
[4] For details of Owen's partnership and his subsequent position as Drinkwater's manager, see Chaloner, *Robert Owen, Peter Drinkwater and the Early Factory System in Manchester*, and *Life*, pp. 30–62. Chaloner corrects some faulty dates in the latter.
[5] Unfortunately, in his autobiography Owen gives no details about the period 1796–1800, and there are no other sources of information.

and wholesome at this point is a matter which I cannot help considering of the utmost importance, whether as regards decency, convenience or humanity'.[1] The fact that Drinkwater's mill was in any sense at all well-run, or humanely run, in a period such as this, is of considerable importance to the examination of Owen's future development. Owen himself claimed that by the time he became Drinkwater's manager he had 'perceived the constant influence of circumstances over my own proceedings and those of others'. He had come to the conclusion that 'man could not make his own organization, or any one of its qualities, and that these qualities were according to their nature, more or less influenced by the circumstances which occurred in the life of each . . . I therefore viewed human nature in my fellow-creatures . . . with far more charity'. This, in his view, enabled him to exert 'complete influence' over the workpeople within six months, and 'their order and discipline exceeded that of any other in or near Manchester'.[2]

This does not mean, of course, that Drinkwater's was a model mill, or that Owen was undertaking a community experiment there. The point is that Drinkwater's ideas and the conditions in the mill were progressive from both the industrial and humanitarian points of view, and that any step beyond the general level of callous industrial conditions cannot have failed to influence Owen into considering the possibility of more substantial steps.[3]

Owen himself repeatedly emphasised later in life the importance of his experience at Drinkwater's. In 1834, for example, during a controversy on the origin of infant schools, he wrote that:

'In consequence of having a large population of the working classes

[1] Quoted in Chaloner, *Robert Owen . . . and the Early Factory System*, p. 90. A German commentator, Adolph Röhl, entirely missed the point in asserting that Owen's activities in Manchester were of no interest because they were the same as in any other well-run enterprise of the time ('Owens Unternehmungen in Manchester vor dem Jahre 1800 unterscheiden sich durch nichts von den anderen gut geleiteten Betrieben seiner Zeit; sie bedürfen darum keiner besondern Betrachtung' (*Die Beziehungen zwischen Wirtschaft und Erziehung im Sozialismus Robert Owens*, Hamburg, 1930, p. 72, note).

[2] *Life*, pp. 41–2.

[3] Chaloner suggests that it would be interesting to know 'whether Drinkwater's sentiments and the conditions in the Piccadilly Factory influenced Owen's later experiments at New Lanark' (*Robert Owen . . . and the Early Factory System*, p. 90), but himself shows the importance of the conditions at the mill. Axon, in *Annals of Manchester*, is categorical: Owen 'became manager of a cotton mill in Manchester, where he distinguished himself by business ability and care for the workpeople' (p. 276).

under my direction in Manchester from 1791 to 1799, and a still larger number at New Lanark from that period . . . I could not avoid seeing the very unfavourable and often very pernicious circumstances in which the children of these classes were placed . . . I was determined to apply this knowledge to practice.'[1]

Even more important is Owen's assertion in the first essay of *A New View of Society* (Owen wrote this essay in 1812, though it was not published for sale until 1816), that his views had arisen 'from extensive experience for upwards of twenty years, during which period its truth and importance have been proved by multiplied experiment'.[2] Allowing for exaggeration and over-enthusiasm, we are left in no doubt that Owen later considered his experiments to have in some sense included his industrial experience in Manchester, so much so that in the second essay of *A New View*, written in the following year, he described himself as succeeding in 'reforming the habits of those under his care' in Manchester 'by the steady application of certain general principles'.[3] He went so far, in fact, as to speak of his experience in Manchester as of his first, though limited, attempt to apply the principles for which by 1816 he was already becoming famous.[4]

Owen's experience at Drinkwater's mill certainly coincided with and reinforced the widening intellectual experience Manchester provided for him, and it is only as a part of a broad pattern of social experience that his industrial career assumes importance. Fortunately, though fragmentary and often circumstantial, the evidence of Owen's participation in the social and intellectual life of Manchester from the early 1790's to his departure for New Lanark at the end of this immensely important decade, is more coherent than for the earlier years.

It is important to remember, however, turbulent though the radical politics of Manchester in the 1790's may have been, that they were certainly not at the centre and were probably not even within the periphery of Owen's concerns. The Manchester radicals, members and

[1] *N.M.W.*, Vol. I, No. 1, November 1, 1834.
[2] *A New View*, p. 15.
[3] *Ibid.*, p. 29.
[4] See *ibid.*, p. 95. For other examples of such a stress in Owen's writings, see *An Address to the Inhabitants of New Lanark*, in *ibid.*, p. 93 ('long before I came to reside among you, it had been my chief study to discover . . .'); *Address* of August 14, 1817, in *Life*, Vol. IA, p. 101 ('devoted nearly thirty years to deep research and active experiment . . .'), and *Address to Infant-School Societies*, January, 1830, *N.M.W.*, Vol. II, No. 66, January 30, 1836 ('from a practice of ten years previously, at Manchester, I had experienced . . .').

supporters of the Manchester Constitutional Society,[1] suffered badly at the hands of the mob with, for example, the shop where the radical *Manchester Herald* was printed, and Thomas Walker's house, being attacked. The *Herald* had to close down in 1793.[2] In September 1792, 186 innkeepers and ale-house keepers, 'afraid of losing their licences, and anxious to secure the custom of the party which was at once the most bigoted and the most thirsty', signed a paper expressing their alarm at sedition and declaring:

> '*we will not suffer* any meeting to be held in our houses of any CLUB or societies ... that have a tendency to put in force what those INFERNALS so *ardently* and *devoutly wish for*, namely, the DESTRUCTION OF THIS COUNTRY ...'[3]

But the activities of the parliamentary reformers, and the social turbulence of the early years of the war with France, were not, so far as we know, of major concern to Owen. His points of social involvement lay elsewhere.[4]

By 1793 Owen's reputation as a spinner of fine cotton stood high, and he had made a number of important local contacts. He tells us that there were two 'popular and celebrated' institutions in Manchester, the Literary and Philosophical Society, and what he calls ' "Manchester College", under Dr Baines'.[5] At this period, 'John Dalton, the Quaker, afterwards the celebrated Dr Dalton the philosopher, and a Mr Winstanley, both intimate friends of mine, were assistants in this college ... and in their room we often met in the evenings, and had much and frequent interesting discussions upon religion, morals, and other similar subjects, as well as upon the late discoveries in chemistry and other sciences—and here Dalton first broached his then undefined

---

[1] Founded in October 1790 to 'effect a reform in the representation of the people in Parliament' (Axon, *The Annals of Manchester*, p. 117), as were societies in a number of cities.

[2] See Archibald Prentice, *Historical Sketches and Personal Recollections of Manchester*, London, 1851, p. 5.

[3] *Ibid.*, p. 8. As late as 1825, says Prentice, inscriptions were seen on Manchester inns proclaiming 'NO JACOBINS ADMITTED HERE' (*ibid.*, p. 7). Axon records that in January 1793 'the effigy of Paine was burnt by the populace' (*The Annals of Manchester*, p. 120).

[4] This foreshadows Owen's life-long lack of interest in parliamentary reform. Owen was as little excited by the persecution of the reformers, it would appear, as he was by the reform movement itself.

[5] This is Manchester New College or Academy, instituted in 1786, and 'Baines' is a mistake for Rev. Thomas Barnes.

atomic theory'.[1] Such contact with the Academy and the discussions of this informal group cannot have begun before 1793 (in which year Dalton was appointed tutor at the Academy[2]), unless the discussions began without Dalton. One of Dalton's sponsors for membership of the Literary and Philosophical Society on October 3, 1794, was Owen.[3]

The group occasionally admitted a friend or two to their circle, and one such guest was Coleridge. With his typically casual immodesty, Owen relates that Coleridge was at this period:

'studying at one of the universities, and was then considered a genius and eloquent. He solicited permission to join our party, that he might meet me in discussion, as I was the one who opposed the religious prejudices of all sects . . . Mr Coleridge had a great fluency of words . . . but my few words, directly to the point, generally told well; and although the eloquence and learning were with him, the strength of the argument was generally admitted to be on my side.'[4]

Owen also relates how he and 'that ultimately ill-used man of genius and high enterprise', Robert Fulton, 'were boarding inmates' together in Manchester, and Owen gives the text of letters from, and a partnership agreement with, Fulton between 1794 and 1797.[5] J. H. Nodal speculated as to whether

'the scheme for a Pantisocracy on the banks of the Susquehannah', which Coleridge planned shortly after leaving college with Southey, Wordsworth, and Lovell, was 'due to conversations with Robert Owen . . .?'[6]

[1] *Life*, p. 49.
[2] See, for example, Sir Henry E. Roscoe, *John Dalton and the Rise of Modern Chemistry*, London, 1895: 'the college in which Dalton became tutor (in 1793) in mathematics and natural philosophy was one established by the Presbyterians of Manchester as a continuation of the Warrington Academy . . .' (p. 49). The Manchester Academy was, in fact, like its Warrington predecessor, a *Unitarian* institution.
[3] *Ibid.*, p. 71 (note).
[4] *Life*, pp. 49–50. For a discussion of Coleridge and Manchester in the 1790's see *Notes and Queries*, 5th series, Vol. vii, March 3, 1877, p. 161 (J. H. Nodal, 'Coleridge in Manchester') and p. 311. The dates are obscure, but Nodal accepts that Owen's statements 'are too circumstantial to warrant their absolute rejection'.
[5] *Ibid.*, pp. 89–97. Owen was always interested in schemes for progress in science, industry and social organisation. Robert Dale Owen, mentions, for example, Owen's interest in Rowland Hill's scheme for postal reform (*Threading My Way*, London, 1874, pp. 309–10).
[6] *Notes and Queries*, Vol. vii, p. 161.

One answer was that it was just as likely that 'the American location was influenced by Robert Fulton, because Owen's notions then were rather in favour of a home site for his world'.[1] The specific point behind both the question and the answer is unimportant here; what is important is that they remind us that Owen had now established contact with a group of people with whom he was involved in a wide-ranging discussion of religious, scientific and social issues.

How he came to be introduced to the Literary and Philosophical Society is again a matter for conjecture. It has been suggested that Dr Barnes, one of the founders of the Society, and principal of the Academy, may have been the one 'who first suggested that Owen might be asked to join'.[2] Owen tells us that the discussions he was having with Dalton and others attracted the attention of Barnes, 'who became afraid that I should convert his assistants from his orthodoxy; and our meetings were required to be less frequent in the college. They were, however, continued elsewhere.'[3] The fact is that by the end of 1793 Owen was well enough known in industrial circles, and had acquired sufficient of a reputation in Manchester, to be admitted to the Society.

The Manchester Literary and Philosophical Society was largely the creation of Dr Thomas Percival, and Owen's contact with Percival himself as well as with the Society was to be of decisive importance in his thinking. Percival had settled in Manchester in 1767,[4] and from the 1770's onwards his home was a centre for discussion among local and visiting men of intellect.[5] The discussions were transferred to a tavern, and became the Literary and Philosophical Society on February 28, 1781, with Percival as its first President.

Percival had been educated at the Warrington Academy, where he knew Joseph Priestley well, had studied medicine at Edinburgh, and was elected a Fellow of the Royal Society at the age of twenty-five. He became a physician in Manchester, already with a wide circle of acquaintances in the world of enlightenment. Thomas de Quincey

---

[1] Hyde Clarke, 'Coleridge: Fulton: Priestley', in *Notes and Queries*, 5th Series, vol. vii, p. 217.

[2] Fraser, 'Robert Owen in Manchester,' p. 36.

[3] *Life*, p. 50. The dates, again, are confusing.

[4] The fullest account of Percival's career is Royden Birtley Hope, 'Dr Thomas Percival, A Medical Pioneer and Social Reformer, 1740–1804', an M.A. thesis of Manchester University.

[5] 'He was in the habit of holding at his house weekly meetings . . . attended by his own friends . . . and by occasional strangers' (Francis Espinasse, *Lancashire Worthies*, Second Series, London, 1877, p. 189).

described him as 'a favoured correspondent of the most eminent Frenchmen at that time who cultivated literature jointly with philosophy. Voltaire, Diderot, Maupertuis, Condorcet, and d'Alembert had all treated him with distinction.'[1] Percival's four-volume *Works*[2] reveal a dedicated, rational man of culture, similar in the breadth of his interests and his vision of a better world through science (in his case, medicine) and early moral training, to his friend Joseph Priestley. Priestley and Percival both recognised the crucial importance of education, with its primary object 'to form valuable characters, and to prepare men for the most important stations in life,'[3] in the tradition of Locke. They were concerned, like Locke, not with *mass* education, but with *correct* education. For Percival reading, writing and arithmetic were favourable not only to 'skill and advancement in the arts', but also 'to subordination, peaceableness, sobriety, and honesty'.[4] The point, however, is not so much that Percival's views on education were in general more limited than his overall philosophy, as that he was interested in education at all. We shall see that, however strongly Percival might have resisted the idea of state intervention in education, his devotion to problems of health reform, particularly in relation to industry, led him into the field of industrial and charity education. A scientist, a rationalist, familiar with the works and in some cases the personalities of the French Enlightenment, on intimate terms with men like Benjamin Franklin and Joseph Priestley,[5] and devoted to work for practical social reform, Percival was clearly an influential figure.

Without any detailed records of the Manchester Literary and Philosophical Society, a certain amount of conjecture goes into any picture of the general atmosphere Owen found in it. The kind of people who joined the Society obviously included many of the more enlightened industrialists and of the professional men of the town. Owen's comments

[1] Quoted from his *Autobiographical Sketches*, in Espinasse, *Lancashire Worthies*, p. 174. Miss Fraser describes him as 'a true eighteenth-century philosopher in the French sense, a believer in science, civilisation, and progress' ('Robert Owen in Manchester', p. 39).

[2] *The Works, Literary, Moral, Philosophical, and Medical, of Thomas Percival, M.D.*, London, 1807.

[3] Joseph Priestley, *A Discourse: The Proper Object of Education in the Present State of the World* (1791), in *The Theological and Miscellaneous Works of Joseph Priestley*, edited by J. T. Rutt 1831, Vol. XXV, p. 421.

[4] *Miscellaneous Communications to a Young Clergyman*, in *Works*, Vol. I, p. 319.

[5] In 1784 Percival persuaded the Society to donate £50 to help Priestley's research.

on his introduction to the Society tell us a little. When he joined he was 'introduced to the leading professional characters, particularly in the medical profession, which at this period stood high in Manchester, and its leading members were the aristocracy of the town. The manufacturers at this period were generally plodding men of business . . . The foreign merchants, or rather the merchants in the foreign trade, were somewhat more advanced . . .'[1] Donald Read describes the leaders of the eighteenth century cotton industry as 'a small, wealthy and exclusive circle of merchants with some pretensions to luxury and culture . . . The more reflective among them participated in the discussions of the famous Manchester Literary and Philosophical Society . . . Their religious and political creeds were those natural to a prosperous, contented class, Anglican and tory.'[2] This may be true of the class of merchants as a whole, but the deduction that such an 'Anglican and tory' would feel entirely at home in the Society would be misleading. Its principal founders were Unitarian and, at least, in philosophy, radical. Manchester's leading parliamentary reformer, Thomas Walker, in the 1780's regularly attended the meetings of the Society where he met his friends:

> 'Dr Ferriar, one of the chief physicians at the local Infirmary, who was an excellent doctor with advanced ideas; Joseph Collier, the surgeon; Samuel Jackson, a progressive cotton merchant like himself; Thomas Cooper, a brilliant lawyer and research chemist in a local bleachers' firm—a dynamic personality whose bitingly witty pen was constantly in action against obscurantism and reaction.'[3]

That in the 1790's the Society fought shy of being identified with Jacobinism is clear. Percival's failure in 1791 to persuade the Society to send a letter of sympathy to Joseph Priestley, after his home was wrecked by a Birmingham mob, is clear enough evidence of this. But prudence and caution do not mean Anglicanism and Toryism. The admission of Owen to membership in 1793, if his religious views were known, and the admission of Dalton (scarcely an Anglican), in 1794, are helpful clues as to the composition of the Society at the time.[4]

[1] *Life*, p. 50.
[2] Donald Read, *Press and People 1790–1850*, London, 1961, p. 7.
[3] Knight, *The Strange Case of Thomas Walker*, p. 13.
[4] The Society's Corresponding Members included Priestley and Benjamin Franklin, Gilbert Wakefield, 'the distinguished classicist who was jailed for supporting the French Revolution, William Hawes the founder of the Royal

Owen tells us (there is no other testimony for this) that he was 'introduced to the *elite* of the . . . Society, for I had not been long a member . . . before I was requested to become a member of its committee, a club which was composed of what were considered the select and most efficient members of the society, and which met always immediately after the regular sittings of the society'.[1] This committee included Dr Percival and Dr Ferriar (a fellow physician of Percival's at the Infirmary, and, as we have seen, a close friend of Thomas Walker).

That Owen was in Percival's circle of close associates can be seen from another, and highly important, development, one which, curiously, Owen does not mention in his autobiography. In 1795, after a series of fever epidemics in the Lancashire mills, including a particularly violent one in a cotton mill near Manchester belonging to Sir Robert Peel, Percival helped to set up a Manchester Board of Health to investigate the cause of the outbreaks. A meeting was called on January 7, 1796 'to consider proper means to secure the general health of the town and neighbourhood of Manchester from the contagion of an infectious fever, which has long prevailed amongst the manufacturing poor'.[2] A committee was appointed at the meeting, including Percival and Owen, and Percival produced for publication on January 25, 1796, a famous set of 'Heads of Resolutions for the consideration of the Board of Health'.[3] There is no further record of Owen's participation in the work of this committee, but that he was associated with the work of the Board of Health is indisputable, and that he therefore encountered at one of its most crucial points the work of social reform is of vital importance. The Manchester Board of Health, and Percival's Heads of Resolutions are an obvious point at which the whole apparatus of eighteenth century radical philosophy and its concomitant humanitarianism became transmuted into social action in Britain. And Owen was present at the event.

Percival's document contains five points, the first of which begins:

Humane Society . . . and a whole host of others . . . of the leading minds which at the end of the eighteenth century were steadily and consistently interested in new developments in society a very high proportion were associated with the Manchester Lit. and Phil. . . .' (Margaret Cole, *Robert Owen of New Lanark*, p. 19).

[1] *Life*, pp. 50–1.
[2] *Proceedings of the Manchester Board of Health*, Manchester, n.d., p. 1. This publication consists of selections from the Journals of the Board, 1796–1805.
[3] *Ibid.*, p. 33.

'It appears that the children and others who work in the large cotton-factories, are peculiarly disposed to be affected by the contagion of fever . . .'

The next two items attack conditions in the large factories as 'generally injurious to the constitution of those employed in them', citing 'the debilitating effects of hot or impure air' and the lack of proper exercise 'which nature points out as essential in childhood and youth', and the harmful physical and social effects of 'the untimely labour of the night, and the protracted labour of the day, with respect to children . . .' The importance of item four in this context can scarcely be over-estimated:

'It appears that the children employed in the factories are generally debarred from all opportunities of education and from moral and religious instruction.'

The document, finally, appeals for support from 'the liberal proprietors' of those cotton factories where 'excellent regulations . . . subsist' in obtaining Parliamentary aid '(if other methods appear not likely to effect the purpose,) to establish a general system of laws for the wise, humane, and equal government of all such works'.

Another member of the Board was Sir Robert Peel himself, and out of this set of resolutions sprang his Act of 1802, the Health and Morals of Apprentices Act, attempting to regulate industrial conditions in this way.[1] Owen was later, in 1815, to impel Peel to introduce a further bill to amend and extend the Act of 1802. Owen was now firmly committed to the idea of state action.

Within the Society, he heard papers and discussion on a wide variety of topics, but a substantial part of the Society's activities related to industrial and scientific questions. Miss Fraser estimated that Owen 'attended not more than forty-one and not less than thirty-seven meetings of the Literary and Philosophical Society during his years at

---

[1] S. E. Maltby, *Manchester and the Movement for National Elementary Education, 1800–1870*, Manchester, 1918, summarises the effects of the work of this Board as follows: 'That Robert Owen was a member of the Board of Health, and likewise the first Sir Robert Peel, a friend of Percival, is of the utmost significance, for in this way the two most successful cotton manufacturers of their day came into touch with the cruelties so bound up with their business, and at once accepted the idea of legal control, regulations and State compulsion on employers to abolish them . . . The seed sown by them (Peel and Owen) was good; but the soil of public opinion was not ready to receive it . . .' (p. 17).

Manchester',[1] and gives an idea, from the Minute Books,[2] of the discussions that took place on:

> 'Many literary subjects, many medical subjects, generally of a humanitarian nature. We note the interest taken in Manchester's staple industry . . . A meeting discusses Daubenton's "Memoirs on the improvement of wool" . . . Public health, citizenship, civilisation —these are the main themes . . . Dr Bardsley on "Party prejudice, moral and political" . . . Dr John Ferriar on "Genius and modern Prophets". "Cursory observations, moral and political, on the state of the poor and lower classes in society" . . . by Dr Bardsley, may well have contained ideas of special interest to Owen . . .'[3]

Owen's own comment is that the meetings were 'pleasant and useful to me; making me familiar with the ideas, habits, and prejudices of a new class in society.'[4]

Dr Ferriar's paper on 'Genius and Modern Prophets' is presumably the one Owen refers to in his autobiography, when he tells us that Ferriar endeavoured 'to prove that any one, by his own will, might become a genius.' Ferriar's paper, according to Owen, was followed by a silence. He had taken Dalton and Winstanley with him as guests, was disappointed that no one was starting a discussion and rose 'merely with a view to induce a debate'. The paper he said, was learned and ingenious:

> ' "But as it was read it occurred to me that I have always had a great desire to become a genius, and have always been very industrious in my application for the purpose, but I could never succeed. I therefore am obliged to conclude that there must be some error unexplained in our learned author's theory." . . . Dr Ferriar . . . stammered out some confused reply . . . and a discussion followed.'[4]

How much discussion Owen heard on the subject of education is not certain. If he heard Bardsley on 'Party Prejudice' in April 1794 he will have heard support for the idea of inspiring youth 'with a rational zeal for the preservation of its liberties and blessings', but also of making

---

[1] 'Robert Owen in Manchester', p. 38.
[2] The papers published in the *Memoirs* necessarily give only a partial picture of the range of discussion.
[3] *Ibid.*, pp. 37–8.
[4] *Life*, pp. 52–3.

them 'acquainted with the history and transactions of its party divisions'.[1] If Owen's account of his reaction to Dr Ferriar's paper is at all reliable, he was in a frame of mind to question and challenge even if only 'with a view to induce debate'.

Having become a member of the Society's committee, Owen wrote his 'expected paper for each session; but on what subjects they were written I do not now recollect'.[2] He did, in fact, present four papers to the Society, none of which was published in the Society's *Memoirs*.[3]

The main question that remains unanswered, however, is the extent to which, and the form in which, radical and rationalist ideas circulated inside the Society during these years when all such ideas lurked under the shadow of suspicion and persecution. We have seen that the Society was extremely careful to avoid any public association with 'Jacobin' ideas, and the *Memoirs* of the Society certainly contain no hint of any discussion of heretical ideas, presenting the image of a Society concerned with literary, industrial and scientific questions. Have we any right to assume that in Manchester, in the Society, and in his association with members of the Society, Owen did, in fact, encounter to any significant extent the liberal ideas of contemporary writers and thinkers?

Any attempt to answer this question, given the absence of details about the Manchester Society, must rely on circumstantial evidence from other sources. It will be helpful to supplement what we know of the Manchester Society and of men like Percival with a picture of another Literary and Philosophical Society about which more relevant information is available.

The Literary and Philosophical Society of Newcastle Upon Tyne, a younger sister of the Manchester Society, began with the publication in 1792, by William Turner, Jun., of some *Speculations on the Propriety of Attempting the Establishment of a Literary Society in Newcastle*, republished with some modifications in 1793 under the title *Plan of the Literary and Philosophical Society of Newcastle Upon Tyne*, which had in fact been instituted on February 7 of that year, twelve years after the

---

[1] *Memoirs of the Manchester Literary and Philosophical Society*, Vol. 5, Pt. I, pp. 7–8.

[2] *Life*, p. 53.

[3] The titles were: 'Remarks on the improvement of the cotton trade', 'The utility of learning', 'Thoughts on the connection between universal happiness and practical mechanics' and 'On the origin of opinions, with a view to the improvement of social virtues' (see Fraser, 'Robert Owen in Manchester', p. 37). Conjecturing from these titles is not very helpful.

Manchester Society.[1] The *Plan* begins with the following indication of
its debt to the Manchester Society:

> 'Among the various causes of the rapid advancement of science,
> which has taken place in modern times, the institution of Philosophi-
> cal Societies in one of the most obvious and important ... in
> England, the Literary and Philosophical Society of Manchester has
> not only been eminently serviceable to that flourishing town, by
> leading the attention of several of its members to pursuits connected
> with improvement of its extensive manufactures, but it has greatly
> contributed to the general instruction and entertainment, by the
> publication of its Memoirs.'

This is certainly the image that the Manchester Society wished to
present of itself, and the founders of the Newcastle Society adapted the
Manchester situation, stressing that the main purpose of the new
Society would be to encourage research into coal and lead, navigation,
and so on, in conjunction with its literary and historical pursuits. Subjects on which papers had already been presented indicates the *Plan*, in
appealing for public support, included, for example:

—The discovery of a species of air possessed in an extraordinary
  degree of the property of exciting and maintaining combustion;
—the cultivation of taste;
—the settlement at Sierra Leone;
—some ancient pigs of lead and remains of antiquity in Cumberland
  and Northumberland;
—the difference between poetry and prose.

Such items and the Society's account of itself at this stage indicate how
closely it modelled itself on the Manchester pattern. By this *Plan*, said
a member of the Society writing in 1809;

> 'The miner, the mechanic, the manufacturer, the agriculturalist, the
> naturalist, the virtuoso, and the classical scholar, were all promised
> a participation in the great advantages expected to flow from this
> newly opened, perennial fountain of science.'[2]

[1] Turner, a Unitarian minister, was educated at the Warrington Academy.
See Brian Simon, *Studies in the History of Education 1780–1870*, London, 1960,
p. 30.
[2] *A Brief Account of the Literary and Philosophical Society and of the New
Institution of Newcastle Upon Tyne*, by a member of the Society, Newcastle Upon
Tyne, 1809, p. 4.

From its foundation, however, the Newcastle Society was beset with difficulties which were much less acute in Manchester. By the time the heresy-hunt of the mid-1790's took place, the Manchester Society was well established, and had a local, national and international reputation which helped it to weather the storms. The Newcastle Society was being founded in the midst of 'the horror of French liberalism and philosophy' which was at the time 'at a pitch of frenzy, which caused many parties to dread the diffusion of knowledge'.[1] The pressure against the Society was very strong, and led to crises and factionalism in the Society,[2] and also to the adoption of an attitude which, though felt more acutely necessary than in Manchester, probably reflected the situation in Manchester also:

'Notwithstanding the catholic and literary spirit in which the Society was founded, accusations were brought against it at the time, which was one of high political excitement, as if the real objects entertained were disguised, and as if political objects had been discussed at its meetings, and jacobinical opinions fostered by its members ... a law was framed (in the Society) to exclude all such subjects of excitement ...'[3]

The attacks on the Society appear also to have been made more acute in Newcastle by the fact that a small Philosophical Society had come into existence on March 15, 1775, 'for the consideration of questions of mental and social philosophy'.[4] It 'would have been unknown to fame if it had not chanced to include amongst them a certain Thomas Spence'.[5] In November 1775, this Society expelled Spence for publishing, without the Society's approval, 'a lecture with the title "Property in Land every One's Right", "which he had delivered at a former meeting, of which they disclaim all patronage".'[6]

The existence of the previous society, and its association with the

---

[1] R. M. Glover, *Remarks on the History of the Literary and Philosophical Society of Newcastle Upon Tyne*, Newcastle, 1844, p. 11.

[2] *A Brief Account* by a Member describes this situation.

[3] Glover, *Remarks*, p. 10.

[4] R. S. Watson, *The History of the Literary and Philosophical Society of Newcastle-Upon-Tyne (1793–1896)*, London, 1897, p. 15. Glover gives the date erroneously as 1777.

[5] *Ibid.*, pp. 15–16.

[6] *Ibid.*, p. 16. Podmore also mentions this incident, relating how Owen's community schemes were popularly associated with Spence's plans for common ownership of the land (*Robert Owen*, pp. 230–1).

name of Spence, proved to be 'the cause of some obloquy being directed by mistake against the Literary and Philosophical Society as if that Institution had been political at its commencement'.[1] The fact that the foundation of this early Society was popularly believed to have been associated also with Jean-Paul Marat, who was at that time living in Newcastle, and wrote his *Chains of Slavery* there, makes the reasons for the obloquy all the more obvious.[2] The Manchester Society cannot have escaped similar attack.

The Member of the Society writing in 1809 makes it absolutely clear that in his view at least the real purpose of the Society was the provision of a library, a service of much greater value than the lectures. The records of the Society show that between March 8, 1793 and March 1801, the amount spent on books for the library was £792 13s. 8d.[3] A *Catalogue of Books* (1798) in the Society's library includes the following items:

> Bentham on Morals and Legislation
> Eden's (Sir Fred.) State of the Poor
> Helvétius on the Mind
> Howard's State of Prisons
> Godwin's Political Justice
> Godwin's Enquirer
> Helvétius on Man
> Price and Priestley on Materialism
> Priestley on Air
> — Lectures on History
> — on Atmospheric Air
> — on Education
> — 's Disquisitions, &c.
> Reports of the Society for bettering the Condition of the Poor
> Wollstonecraft's Rights of Women
> Wollstonecraft's Posthumous Works, 5 vols.

[1] Glover, *Remarks*, p. 7. Watson also adds that the appointment of a Robert Spence as Librarian of the Society in 1797 further complicated the matter (p. 25).

[2] Watson refers to the supposition that Marat was the 'instigator, if not founder, of this Society (p. 16). Marat left England in 1777 (see E. B. Bax, *Jean-Paul Marat: The People's Friend*, London, 1900, second edition 1901, p. 36). Marat, to complete the coincidences, may have for a period been tutor in French at Warrington Academy (see *ibid.*, p. 27, and *The Manchester Guardian*, October 19, 1957, article on 'Warrington—an Origin of New Traditions in Education').

[3] 'Two Volumes of Papers Read and other MSS Records', in Newcastle Reference Library.

Through books like Eden's *State of the Poor* (1797) and the Reports of the Society for bettering the Condition of the Poor (founded in 1796) the Society's members will have been able to acquaint themselves with charitable, 'limiting' and far from unorthodox analyses of major social problems (including, of course, in the case of the latter, popular education). More important, readily available were the works of writers like Price and Priestley on non-scientific as well as scientific subjects. Above all, such names as Helvétius, Godwin and Mary Wollstonecraft appear in the list.

There is no parallel list of library books belonging to the Manchester Society, and we cannot assume that it would contain the same names. Knowing the composition of the Manchester Society, however, and the key role played in it by men like Percival and Ferriar (whose friend Thomas Walker was also a 'sincere friend' of Paine[1]), we can but assume that works like Godwin's *Political Justice* and Mary Wollstonecraft's *A Vindication of the Rights of Woman* circulated and were discussed among members of the Society (however informally), as, of course, they did in radical circles in general during this period.

We have Owen's testimony to the fact that he used to read enthusiastically before he came to Manchester, though we know that in later life he read little. How much he read while in Manchester we cannot guess, but it is evident that the kind of atmosphere Owen found among his acquaintances there was one in which liberal ideas of all kinds will have been anatomised, if not accepted. The position in the Newcastle Society cannot but confirm that it was at the centre of keen discussion in the forum of the Literary and Philosophical Society that Owen must have become familiar with the ideas of thinkers like Paine, Godwin and Mary Wollstonecraft.

(ii) *Mock not their ignorance*

What, then, were the ideas about education available to Owen? Attempts have been made to link his name with distant predecessors, such as More and Campanella[2] and Winstanley.[3] Of the eighteenth

---

[1] See Knight, *The Strange Case of Thomas Walker*, p. 64.

[2] Professor A. Anekshtein, in *Pedagogischeskiye Idei Roberta Owena*, Moscow, 1940, discussing the fact that Owen's educational efforts were directed towards communitarian life, adds: 'Of course, in this respect, More and Campanella are his predecessors' (p. 138).

[3] William Dale Morris, in *The Christian Origins of Social Revolt*, London, 1949, outlines Winstanley's belief in the efficacy of education, and concludes:

century continental philosophers, Morelly was singled out as an influence on Owen by G. J. Holyoake.[1]

None of this ancestry-hunting, however, is of any help. If, while in Manchester, Owen encountered views which helped to mould his own, and encountered a lot of them at second-hand, then the stimuli behind Owen's thinking lay, not in Winstanley or Bellers or Locke, but in the living ideas which were being read, talked about, challenged, revised and absorbed in the 1790's.

What, specifically, were the salient ideas about education which were 'in the air' during Owen's period in the Manchester Literary and Philosophical Society? To try to answer this question we must look in particular at the writers through whose work the kind of assumptions we have seen held by Helvétius came to prominence in Britain.

Godwin's *Political Justice* was, as we have seen, in the library of the Newcastle Literary and Philosophical Society, a fact which is all the more important when we remember that Godwin, unwilling to encourage tendencies towards violent change, published the book at the price of three guineas (a price which saved him from prosecution), and that the book therefore did not circulate as extensively as *The Rights of Man*.[2] It was published in February 1793,[3] shortly after the trial of Tom Paine. The impact of the book was enormous, especially on the younger generation of writers, like Coleridge and Wordsworth,[4] with its clear

'in the influence which his writing exerted on John Bellers, and through him upon Robert Owen, he is linked with the modern Socialist and Co-operative movements' (p. 138). Francis Place introduced Owen to John Bellers' 1696 pamphlet entitled *Proposals for raising a Colledge of Industry*, Owen published an edition of the pamphlet in 1818. See *Life*, Vol. IA, pp. 155–81.

[1] Through the agency of Francis Place, he suggests. See G. J. Holyoake, *The History of Co-operation*, London, 1875–9 (edition of 1908, p. 22). See also J. O. Hertzler, *The History of Utopian Thought*, London, 1922: 'Morelly claimed that evil arose from secondary and not from primary causes, in the maladjustment of social forces as indicated particularly by the environment. It could thus be eradicated and society redeemed . . . Here he foreshadowed Owen' (p. 187).

[2] Godwin had taken care 'that his disquisitions should reach none but educated readers . . . The price was three guineas, to make plain his intention of restricting the influence of the new doctrine to the upper classes' (Cestre, *John Thelwall*, pp. 133–4).

[3] *Enquiry concerning Political Justice and its Influence on Morals and Happiness*, London, 1793. Further editions were published in 1796 and 1798, in which Godwin made important modifications. References here are to the 1946 facsimile edition (based on the 1798 one), edited by F. E. L. Priestley.

[4] See Hazlitt's brilliant essay on Godwin in *The Spirit of the Age*, quoting Wordsworth's 'Throw aside your books of chemistry . . . and read Godwin on Necessity' (London, 1825, World's Classics edition 1928, p. 18).

message of the corruption of social institutions, and of the perfectibility of man by the renovation of government and society.

> 'Education,' said Godwin in the first edition, 'in the sense in which it has commonly been understood, though in one view an engine of unlimited power, is exceedingly incompetent to the great business of reforming mankind. It performs its task weakly . . . Where can a remedy be found for this fundamental disadvantage? where but in political justice, that all comprehensive scheme, that immediately applies to the removal of counteraction and contagion, that embraces millions in its grasp, and that educates in one school the preceptor and the pupil?'[1]

The assumptions behind Godwin's analysis of society and of man's position in it, are, with slight reservations, those of Helvétius. We need not here go into the details of how Godwin modified his initial complete acceptance of Helvétius' view of character as being completely moulded by environment, to a partial acceptance of innate differences. In the 1798 edition his position was still categorical enough: 'I shall attempt to prove that the actions and dispositions of mankind are the offspring of circumstances and events, and not of any original determination that they bring into the world . . . The actions and dispositions of men flow entirely from the operation of circumstances and events acting upon a faculty of receiving sensible impressions.'[2] Virtually using the same language as Helvétius, he throws the major responsibility for differences between individuals on environmental differences. Education, he insists, 'never can be equal. The inequality of external circumstances in two beings whose situations most nearly resemble, is so great as to baffle all power of calculation.'[3] This is Helvétius' 'infinité d'événements', producing the essential differences between individuals; compared with 'the empire of impression', says Godwin, 'the mere differences of animal structure are inexpressibly unimportant and powerless'.[4]

---

[1] *Political Justice*, Vol. III, p. 244.

[2] *Ibid.*, Vol. I, pp. 26–7. Godwin's reservation, a substantial one, is that there are 'real differences' between children at birth' 'Hercules and his brother, the robust infant whom scarcely any neglect can destroy, and the infant that is with difficulty reared, are undoubtedly from the moment of parturition very different beings' (p. 38).

[3] *Ibid.*, p. 39.

[4] *Ibid.*, p. 40. Godwin makes an indirect attack on the more thorough-going position of Helvétius (in the third edition): to claim 'that all minds, from the period of birth were precisely alike', would be 'an incautious statement' (p. 42).

On such a basis Godwin built, here and particularly in *The Enquirer*, a theory of education, of which, from our point of view, two main elements stand out. The first is the typical rationalist stress on the power of truth and reason:

> 'Speak the language of truth and reason to your child, and be under no apprehension for the result. Show him that what you recommend is valuable and desirable, and fear not but he will desire it . . .'[1]

Godwin's emphasis on this power was as strong as at any point in the French Enlightenment. Reason, he proclaimed, 'is the genuine exercise and truth the native element of an intellectual nature'.[2] The second important element is Godwin's interpretation of the educational process itself. He opposed a system of national education on a number of grounds, primarily 'on account of its obvious alliance with national government . . . Government will not fail to employ it, to strengthen its hands, and perpetuate its institutions',[3] but also because it is adverse to individuality, has an 'aversion to change'[4] and instead of inciting men to act for themselves retains them in 'a state of perpetual pupillage'.[5] Under a proper educational process, he suggests no one 'will be expected to learn any thing, but because he desires it, and has some conception of its value'.[6]

In *The Enquirer* Godwin laid considerable stress on this last point, making motivation the mainspring of the educational process. He starts from the hypothesis that 'the true object of education, like that of every other moral process, is the generation of happiness'.[7] He by-passes the issue of the extent of education's power to mould the individual because 'what may be the precise degree of difference with respect to capacity that children generally bring into the world with them, is a problem that it is perhaps impossible completely to solve'. But, he would have us remember, 'if education cannot do everything, it can do much'. Its effectiveness is dependent on 'accomplishment being ardently desired . . . Give but sufficient motive, and you have given every thing'.[8]

---

[1] *Ibid.*, p. 43.
[2] *Ibid.*, p. 48.
[3] *Ibid.*, Vol. II, p. 302. Book VI, Chapter VIII discusses this issue at length.
[4] *Ibid.*, p. 298.
[5] *Ibid.*, p. 301.
[6] *Ibid.*, pp. 512–13.
[7] *The Enquirer, Reflections on Education, Manners, and Literature*, London, 1797, p. 1.
[8] *Ibid.*, p. 3.

'The most desirable mode of education,' he emphasises, 'is that which is careful that all the acquisitions of the pupil shall be preceded and accompanied by desire. The best motive to learn, is a perception of the value of the thing learned . . . According to the received modes of education, the master goes first, and the pupil follows. According to the method here recommended, it is probable that the pupil should go first, and the master follow.'[1]

Godwin set his pedagogy against a backcloth of a philosophy of society. He was not concerned, as were Bell and Lancaster, with expedients and with preparation for a role in society, in habits of subordination, or in habits of anything except independent thought and attention to the happiness of others. The mainspring of correct social action, with Godwin, as with Helvétius, lay in a proper awareness of the self, in an understanding of how the happiness and well-being of others coincide with one's own happiness and well-being.

Godwin, in *Political Justice* and in *The Enquirer*, was, therefore, restating a humanist and liberal approach to both the power and the process of education, elements of which we have already seen in Locke and Helvétius. Both books, we have seen, were in the library of the Newcastle Literary and Philosophical Society, and during Owen's period of membership of the Manchester Society, which began in the same year as the publication of *Political Justice* and ended two years after the publication of *The Enquirer*, Godwin's fame was at its peak. It was primarily through these two works, in the period, let us remember, of the expansion of the Sunday school and the beginnings of the monitorial schools, that older and more expansive theories of human nature and of education returned most directly to the centre of ideological debate.[2]

Godwin's obvious influence on Owen's thinking has been frequently and rightly stressed. As early as 1817 a Congregational Minister in Edinburgh was pointing out that 'Owen's system of morals is substantially the same, or, at any rate, embraces the leading peculiarities of Godwin and his brother philosophists'.[3] A quarter of a century later,

---

[1] *Ibid.*, pp. 78–9.
[2] In the 1793 and 1796 editions of *Political Justice*, Godwin made slight acknowledgment of the influences of Locke, Hartley, Rousseau and Helvétius (see Cumming, *Helvétius*, p. 81).
[3] John Brown, *Remarks on the Plans and Publications of Robert Owen, Esq. of New Lanark*, Edinburgh, 1817, p. 39. For recent references to Owen's debt to

Professor W. Smyth who had believed that the world was in a more settled state and that Godwin's works had become impossible to read, confessed, in fact that he had lived 'to see all the doctrines of Godwin revived—they are the same as those which now infest the world and disgrace the human understanding, delivered by Mr Owen, the Chartists, and the St Simonians'.[1] Though Owen did, in fact, meet Godwin, the acquaintance was too late to be influential.[2] The only real evidence for the contact between Godwin and Owen that we have is a letter from Fanny Imlay to Mary Shelley,[3] a letter which tells us less about Godwin than it does about Mary Wollstonecraft. Fanny was writing to Mary, living in Geneva, about the poverty and suffering in England and Scotland, and outlined for her Owen's *Address to the People of New Lanark*, published in January of that year. She ended her comments with the words:

'So much for Mr Owen, who is, indeed, a very great and good man. He told me the other day that he wished our Mother were living, as he had never before met with a person who thought so exactly as he did, or who would have so warmly and zealously entered into his plans.'[4]

We have seen that 'Wollstonecraft's Rights of Woman' was in the catalogue of the Newcastle Literary and Philosophical Society library, together with *Political Justice* and *The Enquirer*; when Fanny quoted Owen as saying that 'he had never before met with a person who thought

---

Godwin see, for example, Halévy, *The Growth of Philosophic Radicalism*, p. 285, and R. G. Grylls, *William Godwin and his World*, London, 1953, p. 39.

Podmore discusses the similarities between Godwin's and Owen's views (*Robert Owen*, pp. 119–21), commenting that *Political Justice* 'can hardly have escaped (Owen's) notice . . .' (p. 120).

[1] Quoted in H. S. Salt, *Godwin's Political Justice: A Reprint of the Essay on Property*, London, 1890, edition of 1949, p. 31.

[2] Some writers have assumed that Owen met Godwin frequently. See, for example, George Woodcock, *William Godwin: A Biographical Study*, London, 1946, p. 226, and David Fleisher, in *William Godwin: A Study in Liberalism*, London, 1951, p. 53.

[3] The letter, dated July 29, 1816, is in Mrs Julian Marshall, *The Life and Letters of Mary Wollstonecraft Shelley*, London, 1889, Vol. I, pp. 148–50.

[4] She gives a very odd summary, and comments she is 'sick at heart at the misery I see my fellow-beings suffering, but I own I should not like to live to see the extinction of all genius, talent, and elevated generous feeling in Great Britain, which I conceive to be the natural consequence of Mr Owen's plan' (*ibid.*, p. 150).

so exactly as he did' as Mary Wollstonecraft, we must assume that Owen did, in fact, probably while in Manchester, encounter her ideas on the printed page or in discussion.

In one respect, Mary's views were by this stage more acceptable to Owen than Godwin's. Godwin's entire argument led him to oppose state-provided education, whereas Mary's views led her to the opposite conclusion in *The Rights of Woman*, for example, when discussing the need for the establishment of 'proper day-schools' which 'should be national establishments'.[1] At a time when Owen, through the Board of Health, was coming to accept the need for state intervention to regulate social and industrial conditions, encountering her (or perhaps even Paine's[2]) advocacy of 'national education' could well have decisively influenced him to advocate state provision in education.

In two chapters of *The Rights of Woman* ('The Effect which an early Association of Ideas has upon the Character', and 'On National Education') Mary Wollstonecraft presented ideas of character and education along lines with which we are now familiar. She was concerned, particularly, of course, with the position and rights of women,[3] and her commentary was therefore much more specific, more polemical, and in general more subtle, than that of Godwin. Her emphasis was a much more explicitly sensationalist one on association, but her purpose was the same. 'There is an habitual association of ideas,' she wrote, 'that grows "with our growth" ... So ductile is the understanding, and yet so stubborn, that the associations which depend on adventitious circumstances, during the period that the body takes to arrive at maturity, can seldom be disentangled by reason'.[4] Given such an habitual association

---

[1] Mary Wollstonecraft, *A Vindication of the Rights of Woman*, London, 1792, Everyman edition of 1955, p. 180. All references are to this edition.

[2] See, for example, *The Rights of Man*, Part II, 1792, in *The Writings of Thomas Paine*, collected and edited by M. D. Conway, London, 1906 (government consists in 'making such provision for the instruction of youth and the support of age, as to exclude, as much as possible, profligacy from the one and despair from the other', p. 462). Owen frequently used this kind of argument.

[3] '*The rights of man*', said Hannah More, 'have been discussed, till we are somewhat wearied with the discussion. To these have been opposed, with more presumption than prudence, *the rights of woman* ... the next stage of that irradiation which our enlighteners are pouring in upon us will illuminate the world with grave descants on the *rights of children*' (*Strictures on the Modern System of Female Education*, Vol. I, p. 147). She was more correct than she imagined. Godwin and Mary Wollstonecraft were, in fact, undermining the whole situation in which children were considered to have no 'rights' in education.

[4] *The Rights of Woman*, p. 127.

of ideas, women are trapped inside the set of values established for them and with which they grow up:

'. . . the severest sarcasms have been levelled against the sex, and they have been ridiculed for repeating "a set of phrases learnt by rote", when nothing could be more natural, considering the education they receive, and that their "highest praise is to obey, un-argued"—the will of the man . . . how can (men) . . . expect women . . . to despise what they have been all their lives labouring to attain?'[1]

Like Godwin, she attacked rote learning:

'How much time is lost in teaching them to recite what they do not understand? whilst, seated on benches, all in their best array, the mammas listen with astonishment to the parrot-like prattle, uttered in solemn cadences, with all the pomp of ignorance and folly.'[2]

Her remedies were equally specific. In elementary day-schools, she proposed, 'boys and girls, the rich and the poor, should meet together'. They should be dressed alike. The schoolroom 'ought to be surrounded by a large piece of ground, in which the children might be usefully exercised, for at this age they should not be confined to any sedentary employment for more than an hour at a time'. Such relaxation was a part of education, 'for many things improve and amuse the senses, when introduced as a kind of show, to the principles of which, dryly laid down, children would turn a deaf ear'.[3]

That Owen did, in fact, in one way or another meet ideas such as this in Manchester in the 1790's is made abundantly clear, as we shall see, by the very language he came to speak.

There were, of course, other channels through which ideas of this kind made (or re-made) their way into the ideological confrontations of the 1790's. For a full picture of the processes at work it would be necessary to look at, for example, the kind of ideas with which Percival's friend Priestley became familiar through his friendship with the French philosophers, including Holbach,[4] and the way in which the ideas of radicals like Thelwall and Holcroft came to have influence. Holcroft

---

[1] *The Rights of Woman*, p. 128.   [2] *Ibid.*, p. 180.
[3] *Ibid.*, p. 186.
[4] See W. H. Wickwar's article on Helvétius and Holbach in Hearnshaw (ed.), *The Social and Political Ideas of some Great French Thinkers of the Age of Reason*, p. 213.

believed, as we have seen, that 'truth had a natural superiority over error' and he held that 'the best and only effectual means of ameliorating the condition of mankind, is by the gentleness of instruction, by steady inquiry, and by a calm, but dauntless reliance on the progressive power of truth'.[1] This could well be taken as a summary of Owen as educator at New Lanark. To each item—gentleness of instruction, steady inquiry, calm and dauntless reliance on the power of truth—Owen would have explicitly subscribed. There were even links, as Holyoake points out, between the forms of propaganda and organisation adopted by men like Holcroft, and those of Owen and social movements of a later day.[2]

It would be necessary, finally, to look at the thinking and influence of the utilitarian philosophers, though their real impact came later than the period with which we are here concerned. Although Bentham, for example, may have offered 'a truer—or at least a more balanced—interpretation of Helvétius than that given by Godwin and Adam Smith',[3] though 'Bentham on Morals and Legislation' was in the Newcastle Literary and Philosophical Society library, and though claims have been made for a major influence on Owen by Bentham,[4] Bentham did not in fact have any real influence on Owen or on radical or educational thought in the 1790's. 'Until 1802,' points out one commentator, 'Bentham was comparatively unknown.'[5] Not until he

---

[1] Hazlitt (ed.), *Memoirs of the late Thomas Holcroft*, in *Complete Works of William Hazlitt*, Vol. 3, p. 140. H. N. Brailsford, in *Shelley, Godwin, and their Circle*, also quotes a 'striking metaphor' from Holcroft: 'Men do not become what by nature they are meant to be, but what society makes them. The generous feelings and higher propensities of the soul are, as it were, shrunk up, scared, violently wrenched, and amputated, to fit us for our intercourse in the world, something in the manner that beggars maim and mutilate their children to make them fit for their future situation in life' (pp. 31–2).

[2] See *Sixty Years of an Agitator's Life*, edition of 1902, Vol. I, p. 116 (he describes Holcroft as 'a precursor of Mr Owen').

[3] Cumming, *Helvétius*, p. 166.

[4] See, for example, K. Marx and F. Engels, *The Holy Family*, 1844, English translation by R. Dixon, Moscow, 1956 (Bentham derived his system of 'correctly understood interest' from Helvétius, and Owen 'proceeded from Bentham's system to found English communism', p. 176). Professor A. Anekshtein takes up this theme in *Pedagogicheskiye Idei Roberta Owena*, ('Owen's theory had its starting point in the materialistic philosophy of the eighteenth century, which he adopted from Bentham . . .', p. 118). See also Peter Michaels, 'Robert Owen: Visionary of a New Society', *The UNESCO Courier*, October, 1958 ('The early Utilitarian philosophers, Jeremy Bentham, James Mill and Francis Place, were those who most directly influenced Owen', p. 32).

[5] John Plamenatz, *The English Utilitarians*, Oxford, 1949, revised edition of 1958, p. 63.

met James Mill in 1808 was he attracted towards any democratic views. 'Bentham on Morals and Legislation' was not in the 1790's the same kind of focal point of general discussion as 'Godwin's Political Justice'. Bentham was later to become a partner in the New Lanark mills, but, certainly until the 1810's (and in Hazlitt's view still in 1825) Bentham was 'one of those persons who verify the old adage, that "A prophet has most honour out of his own country".'[1] James Mill contributed more firmly than Bentham to the 'more balanced' interpretation of Helvétius' views on education. 'In psychology', John Stuart Mill said of him, 'his fundamental doctrine was the formation of all human character by circumstances, through the universal Principle of Association, and the consequent unlimited possibility of improving the moral and intellectual condition of mankind by education.'[2] Mill's biographer, Alexander Bain, comments on this score that Mill 'goes nearly all lengths with the extreme view of Helvétius, namely, that the mass of mankind are equal as to their susceptibility of mental excellence'.

Mill was convinced of the importance of the power of circumstances over the child from its earliest days. Bain quotes Mill's *Encyclopaedia Britannica* article: 'the works of Helvétius would have been invaluable, if they had done nothing more than prove the vast importance of these circumstances in giving permanent qualities to the mind'.[3] But this article, we must remember, was written in 1818, five years after Owen's *A New View of Society*. Francis Place had in 1816 written to Mill, attacking the belief in 'innate propensities', and commenting that 'the generality of children are organised so nearly alike that they may by proper management be made pretty nearly equally wise and virtuous'.[4] This kind of assumption was commonplace to the utilitarians, but when Owen made contact with people like Place he had already held such views demonstrably for ten, and probably for twenty, years. Owen was a product of the Godwinian radical rationalism of the 1790's, not the utilitarianism of the 1810's.

What he learned in Manchester, through his contact with the industrial system and the Board of Health, through men like Percival, through ideas which circulated in informal discussion with Dalton or in more serious debate in the Literary and Philosophical Society, through

[1] Hazlitt, *The Spirit of the Age*, World's Classics, edition of 1928, p. 1.

[2] J. S. Mill, *Autobiography*, London, 1873, World's Classics edition of 1955, p. 91.

[3] Alexander Bain, *James Mill. A Biography*, London, 1882, p. 249.

[4] Quoted in Wallas, *The Life of Francis Place*, p. 71.

his reading of Mary Wollstonecraft or of Godwin, through conversations with men who knew Holbach or Paine or Priestley, through debate with Coleridge or conversation with Fulton, through the myriad channels in which the ideological shocks of the 1790's were felt, amounted to what H. N. Brailsford described as the 'revolutionary leaven which Godwin's generation set fermenting'. It added up to a message that 'by a resolute effort to change the environment of institutions and customs which educate us, we can change ourselves. They liberated us not so much from "priests and kings" as from the deadlier tyranny of the belief that human nature, with all its imperfections, is an innate character which it were vain to hope to reform.'[1] It was a message that in the mid-1790's was being 'spoken on the house-tops . . . whispered in secret . . . published in quarto and duodecimo . . . and turned the heads of almost the whole kingdom . . .' in the splendid over-statement of Hazlitt.[2]

It was from such starting points, then, that Owen came to formulate his general theoretical framework and detailed thinking about education. His views, however, are inseparable from the developments he introduced at New Lanark from taking over the management of the mills 'about the first of January 1800'.[3] *A New View of Society*, Owen's meteoric first statement of his views, is, in fact, both a theoretical analysis and an account of the New Lanark experiments and plans. In answer to possible criticism that his plans are visionary, he asserts that 'only one reply *can* and *ought* to be made; that *these* principles have been carried most successfully into practice'.[4] Owen was, therefore, not merely continuing an intellectual tradition that we have seen being established; he was making general property ideas which, in his view, were justifying themselves in practice day by day.

Before we look at these ideas, and some relevant aspects of developments at New Lanark, it is important to note that considerable changes in Owen's emphases with regard to social questions were to take place in these crucial twenty-five or so years.

The difference between the Owen of *A New View of Society* in 1813 and his contributions to the discussion of poverty and unemployment in 1817 and after (including the *Report to the County of Lanark* in 1820)

---

[1] *Shelley, Godwin, and their Circle*, p. 251.
[2] *Political Essays*, see Appendix A below.
[3] *Life*, p. 78.
[4] *A New View*, p. 20.

is the difference between a man who, as Max Beer half-truthfully puts it, 'had started as a rationalist educator and psychologist' and now 'became a social economist'.[1] This is only half true because whatever Owen *became* he *remained* a rationalist educator, and although the zig-zags of Owen's future career were to lead him to look in many directions for the solution to the problems of society, his conception of human nature, and of the role of education and environment in shaping human character, remained almost unchanged.

The four essays 'on the principle of the formation of human character' which constitute *A New View of Society* were distributed privately and anonymously from 1813, and under his own name from 1816. They were an analysis of how character is formed, and can therefore be re-formed, and a demonstration of the concomitant social re-formation needed. The formation of character was, of course, no new concern in the history of educational thought, but the implications behind Owen's use of the phrase had nothing in common with those of, say, Lancaster or even Joseph Priestley, when the latter asserted that 'it is the great object of education to form valuable characters, and to prepare men for the most important stations in life'.[2] Owen's less utilitarian theme, the central one of the essays, was expressed in his famous formula that:

'Any general character, from the best to the worst, from the most ignorant to the most enlightened, may be given to any community, even to the world at large, by the application of proper means; which means are to a great extent at the command and under the control of those who have influence in the affairs of men.'[3]

Children, he affirmed, are 'impressed with habits and sentiments similar to those of their parents and instructors; modified, however, by the circumstances in which they have been, are or may be placed, and by the peculiar organization of each individual'.[4] Owen clearly phrased this with some care, and was at this point expressing a viewpoint not unlike that of Godwin's considered statements.

When Owen affirmed that 'the character of man is, without a single exception, always formed for him',[5] he saw this as a collective process: 'the old collectively may train the young collectively, to be ignorant and

---

[1] M. Beer, *A History of British Socialism*, 1919, edition of 1948, Vol. I, p. 166.
[2] Priestley, *The Proper Object of Education*, in *Works*, Vol. XXV, p. 421.
[3] *A New View*, p. 16.
[4] *Ibid.*, p. 22.
[5] *Ibid.*, p. 45.

miserable, or to be intelligent and happy'.[1] But the ambiguity involved in definitions of this kind, between what is achieved socially, collectively, and what exists individually, allowing for individual differences, was to be prominent throughout Owen's life. Here in *A New View* he was anxious to counter, as was Godwin, the objection that the concept of environmental influence ignored the possibility of individual differences:

> 'Children are', Owen insisted, 'without exception, passive and wonderfully contrived compounds; which . . . may be formed collectively to have any human character.'[2]

And in the third essay Owen returned to this theme, to try to make more explicit his view of what it is the individual can be said to have from birth which differentiates him from other individuals. 'Man is born with a desire to obtain happiness', and both this desire and 'the faculties by which he acquires knowledge' are 'not formed exactly alike in any two individuals', because of the dominance of social influence.[3] Such diversity, he stressed in the fourth essay, is but 'the minute differences which are ever found in all the compounds of the creation' and human nature is:

> 'without exception universally plastic, and by judicious training *the infants of any one class in the world may be readily formed into men of any other class* . . .'[4]

If the human being is so malleable, Owen concluded, we must look to two factors if we are to bring about a more rationally-ordered and just society—environment and education. He argued categorically from his experience at New Lanark that 'by far the greater part of the misery with which man is encircled *may* be easily dissipated and removed; and that with mathematical precision he *may* be surrounded with those circumstances which must gradually increase his happiness'.[5] Ultimately it is education which will effect the major change in society, and it is the recognition of (a) the power of education, (b) the limitations of current educational practice, and (c) the major development; and the forms of such development, needed, that makes *A New View* so important a document. Owen, in fact, spelled out more fully and urgently the case for a basic revolution in thinking about education than anyone since

[1] *Ibid.*, p. 64. [2] *Ibid.*, p. 22.
[3] *Ibid.*, pp. 54–5. [4] *Ibid.*, p. 72.
[5] *Ibid.*, p. 20.

Locke. This is not to belittle the role of, say, Helvétius and Godwin, nor to exaggerate the originality of Owen: it is purely that Owen, for the first time, in a critical stage of British social development, made what had been a by-product of radical philosophy (and of radical politics, in the case of Paine, for example) a central feature of the analysis of social problems.

Owen, like his rationalist predecessors, saw that remedial action was not enough. Children needed to be trained 'from their earliest infancy in good habits of every description . . . They must afterwards be rationally educated, and their labour be usefully directed'.[1] Education, therefore, for him, as for Helvétius, meant total education, the direction of the overall circumstances surrounding the human being from birth.

Owen therefore outlined his own plans (not finally implemented until 1816) for the education of the children of the village, starting from their reception into the playground adjoining the new Institution for the Formation of Character 'as soon as they can freely walk alone . . . The child will be placed in a situation of safety, where, with its future school-fellows and companions, it will acquire the best habits and principles, while at meal times and at night it will return to the caresses of its parents.' Owen insisted, as the central principle for the teaching of young children, that each child, right from the start, should 'be told in language which he can understand, that "he is never to injure his play-fellows; but that, on the contrary, he is to contribute all in his power to make them happy".'[2]

In asserting what education should and could be, Owen could not fail to look critically at the limitations of existing forms of education. Owen, an extremely generous man, in spirit and financially, had subscribed to both Bell's and Lancaster's schools. He had given Lancaster a thousand pounds and had offered 'a similar sum to Dr Bell's committee for aiding him, if they would open their schools for children of all denominations, as Lancaster and his committee had done, but only half that amount if they continued to exclude all except those of the Church of England . . . it was decided by a small majority to continue to exclude all dissenters from the Church and to accept only the five hundred pounds'.[3] Though Owen's claim that he was 'Lancaster's first and most confided-in patron as long as he remained in England' is clearly an

---

[1] *Ibid.*, p. 20.
[2] *Ibid.*, pp. 40–1.
[3] *Life*, p. 264. See also pp. 116–17.

exaggeration, Owen had indeed become familiar with Lancaster and in 1812, in fact, chaired a dinner in Glasgow at which Lancaster was the guest of honour.[1]

The first essay of *A New View* made a typically generous gesture to the two founders of the monitorial system, praising them for 'directing the public attention to the beneficial effects, on the young and unresisting mind, of even the limited education which their systems embrace . . . they will for ever be ranked among the most important benefactors of the human race'.[2]

But Owen had grown beyond them. Henceforward, he went on immediately to affirm, 'to contend for any new exclusive system will be in vain'.[3] And by the time Owen came to the fourth essay, and looked at the work of Bell and Lancaster again, this time against the backcloth of his detailed and strongly-pressed vision of human progress, their achievement seemed less grandiose.

> 'The systems of Dr Bell and Mr Lancaster . . . prove the extreme ignorance which previously existed in the *manner* of training the young; for it is in the manner alone of giving instruction that these new systems are an improvement on the modes of instruction which were formerly practised.'

Not, added Owen, that the manner of teaching was unimportant, but, examination would show that 'the matter of instruction which is now given in some of our boasted new systems for the instruction of the poor' is 'almost as wretched as any which can be devised'.[4] Recent attempts to educate the mass of the people had been 'conducted on the narrow principle of debasing man to a mere irrational military machine'.[5] He singled out Bell's system of 'initiating the children of the poor in all the tenets of the Church of England' as an 'attempt to ward off a little longer the yet dreaded period of a change from ignorance to reason, from misery to happiness'.[6] But both systems were at fault:

> '. . . children may be taught, by either Dr Bell's or Mr Lancaster's

---

[1] Owen tells us that he encouraged Lancaster to come to Scotland, that Lancaster insisted that Owen should chair the dinner, and that 'it was in my opening speech, that I first declared in public my sentiments on the true formation of character' (*Life*, pp. 147–8). See also Podmore, *Robert Owen*, pp. 95–6, for a reference to Lancaster in a letter written by Owen in 1813.

[2] *A New View*, pp. 18–19. [3] *Ibid.*, p. 19.

[4] *Ibid.*, pp. 74–5. [5] *Ibid.*, p. 81. [6] *Ibid.*, p. 78.

system, to read, write, account, and sew, and yet acquire the worst habits, and have their minds rendered irrational for life. Reading and writing are merely instruments by which knowledge, either true or false, may be imparted.'[1]

This was certainly an enlightened view at the time, and indeed would have been so at almost any point in the nineteenth century. Professor W. B. Hodgson was still arguing the same point in 1867:

'Ignorance of reading and writing is productive of, or accompanied by, a great amount of crime. Knowledge of reading and writing will, therefore, diminish crime. There may be fallacies more palpable than this; there can be few more gross or serious.'[2]

But Owen was not consistently critical. He would without demur tell the Archbishop of Canterbury in 1818 that the society over which he presided had produced 'an almost miraculous change' on the young mind, and that 'the public look on with amazement at the effects which are daily exhibited by the children at the Central School . . .'[3] Owen's son, Robert Dale Owen, also tells of an incident that appears to have taken place in 1824. He and his father had visited Bell's central school:

'A class was standing up for arithmetic. "Seven times eight are fifty-six," said one boy. "*Is*, not *are*," sternly cried the teacher, dealing the offender such a buffet on the ear that he staggered and finally dropped to the ground; then adding: "Get up! Now perhaps you'll remember that, another time." But whether it was the blow or the bit of doubtful grammar he was bidden to remember seemed not very clear.

I still recollect how my nature revolted against this outrage—for such it appeared to me. "Father," said I, as we left the room, "I'm very sorry you gave any money to this school." He smiled, and apologized for the teacher, saying "The man had probably been treated in the same manner when he was a child, and so knew no better".'[4]

We must not, however, allow the generosity of Owen's doctrine and attitude cloud the fact that he knew, and acted upon his knowledge, that

[1] *Ibid.*, p. 74.
[2] *Exaggerated Estimates of Reading and Writing*, p. 6.
[3] *On the Union of Churches and Schools. To his Grace the Archbishop of Canterbury*, 1818, in *Life*, Vol. I, London, 1857, pp. 363–4. The appendices to Vol. I are not included in Max Beer's edition of 1920.
[4] *Threading My Way*, pp. 249–50.

the monitorial system of both religious camps was inadequate and failed to solve the fundamental question of the *content* of education.

A New View emphasises, then, the power of education and the limitations of current educational practice. It goes on, thirdly, to suggest what developments in popular education were required. Owen came out unambiguously in favour of a 'national system of education'.

The controversy over the role of the state in education was, in the eighteenth century and in the early decades of the nineteenth, primarily a moral issue, centring around concepts of individual liberty and the dangers inherent in submitting men's minds to any agency so powerful as the state. It was not yet bound up with the well-demarcated religious and party politics of the later nineteenth century, and the positions of the educationists in the period with which we have so far been concerned are therefore less predictable than might be supposed. We cannot here trace the history of the battle over state intervention; we can merely see roughly how the field was laid out when Owen entered the battle.

The active church and nonconformist advocates of limited education were mostly against state intervention. Bell, with some restraint, pointing out that 'some ancient and military nations', aware that the 'future strength and prosperity of the state depend upon the youth', had provided a public, prescribed education, declared that 'in a free country, and in the improved state of commerce and the arts, this practice does not admit of being universally adopted, and if it did, would not be productive of general benefit'.[1] Lancaster was even more forthright in defending the 'spirit, breathing the language of independence' which 'is natural to Englishmen, few of whom are disposed to brook compulsion, or submit to the dictates of others . . .' He was aware of the need for reforms in education, to improve charity schools for instance, but disliked talk of doing so

'by a compulsive law; as coercion of any kind grates upon our very hearing, and generally fails of its effect . . . teachers or parents of any spirit will not bear attempts to reform them by force, however respectably sanctioned'.[2]

They were joined in their opposition, however, by more radical thinkers. Joseph Priestley, for example, argued from the standpoint of the necessity to direct attention to the good of the individual, not the good

[1] *The Madras School*, p. 290.
[2] *Improvements in Education*, p. 182.

of the state. In *An Essay on the First Principles of Government*, for instance, he had stated his aim as being to 'shew the inconvenience of establishing, by law, any plan of education whatever'.[1] The need for a state hand in education in order to prevent faction and to secure the 'perpetuity of our excellent constitution, ecclesiastical and civil' had been argued, and Priestley agreed that national education would, in fact, achieve this, but he was concerned not only with 'the tranquility of the state', but with 'the forming of wise and virtuous men'.[2] In the formative stage with which education is concerned, a straight-jacket would be undesirable:

> 'Education ... *makes the man*. One method of education, therefore, would only produce one kind of men.'[3]

This, as we have seen, was also Godwin's position. He saw national education being inevitably in 'alliance with national government ... Government will not fail to employ it, to strengthen its hands, and perpetuate its institutions'.[4] Godwin looked at the problem in greater detail to see *how* a national education would operate. He came to the conclusion that 'all public establishments include in them the idea of permanence', and therefore 'public education has always expended its energies in the support of prejudice'.[5]

The argument in favour of the public provision of education usually began with the need for the state to supplement individual efforts in those spheres where the individual was helpless or weak, and therefore men who in other fields would strongly oppose state intervention, were led to accept it in education. Adam Smith, for example, in *The Wealth of Nations*, was aware that, while in some cases society itself enables men, without any government intervention, to develop the 'abilities and virtues' required by the state, there are other cases where 'the state of the society does not place the greater part of individuals in such situations; and some attention of government is necessary, in order to prevent the almost entire corruption and degeneracy of the great body of the people'.[6]

From this premise Smith argued the case for a national system of

[1] *An Essay on the First Principles of Government*, London, 1771, p. 83.
[2] *Ibid.*, p. 84.
[3] *Ibid.*, p. 91.
[4] *Political Justice*, Vol. II, p. 302.
[5] *Ibid.*, pp. 298–9.
[6] World's Classics edition of 1904, Vol. II, pp. 416–17.

education, as did Bentham and Mill after him, both extremely suspicious of state intervention in other spheres. When people were ignorant and too poor to pay for education, submitted James Mill, 'it was necessary for the State to intervene to give the enterprise a push. To prevent the State abusing the powers which were entrusted to it and establishing a sort of intellectual despotism, one guarantee is enough—the freedom of the press'.[1] There is a passage in a favourable review of Owen's *A New View of Society* by Mill that is extremely revealing of what was involved in his conception of state education (and of the bounds of democracy as the utilitarians conceived it). 'The first object undoubtedly to be provided for in the formation of a government', he postulated, 'is the obedience of the governed'. Such obedience, he continued, was obtained in one of two ways—'force or affection':

> 'Every where, with variation only in degree, the object has been to accumulate force enough . . . To train the minds of the people to a virtuous attachment to their government . . . has every where been left to chance . . .'[2]

It is understandable, therefore, that those who defended state intervention on the basis of premises of this kind, with an eye in one way or another on the influence of the state, did not always support such intervention without reservations. Henry Brougham, for example, introducing his 1825 pamphlet in support of Mechanics' Institutes, divided the educational provision needed into three categories—infant, elementary and adult schools:

> 'It is only with the second of these branches that the Legislature can safely interfere. Any meddling on the part of Government with the first would be inexpedient; with the last, perilous to civil and religious liberty.'[3]

Similarly, in an interesting and comparatively enlightened work at the end of the eighteenth century, George Dyer advocated a scheme for

---

[1] Halévy, *The Growth of Philosophic Racialism*, p. 289.

[2] *The Philanthropist*, Vol. III, No. X, 1813, p. 100. Alexander Bain attributes the article to Mill (*James Mill*, p. 125). Owen described 'the new school of modern political economists' as advocating the principle of individualism, with education according to the then notions of national education for the poor . . .' (*Life*, pp. 178–9).

[3] *Practical Observations*, dedication.

public instruction, which would help to provide the poor with knowledge sufficient for them, at least, to get

'their living, to make them honest men, citizens, and patriots. A state should stop there.'[1]

Paine, who, like Godwin, had immense reservations about government action, ranged himself on the opposite side of the debate from Godwin when it came to education, and put forward a very Adam Smith-like case. 'A great part of what is called government is mere imposition', he asserted, but went on to comment that 'government is no farther necessary than to supply the few cases to which society and civilization are not conveniently competent'.[2] He was less wholeheartedly opposed to state action in general than was Godwin. Discussing the financial and other details of national educational provision, he stressed that 'a nation under a well-regulated government should permit none to remain uninstructed. It is monarchical and aristocratical government only that requires ignorance for its support'.[3] Mary Wollstonecraft also, as we have seen, expressed herself in *The Rights of Woman* in favour of publicly-provided education. She was in favour of the establishment of 'proper day-schools' which 'should be national establishments'.[4] Her case for such a national educational system was, however, very much more rounded and rich than that of her contemporaries, and most of her successors. From the starting point of her analysis of women's position in society, she came to the conclusion that 'day-schools for particular ages should be established by Government, in which boys and girls might be educated together. The school for the younger children, from five to nine years of age, ought to be absolutely free and open to all classes.'[5] She defended this version of a common school, for younger children at least, as encouraging honest relations between the sexes ('educating the sexes together to perfect both')[6] and discouraging

---

[1] George Dyer, *The Complaints of the Poor People of England*, 1793, second edition, p. 19. This is not as extensive a programme as it sounds: Dyer was really advocating that the poor should be taught 'such learning, as may be proper for their respective situations' plus a knowledge of the laws.

[2] *Rights of Man*, Part II, in *The Writings of Thomas Paine*, 1906, Vol. II, p. 407.

[3] *Ibid.*, p. 490.   [4] *Ibid.*, p. 185.

[5] *Ibid.*, p. 192.

[6] After the age of nine, she conceded, there was need for some class differentiation, between the children destined for 'domestic employments, or mechanical trades' and those 'of superior abilities, or fortune' (*ibid.*, p. 186).

'distinctions of vanity' by enabling the children to be dressed alike.[1] Though she was here discussing public education primarily as an instrument for the liberation of women, she was by implication strongly defending it as a practicable institution by which to raise the general level of human decency.

Owen's experience in industry and in the Board of Health in Manchester had taught him the limitations of individual initiative in such spheres as public health and the regulation of the hours of work of children. In *A New View* he took up the call for national education strongly and insistently. His first essay described as the most important object to which the public mind could be directed—'a national proceeding for rationally forming the character of that immense mass of population which is now allowed to be so formed as to fill the world with crimes'.[1] In the second essay, talking of this 'national plan for the formation of character', he added that 'anything short of this would be an act of intolerance and injustice to the excluded, and of injury to society'.[2] In the fourth essay, admitting that it is 'premature to introduce a national system of education' until a population 'can be made conscious of the irrational state in which they now exist', he proclaimed that the time had in fact, come when the British government could safely adopt a national system of education for the poor. 'To create a well-trained, united, and happy people, this national system should be uniform over the United Kingdom . . . the thought of exclusion to one child in the empire should not for a moment be entertained.'[3] It was obvious, Owen commented, that 'at this hour a national system of education for the lower orders, on sound political principles, is really dreaded, even by some of the most learned and intelligent members of the Church of England'.[4] He offered the draft of a bill by which national popular education could be effected. It provided for the creation of a new government department of education ('which will be found ultimately to prove the most important of all its departments'), the establishment of teacher-training seminaries, the provision of the requisite state expenditure, the drawing up of the best possible curricula, and the appointment of teachers.[5]

[1] *A New View*, p. 21. [2] *Ibid.*, p. 37.
[3] *Ibid.*, pp. 73–4.
[4] *Ibid.*, pp. 77–8. In passing, Owen criticised Whitbread's 1807 bill for trying to commit a plan for education to the management of ministers, churchwardens, etc., 'whose present interests must have appeared to be opposed to the measure'.
[5] *Ibid.*, pp. 81–8.

Owen's range of arguments in defence of his commitment to so far-reaching a conception of education took in, of course, many of the limited arguments which others had used in a much less generous framework. He argued, for example, the need for 'efficient corrective measures, which if we longer delay, general disorder must ensue'.[1] But he turned the rescue argument into an attack on the effects of circumstances in society as it was constituted. We must rescue, he constantly implied, because to do otherwise was to behave barbarously, as it was when society surrounded men with circumstances 'which inevitably form such characters as they afterwards deem it a duty and a right to punish even to death'.[2] Owen obviously felt a deep moral involvement in the question of punishment, returning to it again and again:

'. . . such has been our education, that we hesitate not to devote years and expend millions in the *detection* and *punishment* of crimes . . . and yet we have not moved one step in the true path to *prevent* crimes.'[3]

This is an unmistakably different tone of voice from that of the eighteenth century philanthropist anxious to clear the streets of the sight of evil. Owen was tackling a social problem at its root, not because it was *evil*, but because it was *unjust*. When he asked how much longer society was to be allowed to turn people into criminals, and then 'hunt them like beasts of the forest'[4] it was a very different tone of voice from, for example, that of Lancaster asking for sympathy with the 'forty thousand impures . . . in the metropolis' and for benevolence to 'alleviate the consequences of this dreadful profligacy'.[5] Just as Owen absorbed and transformed this typical eighteenth century argument, so did he adapt other of its attitudes. He was convinced, for example, like any rationalist philosopher, that what he hoped to achieve would be accomplished by the sheer force of reason, and this was a theme to which he returned constantly. He looked at all the misguided individuals, sects and parties, and urged:

'Let truth unaccompanied with error be placed before them; give them time to examine it and to see that it is in unison with all previously ascertained truths; and conviction and acknowledgment of it will follow of course'.[6]

[1] *Ibid.*, p. 14. [2] *Ibid.*, p. 17.
[3] *Ibid.*, p. 21. [4] *Ibid.*, p. 25.
[5] *Improvements in Education*, pp. 116–17.
[6] *A New View*, p. 24.

Convinced of the rationality of human behaviour, once exposed to the revelation of truth, Owen at this stage pinned his faith on being able to convince the men of authority and power. He believed that 'neither prince, ministers, parliament, nor any party in Church or State, will avow inclination to act on principles of such flagrant injustice'.[1] Once everyone had realised that what he advocated was for the benefit of the whole human race his principles 'must ultimately and universally prevail'.[2] Owen therefore submitted his essays to the great of the land for approval, and worked enthusiastically to persuade them to act upon his principles.[3] A New View and New Lanark, had made him well known 'among the leading men of that period'.[4] He describes, for example, the consideration given to his essays by the Prime Minister, Lord Liverpool, and by the Home Secretary, Lord Sidmouth, both of whom received him, and for a time treated him with respect. Liverpool and his Cabinet, the Archbishop of Canterbury, and the English and Irish Bishops 'were favourable to my views and friendly to myself'.[5] He persuaded the government to send a copy to all the sovereigns, governments, universities and 'learned individuals' of Europe,[6] and one appears to have reached Napoleon in Elba, who, Owen would have us believe, 'studied this work with great attention' and determined, on returning to power, to work for peace and progress.[7] Be this as it may, Owen was convinced that he had only to speak rationally to the powerful, and they would respond rationally. He was, therefore, again like Godwin, led to proclaim the need not to act hastily, recklessly, the need to let truth take its inevitable path at its own speed, for change to be 'so gradual as to be almost imperceptible, yet always making a permanent advance in the desired improvements'.[8] 'Of all the men I know,' said the Honorary Physician to the Duke of Kent, after visiting New Lanark, 'he is among those incapable of being practically advocates for disorder'.[9]

[1] Ibid., p. 36.　　　　　　　　　　[2] Ibid., pp. 53–4.
[3] For a delicious passage on the score of Owen's attempt to win over the great to his schemes, see Hazlitt, Political Essays, Appendix A below.
[4] See Life, pp. 142–3.
[5] Ibid., p. 149. For the closeness of his relations with Sidmouth in particular, see ibid., pp. 152 and 164–6.
[6] Ibid., p. 152.　　　　　　　　　　[7] Ibid., p. 155.
[8] A New View, p. 36. See also p. 65.
[9] Dr Henry Gray MacNab, The New Views of Mr Owen of Lanark Impartially Examined . . . also Observations on the New Lanark School, and on the Systems of Education of Mr Owen, of the Rev. Dr Bell . . ., London, 1819, p. 25. MacNab visited New Lanark at the request of the Duke, and was converted from scepticism to active advocacy of Owen's views.

Owen remained inflexibly devoted to this viewpoint throughout his life, asserting in his autobiography, for example, that the defects of government can be overcome, but not 'by force, or by abusive language. Reason and common sense are the true and only weapons which can ever succeed.'[1]

Once again, however, adopting the eighteenth century view, he transmuted it. Reading any of Owen's many pronouncements one feels that he does not *hope* something will be done, he has willed it into existence, it *shall* be done. One cannot but be aware of the fact that the moments of real sympathy with the poor, the deprived and the victims of injustice, which one finds occasionally in Helvétius, for example, have become intense and dominant in Owen.

The voice of Owen's indignation is as real as the voice of his reason or of his generosity. His road to 'intelligence and true knowledge' was not 'a narrow or exclusive path; it admits of no exclusion: every colour of body and diversity of mind are freely and alike admitted. It is open to the human race . . .'[2] His thesis rests on the rock of his feeling for those who suffer the injustice he describes:

> '. . . important as are considerations of revenue, they must appear secondary when put in competition with the lives, liberty and comfort of our fellow-subjects'.[3]

His compassion produced two of the most eloquent passages of *A New View*. While politicians, agricultural and commercial interests argued over the pecuniary profit, would 'the well-being of millions of the poor, half-naked, half-famished, untaught, and untrained, hourly increasing to a most alarming extent in these islands, not call forth *one* petition, *one* delegate, or *one* rational effective legislation measure?'[4] And at another point, after his reference to the work of Bell and Lancaster, and the need to adopt the best matter as well as the best manner of education, he made this plea:

> 'Either give the poor a rational and useful training, or mock not their ignorance, their poverty, and their misery, by merely instructing them to become conscious of the extent of the degradation under which they exist. And, therefore, in pity to suffering humanity, either keep the poor, if you now can, in the state of the most abject ignor-

[1] *Life*, p. 146.
[3] *Ibid.*, p. 38.
[2] *A New View*, p. 80.
[4] *Ibid.*, p. 21.

ance, as near as possible to animal life, or at once determine to form them into rational beings, into useful and effective members of the state.'[1]

It is at a point such as this, especially in the language of 'mock not their ignorance, their poverty, and their misery', that Owen marked himself off most distinctly from previous educators, and even from the language of the 1790's and Godwin. Owen had, indeed, adopted their assumptions and vocabulary, and gone beyond. There is embodied in passages such as these not only the rationalist message and the certainty of a practical programme, but a new kind of humanitarian call—from close quarters to the point of suffering. From within the cotton industry, the nerve centre of the industrial revolution, a voice was being raised to show that the new industrialism of Britain and the energy of rationalism had met. The understanding and emotion of Owen ultimately, as we shall see, helped decisively to make it possible for the rationalist statement about man and society to reach out in a new environment and make an impact of a kind and at a level that Owen himself did not foresee.

(iii) They acted rationally

When Owen, as manager of the Chorlton Twist Company, visited the New Lanark Mills, near Glasgow, he saw it, he tells us, as the site where he would like to try an experiment he had 'long contemplated' and 'wished to have an opportunity to put into practice'.[2] Owen and his partners bought the mills from David Dale,[3] and Owen married Dale's daughter. He left Manchester at the beginning of 1800, intending 'not to be a mere manager of cotton mills . . . but to introduce principles in the conduct of people, which I had successfully commenced with the workpeople in Mr Drinkwater's factory'.[4] The body of ideas he had encountered and adopted, and the experience of industry and social organisation he had obtained in Manchester, were to find expression on a vaster scale and in a more deliberate form in his quarter-century at New Lanark.

[1] Ibid., p. 75.
[2] Life, p. 63.
[3] Owen heard a rumour that the mills might be for sale, and pressed his partners to a successful purchase. Dale was not unwilling to sell, says Owen, because they were not being managed 'with the success that he had expected' (ibid., pp. 69–70).
[4] Ibid., p. 78.

The New Lanark mills had a reputation of which Owen must have been aware before he paid his first visit to them in 1797.[1] David Dale had established the mills in 1784, at the time in partnership with Richard Arkwright. By 1792 *The Annual Register* could describe how Dale had 'reared a village on the banks of the Clyde, containing 2000 persons'. There were five cotton mills, each containing 6000 spindles. Dale ('this extraordinary man') had made provisions for the health of the children employed by him:

'They have every day some hours allowed to them for exercise in the fields; and their looks bespeak health and vigour. These hours of relaxation the boys enjoy in succession. Their apartments are likewise clean and well-aired, and ten school-masters are daily employed in their tuition.'[2]

Dale, a fervent leader of a break-away sect from the Church of Scotland,[3] established a reputation as a humane employer which was known among the circles in which Owen moved in Manchester. The *Proceedings of the Manchester Board of Health* reprinted a copy of a letter from Dale in 1796, in answer to a questionnaire from the Board itself. Dale asserted that employment in the mills was 'as favourable to healthy as any other employment' and that the parents of the children who work at my mills for wages considered 'that the part of their family which works at the mills, is more healthy than the part that is at home'. Morals, he maintained, were 'as correct as will be found among an equal number in any manufacturing business'. The majority of pauper children in the 'boarding house' of the mills consisted of

'destitute orphans, children abandoned by their parents, some of whose parents are transported as felons, many who know not who were their parents . . .'

With such children, 'it gives me great pleasure to say, that by proper

---

[1] See *ibid.*, p. 74.

[2] *The Annual Register . . . for the year 1792*, Chronicle, p. 27. *The Proceedings of the Manchester Board of Health* (p. 79) also reprinted an 'Extract of a Letter from James Currie, M.D. of Liverpool, to Dr Percival' dated May 13, 1792, containing a description of New Lanark similar enough to that in *The Annual Register* to show that Currie wrote both accounts. The only discrepancy is that Currie refers to six, not ten, school-masters in the *Proceedings*.

[3] The Old Scotch Independents. See Podmore, *Robert Owen*, p. 50, and *Life*, p. 69.

management, and attention, much *good*, instead of *evil*, may be done at cotton-mills'.[1]

Dale's case was not especially enlightened. His defence of cotton-mills as being uninjurious to health, remembering the age of the children employed,[2] was little different from the viewpoint of most mill owners of the period, and Dale's claim that the standard of morality was *as correct as* that in other manufactories was in itself no commendation. The distinguishing feature of Dale's administration, however, lay in the details of the measures covering health and education. The rooms in the mill were ventilated, walls and ceilings were 'washed at least once a year with new slacked lime' and there were 'weekly washings of machinery and floor'. More important was the fact that some kind of education was attempted. Working hours were $11\frac{1}{2}$ daily[3] and the children had their supper at 7. From about 7.30 to 9 classes were held:

'The schools at present are attended by 507 scholars, in instructing whom there are 16 teachers employed; 13 in teaching to read, two to write, and one to figure . . .'

There was a person to teach sewing, and another occasionally to teach church music. There were eight classes 'according to the progress of the scholars'. The teachers were told in writing how far they had to 'carry forwards' their scholars, and when the prescribed course was completed the children were transferred to a higher class and the teacher received 'a small premium for everyone so qualified'. Lessons were given on Sundays, since the church would hold only 150 at a time, and the remaining children had to be kept busy. There were, in addition, two 'day-schools' for children too young for work.[4] Owen acknowledged Dale's 'unwearied benevolence' in feeding, clothing and educating the

---

[1] *Proceedings of the Manchester Board of Health*, p. 55. (Also in Maltby, *Manchester and the Movement for National Elementary Education*, p. 124.)

[2] '. . . ages appeared to be from five to ten,—but said to be from seven to twelve' (*Life*, p. 83).

[3] '6 A.M.—7 P.M., with intervals, 9-9.30 breakfast, 2-3 dinner' (*Proceedings*, p. 58).

[4] *Ibid.*, pp. 58–60. An account written in 1797 states that for the 'day-schools' Dale had 'engaged three regular masters, who instruct the lesser children during the day. In the evening they are assisted by seven others . . .' (Thomas Barnard, quoted in W. R. Croft, *The History of the Factory Movement, or Oastler and his Times*, Huddersfield, 1888, pp. 6–7). There is some confusion about the number of teachers employed. Owen adds to it by referring to 'the master'—'a good obstinate "dominie" of the old school' (*Life*, p. 192). Perhaps this was the teacher *in charge*.

children, though he described the population of the village under Dale as living 'in idleness, in poverty, in almost every kind of crime; consequently, in debt, out of health, and in misery'.[1] Some critics, in Owen's lifetime and since, have suggested that Owen represented 'the state of society at New Lanark as considerably worse than it really was when he came to it',[2] in order to exaggerate his own achievements.[3] The important fact is that Dale was extending relatively benevolent treatment to some 500 pauper children, necessary as they were to the running of the mill, and though they were given an education from 7.30 to 9 p.m., 'few were able to profit by the teaching received at the evening classes'.[4]

Owen was not only to discontinue the practice of using pauper children; he was to alter the whole basis on which the enterprise and the community were run. Dale's amenities, by comparison, were no more than well-intentioned palliatives.

We are concerned at this point, of course, with education at New Lanark, but it is important to understand that Owen's work in this area was part of an overall programme of change. In addition to the care and education of the children, he tackled three other basic problems—the organisation of the mills themselves, the living conditions of the inhabitants, and the attitudes of the people.[5]

So far as the mills were concerned, he replaced and rearranged machinery, and reorganised, for example, the carrying of material.[6] He undertook an extensive repairs programme and introduced management decentralisation, so that the mills were able to run efficiently during his long absences.[7] He discovered large-scale theft, but since the people

[1] A New View, pp. 26–7.
[2] Brown, Remarks on the Plans and Publications of Robert Owen, Esq. of New Lanark, p. 42.
[3] See also Aiton, Mr Owen's Objections to Christianity, p. 14, and F. A. Packard, Life of Robert Owen, Philadelphia, 1866, pp. 61–2.
[4] Alexander Cullen, Adventures in Socialism. New Lanark Establishment and Orbiston Community, Glasgow, 1910, p. 17. Cullen, without indicating his source, also states that Dale 'confessed that not more than ten per cent. of the children under his care could read and write'. Owen described the children as 'exhausted ... none of them understood anything they attempted to read, and many of them fell asleep during the school hours' (Life, p. 83).
[5] For accounts of the changes introduced by Owen at New Lanark see Owen's Life (pp. 83–190 passim), A New View (second and third essays), Podmore, Robert Owen (particular Chapter V), and Margaret Cole, Robert Owen of New Lanark (Chapters VII–IX).   [6] See Life, p. 188.
[7] See ibid., p. 191. Dr MacNab doubted this, but after a visit to New Lanark wrote: 'It is with pleasure I acknowledge my error' (The New Views of Mr Owen, p. 128).

concerned were 'the creatures of ignorant and vicious circumstances' he did not proceed against them—he changed the circumstances, devising a system of daily returns and frequent balances in every department, making theft difficult.[1] This, of course, was Owen the experienced, efficient, common-sense organiser at work, but such arrangements were part of a comprehensive scheme for long-term improvements.

He let Dale's arrangements with the parishes for a supply of pauper children run out.[2] He reduced working hours substantially, so that a visitor in 1818 or 1819 could comment that the mills closed 'uniformly at half past six; hence none of that overstraining by which the health of children and young people are so much injured in other manufacturing towns, is here permitted'.[3] A 'silent monitor' he introduced 'was the preventer of punishment. There was no beating—no abusive language.' The monitor was a four-sided piece of wood, each side being a different colour, denoting excellent, good, indifferent or bad. The superintendent turned the relevant colour of each worker's monitor to the front, and the master of the mill regulated those of the superintendents. A register of each worker's record was kept. 'It was gratifying', says Owen, 'to observe the new spirit created by these silent monitors.' At the beginning the majority indicated bad, but these gradually diminished.[4]

An anonymous writer in 1839 described in detail how Owen set about remodelling the village itself. Having collected masons and joiners from the surrounding country, he built second storeys on the one-storey dwellings, had dunghills removed from the streets, and had the streets swept daily. He drew up rules which required houses to be cleaned once a week and whitewashed once a year by the tenant. It was forbidden to throw ashes and dirty water into the street, or to keep cattle, swine, poultry or dogs in the houses. Committees were elected to 'inspect houses ('bug hunters' as they were nicknamed), not a popular measure, but one which ultimately established itself. 'In a short time New Lanark, emphatically speaking, was reared upon the ruins of the Old.'[5]

---

[1] *Life*, pp. 79–80 and 111. [2] *Ibid.*, p. 84.

[3] John Griscom, *A Year in Europe*, quoted in C. A. Bennett, *History of Manual and Industrial Education up to 1870*, Illinois, 1926, p. 173. The 1819 Committee under the presidency of the Duke of Kent to 'investigate and report upon Mr Owen's Plan' reported that 'the hours of labour have been shortened from sixteen in the twenty-four to ten and a half' (*Life*, Vol. IA, p. 243).

[4] *Ibid.*, pp. 111–12. Podmore suggests that Owen may have borrowed the idea from Lancaster (*Robert Owen*, p. 91, note).

[5] *R. Owen at New Lanark; with a variety of Interesting Anecdotes . . .* By one formerly a Teacher at New Lanark, Manchester, 1839, p. 4.

He eliminated the high-price retail shops by establishing 'superior stores' which supplied items like fuel and milk at cost price, and other items at a small profit which, after covering the expenses, was 'devoted entirely to the maintenance of the schools'.[1] Changes such as this led to substantial improvements in conditions of life in the village, but in introducing his paternalistic changes Owen met with considerable resistance from the population of the village.

They were prejudiced, Owen explains, against strangers in authority over them, particularly the English, and against him personally because he succeeded Dale, 'under whose proprietorship they acted almost as they liked', because he did not share their religion, and because they expected his new laws and regulations 'to squeeze, as they often termed it, the greatest sum of gain out of their labour'. For the first few years he made no headway.[2]

Suspicion and resistance came from the inhabitants themselves, from the local clergy, and from his partners. Writing in 1824, William Maclure, an American who was to be closely associated with Owen's community venture at New Harmony, described a few days spent at New Lanark as 'the most pleasant in my life . . . contemplating the vast improvement in society effected by Mr Robert Owen's courage and perseverance in spite of an inveterate and malignant opposition'.[3] Owen, as always, laid the blame for such resistance at the door of circumstances. It was evil conditions, ignorance, bad housing, prejudice, that led the people to oppose change. He was patient, explained his intentions to the influential ones among them, and saw his principles prevail year by year.[4] Gradually they gave him their confidence. 'They were taught to be rational, and they acted rationally.'[5] Health and dress improved, drunkenness declined and religious tolerance among sects increased. Finally, in 1806, when the United States laid an embargo on the export of cotton, causing prices to soar, and placing manufacturers in the dilemma of whether to discharge their workers or continue hazardously to work up material at high prices, Owen decided to stop the machines, but continue to pay full wages for keeping them clean and in good working condition. The embargo lasted four months, during

[1] Podmore, *Robert Owen*, p. 86. See also *Life*, p. 87, and *A New View*, p. 33.
[2] *A New View*, p. 29.
[3] Quoted in A. E. Bestor (ed.), *Education and Reform at New Harmony*, Indianapolis, 1948, p. 307.
[4] *Life*, pp. 85–7.
[5] *A New View*, p. 30.

which time the population 'received more than seven thousand pounds sterling for their unemployed time ... This proceeding won the confidence and the hearts of the whole population.'[1]

The reputation of the mills and the village began to spread. Visitors commented on the intelligence and contentedness of the people, the lack of crime, the superior arrangements in general.[2] An astonishing number of visitors came to New Lanark, including the future Czar of Russia, ambassadors, bishops, British and foreign nobility, is learned men of all professions from all countries—and wealthy travellers for pleasure or knowledge of every description'.[3] Certainly until 1817, and to a large extent well beyond that date, praise came from all quarters. Such criticism as there was tended to be associated with religious sectarianism.[4]

Owen himself was never satisfied with what he accomplished 'under the circumstances of an ill-arranged manufactory and village',[5] and told a deputation from Leeds in August 1819 that he had advanced 'only two points towards twenty, supposing the latter to be the number of perfection'.[6] Owen was to make many extensions of ideas out of his experience at New Lanark, and, in a different situation, the reception accorded to his ideas was to change. For Owen, however, his firm belief that reason must prevail was immeasurably strengthened by the fact that the population of New Lanark 'were taught to be rational, and they acted rationally'.[7]

The difficulties Owen encountered as a result of his partnerships are important only in that, with the first two, they delayed the application

[1] *Life*, pp. 87–8. Dale had behaved similarly when a mill was burned down in 1788 (see R. D. Owen, *Threading My Way*, p. 15).

[2] See *Address of the Committee* appointed by a public meeting in London in 1819 to examine Owen's community plans and report on New Lanark, *Life*, Vol. IA, p. 243, and Frederic Hill, *National Education*, London, 1836, p. 298.

[3] *Life*, p. 203. See also James Smith, *Notes taken during an Excursion in Scotland in the year 1820*, reprinted in *N.M.W.*, Vol. II, No. 80, May 7, 1836.

[4] See, for example, Aiton, *Mr Owen's Objections to Christianity* (describing the visitors to New Lanark as 'benevolent individuals and committees of philanthropic societies, speculative regenerators of mankind, gossiping justices, and jail-gadding ladies . . .', p. 13). See also Mary Howitt, *An Autobiography*, London, 1889, Vol. I, p. 170.

[5] *Life*, p. 109.

[6] *Report of a Deputation from Leeds*, in *Life*, Vol. IA, p. 257.

[7] Edmund Wilson thinks Owen was too modest: '. . . it had never occurred to him that he himself was a man of exceptionally high character and that it was he and not the natural goodness of the children of those ill-conditioned parents who had made New Lanark a model community' (*To the Finland Station*, London, 1942, p. 93).

of his plans for education. The first, a product of his period in Manchester, gave him a one-ninth interest in the partnership and a thousand pounds a year as sole manager.[1] His partners disapproved, however, of his plan to erect what he later called the Institution for the Formation of Character, and agreed to sell their share.[2] Under the second partnership, formed in 1809, he held the greatest share, but the new partnership was even less successful than the first, with his partners trying to prevent further work being undertaken on the schools. The partnership was dissolved, the others tried to win control of the mills from Owen at an auction in 1814, but failed.[3] It was only at this point that Owen was given the green light to go ahead with his educational plans; he had canvassed financial support in the new partnership precisely on the basis of those plans. The new partners consisted of John Walker, a wealthy Quaker, 'a most disinterested benevolent man, highly educated, possessing great taste in the arts . . . well versed in the sciences', Joseph Foster, also a Quaker, 'a man without guile, possessed with the genuine spirit of charity and kindness, and who had one of the most expanded and liberal and well-informed minds,' William Allen, another Quaker, and well-known scientist, Joseph Fox, a wealthy dissenter and dentist, Michael Gibbs, subsequently Alderman and Lord Mayor of London, 'a Church of England man, a conservative, and a man, as I believed, of good intentions, fair abilities, and business habits', and Jeremy Bentham.[4] It was therefore not until 1816 that Owen was able to open the Institution for the Formation of Character, which was to house the schools, although, of course, the development of the educational facilities at New Lanark had been going ahead on a limited basis right from the beginning.

The major measure which made educational expansion possible was Owen's refusal to accept children into the mills below the age of ten, and he tried to persuade parents to keep the children at school until twelve.[5] The articles drawn up in advance for the third partnership laid

---

[1] *Life*, pp. 107–8.

[2] They had bought the mills from Dale for £60,000, and accepted Owen's valuation now at £84,000 (*ibid.*, p. 73).

[3] At a cost of £114,100. For the story see *ibid.*, pp. 121–35.

[4] *Ibid.*, pp. 130–3. Sir Samuel Romilly tried to dissuade Bentham from joining the partnership, among other reasons because he thought Owen, 'though very well-intentioned, was really a little mad' (quoted in R. H. Harvey, *Robert Owen, Social Idealist*, California, 1949, p. 27).

[5] *A New View*, p. 32. See also *An Outline*, p. 31. Some writers have mistakenly believed that Owen kept *all* the children in school until the age of twelve. Donald

down that 'the children shall not be employed in the mills belonging to the partnership, until they shall be of such an age as shall not be prejudicial to their health.'[1] By extending the school age downwards at the other end by the opening of the infant school, and making more viable evening facilities available beyond the age of ten, Owen made education not an adjunct, but a central feature of the New Lanark community.

(iv) A spectacle worth the seeing

The Institution for the Formation of Character was formally opened by Owen with an address on January 1, 1816.[2] It was described by John Griscom as a 'neat and commodious building . . . erected for the purpose of instruction, in a pleasant spot near the centre of the village'.[3] There were two storeys. Upstairs were two large rooms, twenty feet high (one, ninety feet by forty, the other forty-nine by forty[4]), the first with desks and forms, used for lectures, dancing and singing lessons, and as a ballroom. The lower storey was divided into three rooms of equal dimensions, twelve feet high. The headmaster of the school wrote to MacNab in 1819, giving details of the use to which these rooms were put:

> 'The centre room on the ground floor is set apart for the exercise and amusement of children from two to four years of age . . . This class is called the infant school . . . The room on the left is occupied by children from four to six years of age . . . The room to the right hand is occupied by children from six to eight years of age.'[5]

Owen's son later expressed a regret that the space had not been divided into even smaller rooms, since 'the facility of teaching the older classes particularly, would have been greatly increased, had some part of the building been divided into smaller apartments, appropriating one to

---

Read, for example, says that Owen 'set up schools for all children under twelve, at which age they could enter the factories' (*Manchester Guardian*, November 17, 1958).

[1] *Life of William Allen, with Selections from his Correspondence*, p. 183.

[2] At an initial cost of at least £5,000, and involving an annual outlay of over £700 (Podmore, *Robert Owen*, p. 86: see also *Life*, Vol. IA, p. 243 and the anonymous author of *R. Owen at New Lanark*, p. 13).

[3] Quoted in *Bennett, History of Manual and Industrial Education up to 1870*, p. 173.

[4] *An Outline*, p. 29.

[5] MacNab, *The New Views of Mr Owen*, pp. 221-3.

each class of from twenty to thirty children'.[1] The division made, however, was an advance on previous practice. Alexander Cullen stressed the fact that Owen 'did not approve of teaching several classes in a large room, and advocated, instead, a series of small class-rooms providing accommodation for from thirty to forty scholars'.[2] The upper storey was supported by 'hollow iron pillars, serving, at the same time, as conductors, in winter, for heated air'.[3] There was also, according to the anonymous former teacher, 'a large apartment fitted up with elegant and usefully constructed bathing machines, for the purpose of promoting the health and cleanliness of the children'.[4]

Owen describes the infant schoolroom as being 'furnished with paintings, chiefly of animals, with maps, and often supplied with natural objects from the gardens, fields, and woods',[5] and his son describes the smaller of the two upper apartments as being 'hung round with representations of the most striking zoological and mineralogical specimens; including quadrupeds, birds, fishes, reptiles, insects, shells, minerals, &c. . . . and . . . very large representations of the two hemispheres; each separate country, as well as the various seas, islands, &c., being differently coloured, but without any names attached to them'.[6]

Outside the building a playground was laid out, 'regularly walled in, and kept shut during the hours of teaching'.[7] This playground was also described as 'a very large space of ground . . . all seated round for the accommodation of children from two years and a half to four years of age' where the children 'were all furnished with balls, trundling hoops, marbles, tops, &c. for outside amusement, with nurses adequate for the number of children'.[8] Into this playground, says Owen, children were received 'as soon as they can freely walk alone',[9] and children were, in fact, admitted to the infant school from the age of about two.[10]

<hr />

[1] *An Outline*, p. 30.

[2] Cullen, *Adventures in Socialism*, p. 51.   [3] *An Outline*, p. 30.

[4] *R. Owen at New Lanark*, p. 13. He gives no other details, and no other writer refers to this apartment.

[5] *Life*, p. 193.   [6] *An Outline*, p. 29.

[7] Letter from headmaster to Macnab, in *The New Views of Mr Owen*, p. 221. Robert Dale Owen describes it as a 'large paved area in front of the Institution' (*An Outline*, p. 32).

[8] *The Working Bee and Herald of the Hodsonian Community Society*, Vol. I, No. 34, March 7, 1840 (CUL/1250), a letter from Alexander Ross, who describes himself as having 'spent some of my happiest days at New Lanark, in Scotland, under the auspices of Robert Owen . . .'

[9] *A New View*, p. 40.

[10] In his evidence to a Committee of the House of Commons in 1816, Owen

We have seen that Owen gave instructions that each child, right from his introduction into the infant school, was to be persuaded 'never to injure his play-fellows' and the arrangements in the infant school were clearly designed to secure the type of environment which would counter-act the harmful influence of the old, irrational ways of society. In 1819 there was one teacher and three female attendants for the infants, who played in the playground in fine weather. Sir William de Crespigny described the atmosphere as one of 'harmlessness, of fondness, and of attention to each other, which we do not often witness in this country'.[1] Such an atmosphere was created by affection, play and consideration for the children *as children*:

> 'When . . . any infant felt inclined to sleep, it should be quietly allowed to do so.'[2]

On the basis of the need to take *active* steps towards the formation of the infant character, a small amount of formal tuition was included in the programme of the infants. 'As soon as they have acquired habits of speaking', said the headmaster, they are taken 'in rotation in classes of ten or twelve' and 'taught the letters of the alphabet, monosyllables, &c.',[3] though Robert Dale Owen later maintained that 'no attempt was made to teach them reading or writing'.[4] If there was at any stage such a formal element in the programme, it can have been but an extremely minor one. Owen emphasised in 1816 that the children were taught 'by example and practice . . . whatever may be supposed useful, that they can understand; and this instruction is combined with as much amuse-ment as is found to be requisite for their health, and to render them active, cheerful, and happy, fond of the school and of their instructors'. It was, in fact, this spirit, pervading the schools as a whole, that dis-tinguished education at New Lanark from that provided in any of the types of the school that we have previously discussed, and that made New Lanark such a place of pilgrimage.

The children moved up from the infant school after two or three years, but for the remainder of their schooling they continued to be

---

gave the age as three (*Westminster Review*, Vol. XLVI, No. 1, October 1846, p. 221). Sir William de Crespigny, in 1822, described 'little children a year and a half old, and some a little older, in a sort of play-ground' (*Proceedings of the First General Meeting of the British and Foreign Philanthropic Society*, p. 13).

[1] *Ibid.*, p. 13.   [2] *Life*, p. 241.
[3] MacNab, *The New Views of Mr Owen*, p. 221.
[4] *Threading My Way*, p. 90.

'instructed in healthy and useful amusements for an hour or two every day'.[1] The 4–6 age group, for example, 'are permitted to amuse themselves, and to receive lessons alternately during the day',[2] and the time-table was organised throughout to ensure variety and prevent boredom. The headmaster described, for example, a typical day for the 6–8-year-old children. The boys were first taught arithmetic while the girls sat drawing or doing sums on slates; then, after three quarters of an hour, the girls were attended to by the teacher while the boys got on with their work. 'In the forenoon they are all employed in reading, writing, and spelling, and also nearly in the same manner in the afternoon. They attend alternately the singing and dancing master.' The 8–10-year-olds, learning geometry, English grammar, arithmetic, dancing, singing, vocal and instrumental music, changed 'often the objects of study during the day'.[3] Lessons never exceeded three-quarters of an hour and were made as interesting as possible; inattention on the part of the children led the teacher to look 'to the lecture itself, and to his manner of delivering it, rather than to the children, to discover the cause'.[4] The atmosphere in the upper classes, continued, therefore, to be one of generosity and kindliness.

Owen would have preferred to eliminate books altogether from the classroom at least until the age of seven or eight, but reading was, in fact, taught earlier to meet the parents' wishes.[5] He told the teachers in the infant school, however, that 'the children were not to be bothered with books; but were to be taught the uses and nature or qualities of the common things around them, by familiar conversation when the children's curiosity was excited.'[6]

After the 'limiting' views on education we have examined, the curriculum at New Lanark looks almost unbelievable. Robert Dale Owen's account covers content and method in the teaching of reading, writing, arithmetic, sewing, natural history, geography, ancient and modern history, religion, singing, and dancing.[7] This was not, of course,

[1] Owen's evidence to the 1816 committee, *The Westminster Review*, Vol. XLVI, No. 1, October 1846, p. 221.
[2] Headmaster to MacNab, in *The New Views of Mr Owen*, p. 222.
[3] *Ibid.*, pp. 222–3.   [4] *An Outline*, pp. 25–6.
[5] *Ibid.*, p. 34.   [6] *Life*, p. 193.
[7] See *An Outline*, pp. 35–77. An appendix (pp. 81–103) gives the scheme of the 'Introduction to the Arts and Sciences' used with the children, a survey which covers The Earth (how animals, vegetables and minerals change, live, move and think), Astronomy, Geography, Mathematics, Zoology, Botany, Mineralogy, Agriculture, Manufactures, Architecture, Drawing and Music.

some encyclopaedic cram course; it was the range within which skills were taught and curiosity aroused.

Reading, for which it was difficult to find suitable text books, was taught not as a mechanical exercise, but with a stress on understanding: 'children should never be directed to read what they cannot understand'.[1] Writing was taught by copying 'short sentences, generally illustrative of some subject connected with history or geography', and later passages 'that may be considered as difficult, and at the same time important to be retained in their memory'. In arithmetic, an attempt was made to teach the children to understand the processes they were expected to use.[2]

Natural history, geography and history were all taught by 'familiar lectures, delivered extempore, by the teachers' and the attempt was made to balance what was necessary with 'distracting detail'. Outlines were given first, the detail filled in later. Large drawings and charts were fastened to the walls on rollers, and the children were at all times encouraged to 'express their opinions . . . freely, and to ask any explanation'. In subjects like history and geography Owen's theories of character training for an improved society found direct embodiment. Geography, for example, was used to 'repress illiberal or uncharitable sentiments' and combat irrationalism by widening the children's horizons so that they did not suppose their own country equalled perfection.[3] The children were led to realise that if they had been born elsewhere they might have been 'Cannibals or Hindoos', thus encouraging greater tolerance.[4] Owen describes a geography lesson given to a number of classes joined together, about a hundred and fifty children—as many as could be gathered round a huge map of the world, without names, 'so large as almost to cover the end of the room'. A long wand was given to one of the children, and the others asked him to point to a given place, and 'when the holder of the wand was at fault, and could not point to the place asked for, he had to resign the wand to his questioner'. This, Owen tells us, 'became most amusing to the children' and was particularly fascinating to visitors.[5]

History, similarly, had its visual aid—a huge arrangement of 'seven

---

[1] *Ibid.*, p. 36.

[2] *Ibid.*, pp. 39–40. Robert Dale Owen states (writing in 1823) that the elder classes were 'just beginning a regular course of mental arithmetic, similar to that adapted by M. Pestalozzi of Iverdun'. For Owen and the continental reformers, see Chapter III (iii) below.

[3] *Ibid.*, pp. 41–6.   [4] *Ibid.*, pp. 47–8.   [5] *Life*, p. 199.

large maps or tables, laid out on the principle of the Stream of Time',
illustrating the principal events in the history of the different nations.[1]
Singing and music were a prominent feature of the school:

> '. . . One hundred and fifty would sing at the same time—their voices
> being trained to harmonize; and it was delightful to hear them sing
> the old popular Scotch songs.'[2]

Music, in Owen's words, was part of the 'diversified innocent amusement'[3] offered in the school, but dancing had an even stronger justification—it was 'for the benefit of the health and spirits of the children both
boys and girls'.[4] Visitors were charmed by 'the little children, who at
other times are running about in the dirt, without shoes or stockings,
dancing quadrilles in the most elegant style'.[5] The more puritanical
visitors, and some of Owen's partners, however, were perturbed by such
pagan practices, and even more so, in the case of the Quakers, by the
military exercises Owen introduced.

His partners had no cause to be surprised by this innovation, since
Owen had announced his views on this score in *A New View*. Were all
men trained to be rational, he had said, the art of war would be rendered
useless, but so long as men are trained to be irrational and 'acquire
feelings of enmity . . . even the most rational must, for their personal
security, learn the means of defence'. The specific plan he had announced
for New Lanark, therefore, was the training of the boys[6] in the art of
defence, including drill, the use of fire-arms and 'the more complicated
military movements'.[7] The children, in fact, learn such manoeuvres as
'facing, to the right about, &c. and marching to the music of the fife,
performed by the boys of the school'.[8]

[1] R. D. Owen, *An Outline*, p. 50. Miss Whitwell, 'the lady who had painted
the "stream of time" and assisted in the New Lanark schools' was later in
charge of the education of the children under twelve at Orbiston (Cullen,
Adventures in Socialism, p. 277). In 1824 Owen's partners caused 'Miss Whitwell
to cease to be a servant of the company'. (See Sargant, *Robert Owen and his Social
Philosophy*, pp. 190–1.)

[2] *Life*, p. 198. They were taught to sing 'spirited songs in the bravura style'
(R. D. Owen, *An Outline*, p. 70).

[3] *Address at New Lanark*, in *A New View*, p. 99.

[4] *Ibid.*, p. 98. See also *Life*, p. 320 and R. D. Owen, *An Outline*, pp. 70–1.

[5] From the journal of Chandos Lord Leigh, dated 1827, quoted in Bennett,
History of Manual and Industrial Education, p. 174.

[6] In fact 'both sexes . . . were drilled' (*Life*, p. 195).

[7] *A New View*, pp. 57–8.

[8] Headmaster to MacNab, in *The New Views of Mr Owen*, p. 2. See also *Life*,
pp. 195 and 198, R. D. Owen, *An Outline*, p. 71, and J. Smith, quoted in *N.M.W.*

The overall effect of the arrangements in these day schools was obviously such as to arouse among visitors an enthusiasm that no other school in Britain at the time was capable of arousing. Lord Lytton, for example, visited the schools in the company of Owen:

'It was a spectacle worth the seeing. The education seemed to me admirable. Never in any more aristocratic school have I beheld so many intelligent faces, or witnessed the same general amount of information. And the children, in their neat, uniform dresses, looked so clean and so happy. I stood by his side observing them, with the tears starting from my eyes'.[1]

James Smith was impressed above all by the 'delighted looks' of the children when they received Owen, and the fact that in all his observations he 'did not see one angry look or gesture'.[2] Such accumulated reports built up to an enormous reputation for Owen's work with the New Lanark children, so that the Duke of Kent, speaking from the chair at a meeting in 1819, could refer to the 'universally admitted success of his great 'experiment at New Lanark'. There were people present, he said 'of high respectability' who had visited the establishment in Owen's absence. They had stated that 'the happiness of these children, even from three years of age, exceeds everything of the kind they ever witnessed; and that their conduct in all respects was equal to their happiness'.[3]

The importance of this achievement lay primarily in the fact that the principles behind it ran counter to all the theories of education being practised in either the monitorial schools, or in what Lytton called the

---

Vol. II, No. 81, May 14, 1836 ('marching and counter-marching, and scarcely exceeds what is usually practised in schools, and on the Lancasterian plan). Aiton's characteristic comment was that the world would be indebted to New Lanark 'for a liberal supply of expert dancing-masters, agile opera-girls, active drill-sergeants, strolling jugglers . . .' (*Mr Owen's Objections to Chrstianity*, p. 24).

[1] Lytton, *The Life of Edward Bulwer, First Lord Lytton*, Vol. I, p. 92. The 'uniform dresses' were provided for day children. R. D. Owen describes them as being of 'strong white cotton cloth . . . in the shape of the Roman tunic' (*An Outline*, p. 33). The author of *R. Owen at New Lanark*, however, describes them as 'a beautiful dress of tartan cloth, fashioned in its make after the form of the Roman toga' (p. 13).

[2] *N.M.W.*, Vol. II, No. 80, May 7, 1836. MacNab declared himself incapable of describing 'the young, innocent, and fascinating countenances of these happy children and youths. The pen of a Milton and the pencil of a Rubens could not do justice to such a picture' (*The New Views of Mr Owen*, p. 137).

[3] *Life*, Vol. IA, p. 238.

'more aristocratic schools'. No one was being hoisted up to the ceiling in a basket or being shackled to someone else or to the desk. There was no elaborate system of punishments and rewards—Owen was opposed to both on principle. 'Punishment', he wrote, 'in a rationally conducted infant school will never be required . . . No marks of merit or demerit should be given to any; no partiality shown to any one.'[1] Coercion was not used in the schools at New Lanark, and chaos was not the result.[2]

The extent to which Owen's mode of education tampered with established assumptions about the individual and society is shown, however, by the quarter in which its very efficacy was seen to be dangerous. After all, it was realised, the absence of punishment and reward in the classroom was merely an aspect of Owen's more general belief that punishment and reward in society at large were wrong, since no man forms his character, and is therefore absolved of praise or blame. A most forthright statement of this realisation of the implications of Owen's views on punishment came from a writer in *Blackwood's* in 1823. 'Punishments and rewards have, in all ages', he said, 'constituted the chief instruments which men have employed in forming the characters, and regulating the conduct, of their fellow-creatures. But these are to form no part of the "circumstances" of new society, as controlled by Mr Owen and his friends.' Man, according to Owen, is as Nature made him and circumstances modified him, and he therefore cannot be blamed or punished. It is not necessary to try to argue the doctrine of moral liberty, the writer contended, in order to show Owen's fallacy. 'We leave Mr Owen', he indignantly added, 'to settle with his own conscience the matter of his accountableness in the *next* world. But we tell him, that whether his character has been formed *for* him or *by* him, he, in common with all mankind, may be a fit subject both for punishment and reward, in *this*.' The crux of such hostility lies in the fact that Owen was *successful*. 'He tells the children of his establishments to be good, and kind to each other, and avoid selfishness', says the *Blackwood's* writer, 'but parents, ministers of religion, and teachers of youth, do the same in old society. Now what peculiar charm are these good advices to acquire by issuing out of his mouth . . .?'[3] This question and the whole

[1] *Life*, pp. 241–2.
[2] Mary Howitt, in a very self-contradictory account thought coercion probably *was* used (*An Autobiography*, Vol. I, p. 170). The weight of the evidence is against her.
[3] 'Remarks on Mr Owen's Plan', in *Blackwood's Edinburgh Magazine*, Vol. XIII, No. LXXIV, March, 1823, p. 340.

article are directed specifically against Owen's plan for the establishment of communities, and there was some justification for wondering how Owen's 'advices' would act on communities of *adults* trained in old society; phrased in terms of *children*, however, the question merely shows how deep-rooted was the conservative belief that children were inevitably corrupt. It showed how difficult it was, in the final analysis, for people in the most entrenched positions (whom *Blackwood's* certainly represented) to accept the fact that Owen did not tell the children to be good in the same way as old-society parents and ministers did; he did so in a situation in which the words had meaning, in which change was demonstrably taking place, and in which it was not the delivery of the precept that mattered.

Other aspects of education at New Lanark do not radically alter the implications of the picture we have so far examined. The evening schools, for example, offering continued education to the children who left school at ten were immensely successful, and, said Owen, 'it is found that out of choice, about 400 on an average attend every evening'.[1] The range of evening activities covered the subjects we have already seen taught in the day. The adults who worked in the mills, says one ex-resident of New Lanark, 'had the same advantages of education, from the hours of seven till nine o'clock every night, and the girls had the benefit of learning needlework of every description, and the whole was conducted at Mr Owen's private expense'. There were in addition 'weekly lectures on chemistry and mechanism, for the benefit of old and young of the community'.[2] There were also facilities for adult entertainment, including—prominently—music and dancing.[3] The evening classes were for Owen an important continuation of the education begun in the earlier years, though there is no doubt that they were an ad hoc substitute for the full-time education he would have preferred to continue giving the children. His central concern, in his programme for the formation and re-formation of character, was with the children. Considering the prevalent attitudes towards the child in this period,

[1] Evidence to the 1816 committee, *The Westminster Review*, Vol. XLVI, No. 1, October, 1846, p. 221.

[2] Alexander Ross in *The Working Bee*, Vol. I, No. 34, March 7, 1840 (CUL/ 1250).

[3] For a description of a typical Ball and Concert, see *The Economist*, No.13, April 21, 1821. The deputation from Leeds (*Life*, Vol. IA, p. 255) mentions the evening classes and pays tribute to the exemplary deportment of the young people.

and the monumental resistance New Lanark represented to the callousness built-in to the new industrial situation, it is all the more astonishing that Owen's place in the histories of education should have been so insecure.

(v) The legitimate object of society

The Institution for the Formation of Character, then, represents the triumph of eighteenth century rationalism and the 'revolutionary leaven' of the Godwinian '90s. To see what became of the ideas of *A New View of Society* and the experience of education at New Lanark, it is essential to see briefly what Owen himself became between 1816 and the virtual end of New Lanark as his field of operations in 1824.

Although he continued to affirm his basic views about human nature and education, and did so to the end of his life, important changes of emphasis in his general expression of opinion had already begun to take place. The outstanding one was his advocacy of the establishment of communities.

He continued, amidst political and social hurly-burly, to pin his faith on reason and persuasion, the inevitable success of the rational statement of truth. New Lanark had strengthened this belief. In the first of a famous series of public addresses in 1817, for example, he explained that he had attempted 'to make the still small voice of truth heard among my fellow-men. It was gone forth, like the dove from the ark . . . This truth will not rest in its progress until it has visited and pervaded all parts of the earth.'[1] He announced the following month the forthcoming publication of a journal called *The Mirror of Truth*, which would ensure that 'none shall remain in darkness'.[2]

If, as Owen believed, one had only to proclaim the truth for it ultimately to prevail, it is not surprising to find him reiterating the same truths time and again. From 1816, Owen was, in fact, pursuing ways of propagating his rapidly hardening views on the causes of social distress and the solutions to be applied, appearing on committees, calling meetings, distributing copies of newspapers containing reports of his speeches, and elaborating detailed proposals for community and similar schemes.

---

[1] Address of August 14, 1817, in *Life*, Vol. IA, p. 92.

[2] Address of September 19, 1817, in *ibid.*, p. 140. Margaret Cole, in *Robert Owen of New Lanark* (p. 125), states that this journal never appeared. Two issues did, in fact, appear, on October 10 and November 7, 1817.

Edmund Wilson has stigmatised education as 'the last hope of the liberal in all periods'.[1] The interesting fact about Owen, dedicated to the cause of education, is that throughout his career he never in any sense fell back on it as his last hope. In the propaganda methods he adopted in the late 1810's, and in all the successes and defeats of later years, education for him, as for his followers, was part of a wider scheme of social action, associated with the actual needs of men. In *A New View* he was concerned about problems of unemployment, for example, in discussing his plans for national education.[2] In his *Observations on the Effect of the Manufacturing System*, and in his work in connection with what finally became the 1819 Act on cotton mills and factories, he set education in the context of the reform of industrial conditions (although even the minimal educational provisions Owen pressed for inclusion in parliamentary legislation did not appear in the final version of the 1819 Act, an Act which was the direct outcome of his efforts). From 1817, with his *Report*[3] advocating the establishment of communities to settle the poor, education became increasingly bound up with his general plans to provide employment. Education was one of the factors which could help towards a long-term solution to poverty. Means should be devised, he urged, 'to give the most useful training and instruction to the children of the poor'.[4] His *Report to the County of Lanark* in 1820 affirmed that 'training and education must be viewed as intimately connected with the employments of the association. The latter, indeed, will form an essential part of education under these arrangements.'[5]

The twin targets of employment (at this stage through the foundation of communities) and education remained inextricably linked for Owen and his followers. The first issue of Owen's first newspaper, *The Crisis*, in 1832, for example, stated that its object was to show the industrious classes how they 'can be placed under better circumstances to be well educated and beneficially employed'. Error and misery would be removed, and truth and happiness promoted 'by Education and

[1] *To the Finland Station*, p. 31.
[2] See *A New View*, p. 86.
[3] *Report to the Committee of the Association for the Relief of the Manufacturing and Labouring Poor*, March 1817, in *Life*, Vol. IA, pp. 53–64. This Committee, finding the *Report* too startling in its proposals, referred it to the Committee of the House of Commons sitting on the Poor Laws.
[4] *Ibid.*, p. 56.
[5] *Life*, Vol. IA, p. 297.

Employment'.[1] In 1843 we find groups of Owenites organising petitions to Queen Victoria, placing the two equally firmly together:

'... the most essential highest and by far the most important duty of all Governments (is) to form permanent National Arrangements, to ensure regular advantageous employment, and a superior practical education for the governed'.[2]

An Owenite, writing to Owen in 1848, told him of a visit to Lord Ashley's home 'during which I endeavoured to urge upon him the necessity of the Govt. adopting measures to employ and educate the people'.[3]

Owen also continued to believe that educational provisions were best and most justly made for the working classes 'by the country which gives them birth and to which they are afterwards to lend their aid and support',[4] and would have preferred his plans for the co-operative communities he sought to establish to be nationally rather than privately sponsored.[5] The communities he proposed were initially intended to resettle groups of 500–1,500 of the poor population in self-supporting villages which would provide adequate employment and living standards for the inhabitants.[6] All such plans contained detailed proposals for the provision of schools, as for example in the 1817 *Report*, which provided for 'a building, of which the ground-floor will form the infant school, and the other a lecture-room and a place of worship'. Another building contained 'a school for the elder children' and 'a library, and a room for adults'. In these schools the children were to be 'well instructed in

[1] Vol. I, No. 1, April 14, 1832. Owen had already in 1831 launched an Association of the Intelligent and well disposed of the Industrious Classes for removing the causes of Ignorance and Poverty, by Education and Employment. For later expressions of the same twin theme, see, for example, *The Signs of the Times; or, the Approach of the Millennium*, London, 1841, p. 3, and a speech reported at a conference on strikes and lock-outs in *The Journal of the Royal Society of Arts*, Supplement to Vol. II, No. 63, February 3, 1854, p. 200.

[2] MS 'Address of the Members of Branch 63 of the Rational Society and the Inhabitants of the Tower Hamlets ... Whitechapel on April 10, 1843' (Pare MS 578/121).. For a similar address from the unemployed of Halifax, see Pare MS 578/123.

[3] A. Campbell to Owen, June 22, 1848, in CUL/1634.

[4] *Observations on the Cotton Trade*, 1815, in *Life*, Vol. IA, p. 18.

[5] 'If such should be the conviction of Government, the change proposed in the management of the poor and unemployed working classes will be much better directed nationally than privately' (*Report*, 1817, in *Life*, Vol. IA, p. 62).

[6] For the most detailed plans of such community settlements see *Report* (1817) in *Life*, Vol. IA, pp. 53–64, and *Report to the County of Lanark*, in *ibid.*, pp. 263–310.

all necessary and useful knowledge', but exercise and recreation were not forgotten.[1]

The important fact is that in relation to the communities (occasionally advocating the separation of children from parents, largely because of prevalent parental neglect) Owen continued to express a highly-developed commitment to social action and responsibility. In a speech at Holkham in 1821, Owen began his exposition of his plans for communities with the words:

> 'The legitimate object of society is to improve the physical, moral, and intellectual characters of men . . . and in the most convenient manner to supply all their wants, in order that they may experience the least suffering and the greatest enjoyment.
>
> Society, as it is now constituted, is not calculated to produce these results.'[2]

His schemes for communities began in answer to the specific problem of unemployment and destitution, but they evolved into a much broader concept of the reorganisation of the whole pattern of society.[3] The planned community settlement became for Owen the point at which most affirmatively to begin to pursue society's 'legitimate object' of improving character, and the urgent problems of poverty gave the question its sharpest focus.

Throughout this period he continued also to reaffirm his analysis of the perfectibility of human character through a change of circumstances. He continued to assert the predominant role of circumstances, but at the same time became increasingly concerned, partly in an attempt to answer criticism of his position, to insist that he did not deny the role of the original make-up of the individual. In 1815 we find him stating that children 'may be taught any habits and any sentiments; and that these, with the bodily and mental propensities and faculties existing at birth in each individual, combined with the general circumstances in which he

---

[1] *Ibid.*, pp. 58–9.

[2] R. N. Bacon, *A Report of the Transactions at the Holkham Sheep-Shearing, on . . . July 2, 3, 4, and 5 . . .*, Norwich, 1821, p. 118. This contains Owen's speech in reply to a toast and the paper he read. Owen's reply to the toast is also in *The Economist*, No. 29, August 11, 1821, and his paper, under the title *An EXPLANATION of the CAUSE of the DISTRESS which pervades the Civilized Parts of the World*, in No. 32, September 1, 1821.

[3] See W. H. G. Armytage, *Heavens Below*, Chapter II, for a survey of the thinking behind the community plans, and the experiments made.

is placed, constitute the whole character of man'.[1] It is true, he conceded that the power of society over the individual is not without limit:

> 'It cannot recreate and altogether change the natural faculties and qualities which are given to children at birth . . . Such, indeed, is the overwhelming influence which experience has now given to society over the rising generation, that it may surround children from their birth with new circumstances, which shall form each of them bodily and mentally, in such a manner that his habits, dispositions, and general character, shall be greatly superior to the habits, dispositions, and general character which the circumstances of birth have yet formed for man in any part of the world.'

This remained Owen's basic, carefully considered position.[2]

One of the curious facts about Owen in this period is that he established for himself a balance between an intense desire for the total reorganisation of society and a conviction that change needed to be gradual. It was not a compromise position between the two that he adopted; he simply held both views, placing the emphasis according to the situation. The total-reorganisation thread lies in the intensive activity on behalf of his community schemes; the 'gradualist' thread finds constant expression in what came ultimately to be his opposition to political radicalism, to Chartism, to mass action which aimed to alter the balance of society (however unjust) at the expense of the interests of any one section. Owen wished to change society by stepping outside it and demonstrating to it from the detached position of his community experiments that there was a more favourable option than the current organisation of society; he opposed the inflamation of passions to make what he considered minor rectifications in the social structure. Circumstances needed to be altered fundamentally (and in this Owen's views

---

[1] *Observations on the Effect of the Manufacturing System*, in *Life*, Vol. IA, p. 44. In 1817 he felt it necessary to defend himself against the charge that his views, if implemented, would 'produce a dull uniformity of character' (Letter of July 25, 1817, in *ibid.*, p. 72).

[2] *Memorial to the Governments of Europe and America*, 1818, in *ibid.*, p. 217. Owen had to make an occasional retreat in his definitions and confuse his position (see MacNab, *The New Views of Mr Owen*, p. 227). For further discussion of it see *N.M.W.*, Vol. II, No. 78, April 23, 1836. Owen and G. A. Fleming defend it against attack by the phrenologist, George Combe, in *N.M.W.*, Vol. III, No. 128, April 8, 1837, and No. 135, May 27, 1837. See also *Robert Owen's Weekly Letter to the Human Race*, No. XIV, March 1850.

were strongly paternalistic) and men needed to be changed, and prepared for change.

It was this view which led him into direct opposition to what he in 1817 called the 'premature Reformists'[1]—those who believed that the mass of the people could then and there be recruited into a struggle for a larger measure of political justice. Opposition to political reform was to remain a constant feature of his position. Owen believed, in fact, that the improvements he wished to see brought about in the conditions of the poor could only come through an appeal to the interests of *all* classes. He could not see how the rational and reasonable could possibly be against anyone's interests, economic or otherwise. The rational ordering of human affairs would benefit all 'without a single exception',[2] and would bring that improvement in the condition of the poor 'which all classes have so great an interest in promoting'.[3] Owen continued to believe that the men of power and influence would ultimately prove amenable to his persuasion.[4]

He was appealing, therefore, throughout this period, for help in repeating on a wider national basis what he had attempted at New Lanark—to change circumstances and provide education. The *Report to the County of Lanark* (1820) was Owen's most consummate statement of the two aims, and contains one of his clearest expositions of the purpose and value of education, interpreted boldly and broadly.

By the age of twelve, Owen tells us, a child 'may with ease be trained to acquire a correct view of the outline of all the knowledge which men have yet attained'. By this means, therefore, 'he will early learn what he is in relation to past ages, to the period in which he lives, to the circumstances in which he is placed, to the individuals around him, and to future events. *He will then only have any pretensions to the name of a rational being.*'[5] The sort of 'whole man', as Owen himself described him elsewhere,[6] who would know himself in relation to the history, sociology, economics and psychology of his society, was a man such as no other

[1] See Letter of August 16, 1817, and Address of August 21, 1817, in *Life*, Vol. IA, pp. 107 and 109.
[2] Letter of August 9, 1817, in *Life*, Vol. IA, p. 84.
[3] *Report* of 1817, in *ibid.*, p. 59.
[4] See Letter of August 9, 1817, in *ibid.*, p. 88, and *Report to the County of Lanark*, in *ibid.*, p. 287.
[5] *Ibid.*, p. 298.
[6] *Address at New Lanark*, in *A New View*, p. 94 ('. . . the whole man must be re-formed on fundamental principles the very reverse of those in which he had been trained . . .').

educator had previously postulated as a model, and this was not for an isolated, self-contained Emile, but for every member of society, and *particularly* for the dependent and deprived.

By the 1820's, then, Owen had developed an uncompromising, total vision of popular education for rational beings. The proclamation of his vision of a renovated society, he felt, had to be made in increasingly strident terms. It was the herald of a new era. From now on he was to announce that the millennium was at hand, to make apocalyptic announcements of the causes of human error, especially religion. But in doing so, Owen was doing little more than participate in the early nineteenth century search for panaceas. The pressures of unemployment, poverty, crime, disease, growing hostility to privilege and degenerate political institutions, led to a widespread search for solutions, and inevitably in this situation possible improvements were quickly taken up as overall remedies. Immediate benefits might be sought, but for many people the answer to the fundamental problems of society lay in speedy delivery from the mentality of an outdated and evil society. In every reformer lurked the messianic hopes of a Joanna Southcott. Every medical, physiological, political, industrial, economic, financial or social innovation *might* usher in a new world.

Owen's prophetic vein,[1] therefore, was part of a widespread social disturbance. The millenarian elements in his philosophy, however, were kept, certainly until he opted for the New Harmony experiment in America in 1824, under general control. They contributed, in fact, to his enthusiasm for the American site, as a further stage in the dissemination of the influence he had begun to exert from New Lanark. The conditions of the American experiment would be much purer, the possibility of influential success greater. Given the opportunity to purchase the colony belonging to the Rappites in Indiana, therefore, he readily purchased it.

In the late 1810's, what is more, Owen had begun to encounter opposition, and even, in quarters where he had hitherto found support— neglect. He was never able to raise enough subscriptions for the establishment of a model community, and government circles, at least, lost interest in Owen's plans for community settlements as their attitude on the question of the poor and unemployed hardened. He began to encounter opposition from 'the most bigoted and professedly religious

---

[1] For some typical examples see *Life*, Vol. IA, pp. 93 and 126.

of all sects'.[1] The radical economists attacked him for evading, among other things, the basis social issue of preventing an increase in population. 'Mr Owen's plan', said Malthus in 1817, 'not only does not make the slightest approach towards accomplishing this object, but seems to be peculiarly calculated to effect an object exactly the reverse of it.'[2] And finally, from within his third partnership emerged opposition, in the shape of the Quaker William Allen, tormented with doubts about some of Owen's more worldly views, and aspects of the curriculum at New Lanark.[3] In January 1824, Owen had to sign a new agreement under which Allen and his fellow Quakers appointed a new master who would teach the children of six and over on Lancasterian lines, and, among other things, discontinued dancing lessons.[4]

In the summer of 1824, a visitor on behalf of the Rappite community at New Harmony offered the village and twenty thousand acres of land for the sum of a hundred and fifty thousand dollars. The purchase was completed in April 1825.[5]

From 1817, then, Owen had lost support among influential circles. But this very fact also helped ultimately to attract support elsewhere. Hazlitt had very shrewdly said, in his 1816 review of *A New View*, that if Owen's plan 'for governing men by reason, without the assistance of the dignitaries of the church and the dignitaries of the law, but once get wind and be likely to be put in practice, and his dreams of elevated patronage will vanish'. At that point, 'when we see Mr Owen brought up for judgment before Lord Ellenborough, or standing in the pillory, we shall begin to think there is something in this *New Lanark Scheme* of his'.[6] 1817 was the point at which these things in a sense began to happen, and, as we shall, the early co-operators in particular, given Owen's alienation from the 'dignitaries', began to think there was something, in fact, in this 'New Lanark scheme of his'.

---

[1] *Life*, p. 181.
[2] T. R. Malthus, *An Essay on the Principle of Population*, 1798, *Additions to the Fourth and Former Editions*, 1817, p. 263.
[3] See *Life of William Allen*, Vol. I, p. 244.
[4] See Cullen, *Adventures in Socialism*, pp. 83–4.
[5] R. D. Owen, *Threading My Way*, pp. 208–10.
[6] See Appendix A, below.

CHAPTER III

The Fate of an Idea

SOME NOTES ON IDEAS IN THE HISTORY OF EDUCATION

HOW DO ideas come to be held? What is their fate in the processes of social development? Such questions, we suggested at the beginning of this enquiry, are of relevance in the analysis of motives behind educational provision and withholding, behind the variety of concepts that infuse the single concept of popular education. We are involved here, not in an epistomological analysis, but a historical one. We are concerned with the way in which ideas become commonly enough held to be ideologies. The following case histories, arising directly out of the discussion so far, are intended to illustrate ways in which ideas are formed, attitudes adopted, distortions introduced, and, above all, new views absorbed into old ideological patterns.

(i) On looking at Owen

In the previous chapter we looked at evidence, a good deal of it circumstantial, it is true, about Owen's contact with the world of ideas before the end of the eighteenth century. It was necessary to piece together the fragmentary clues, because without this picture, however incomplete, of the processes of ideological debate in this period, there is no perspective from which to begin to look at Owen's thinking, work and impact in terms of education.[1] Without such a picture, one is forced into one of three positions.

The first sees Owen's ideas as nothing but a collection of unacknowledged and fortuitous borrowings. This is the position established by one early critic of Owen:

[1] There is a parallel with the case of Tom Paine. See A. O. Aldridge, *Man of Reason. The Life of Thomas Paine*, London, 1960, quoting Paine's denial that he took his ideas 'from Locke or from anybody else' and describing the situation in America, in which Paine 'ran about picking up what information he could concerning our affairs . . .' (pp. 40–1). Owen, in a sense ran about picking up what information he could, building up a system of ideas, the sources of which later seemed irrelevant to him.

'Were it worth while, Mr Owen's whole system might be shown to be a mere thing of shreds and patches. In More's Utopia, Godwin's Inquiry concerning Political Justice . . . and in the History of the Moravian Establishment in America, are to be found, not only an outline, but much of the filling up of Mr Owen's general plan. His ideas of regenerating society by gentleness and kindness, and of children acquiring facilities in the exercise of combined movement belong to Fellenberg. His mode of education is a jumble of Dr Bell's and Mr Lancaster's; with hints from M. Fellenerg, Père Girard, Pestalozzi and others.'[1]

Where in Owen is More? *Could* Owen have plucked berries from America and Switzerland? Why *these* shreds and patches? It is always easy, even in Edinburgh in 1824, not to ask questions.

Or, secondly, one joins in the apparently serious exercise of looking for 'precursors', with little attention to the processes which might link the ideas of the precursor with his descendant. This is the case with the Soviet writer, Anekshtein:

'It is difficult to assume that Owen, who was exceptionally interested in educational questions, and whose views were based on the philosophy of the eighteenth century, knew nothing at all of the educational thinkers of this and previous times. We must assume, therefore, that he was acquainted with the views of his predecessors in this field, although it is most likely that he became acquainted with them not systematically, but largely at second-hand . . . in so far as Owen borrowed individual, valuable ideas from his predecessors, he transformed them in accordance with his own observations and reflections on the effects of the industrial revolution . . .'[2]

Who these predecessors were, and *why* we must assume that Owen was acquainted with their views, is not clear. And we are taken from the speculation to the certainty—'we must assume that he was' becomes 'Owen borrowed' and 'he transformed'. It may be true, it may not. This is the fairy-land of history.

The third position is the history that negates history. There *are* no sources, no cross-links of ideas, nothing but the isolated individual alone with his ideas, without antecedents:

[1] Aiton, *Mr Owen's Objections to Christianity*, p. 10.
[2] Anekshtein, *Pedagogicheskiye Idei Roberta Owena*, pp. 118–19.

'Owen ne cite aucune source, on ne rencontre le nom d'aucun philosophe et d'aucun économiste auquel il se rattache, soit par la filiation des idées, soit par la convergence des doctrines. L'oeuvre sociologique du réformateur apparaîtrait comme isolée, comme née sans antécédents, s'ill ne fallait y voir un effort constant pour interroger directement la nature.'[1]

J. W. Adamson also flirts with this position of ideological spontaneous combustion:

'Owen may have learned these two principles from a foreign source; but it is equally possible that they were the child of his own mother-wit or of a study of Locke.'[2]

By-passing the questions of the reality of the foreign sources, and of the evidence for Owen's having read Locke, the thesis is, in fact, that it doesn't matter—there is something called mother-wit that does just as well. Whatever Owen's mother-wit was, Manchester made it.

(ii) Infants

'A razor is a useful instrument, when used for its customary purpose, but it is by no means so when it cuts a throat', wrote Owen's *The New Moral World* in 1838. 'The latter kind of use, or rather abuse, has been the general fate of infant schools. They have been prostituted to the purposes of the vilest sectarianism.'[3] Between 1816 and the 1830's a complete change did, in fact, take place in the organisation and aims of the infant school movement, or to be more precise, movements, that arose in Britain.

Owen's own motives in founding his infant school were questioned, even, perhaps especially, in his lifetime. It was being suggested in 1838, for instance, that the idea of forming an infant school arose from the 'danger the little children were in . . . of falling into the stream of water which works the machinery of the mill'. Owen's teacher, Buchanan, had undertaken 'the task of collecting them together . . . He succeeded, partly with the assistance of Mr Owen, who described what he had

---

[1] Hector Denis, *Histoire des Systèmes Economiques et Socialistes*, Paris, 1904, Vol. II, p. 397.

[2] *English Education, 1789–1902*, London, 1930, p. 101.

[3] *N.M.W.*, Vol. IV, No. 197, August 4, 1838, p. 321.

witnessed on the Continent.'[1] Owen did not, in fact, visit the Continent until *two years after the infant school was opened*. The motive is divorced from Owen's philosophy, publicly announced and debated from the early 1810's.

The Institution for the Formation of Character was opened at the beginning of 1816. A group of sponsors, led by Henry Brougham and including James Mill, the Marquis of Lansdowne and John Walker (one of Owen's partners), opened an infant school at Brewer's Green, Westminster, in February 1819. Brougham had had the benefit of discussions with Owen himself and with many people familiar with the New Lanark schools and principles, and at the request of the committee Owen 'kindly furnished them with a master, J. Buchanan, who had been superintendent of his Infant School'.[2] Brougham later insisted to Owen that the London group had undertaken something new, in that 'the Westminster school was an extension of the plan to a town population', de Fellenberg's school at Hofwyl being 'strictly speaking, an infant school, but it is agricultural—yours manufacturing'.[3] In 1819 there was nothing at Hofwyl that could be described, in fact, as an infant school, the poor children being in an 'école de travail', centred of course on agriculture. To suggest, however, that the infant school at New Lanark was in some similar way a 'manufacturing school' was another mistake. It contained no vocational element, and was open to all children in New Lanark *and the surrounding district*. It is, of course, true that the Westminster school was the first infant school in an urban environment, but there its novelty stops. In 1823 it could still be seen clearly that the Westminster school was a result of reports from New Lanark, and though Brougham had always believed that education was begun too late, 'he is convinced that Robert Owen was the first person who made the experiment'.[4]

James Buchanan's transfer to the Brewer's Green school makes him the one teacher at or from New Lanark of whom we know anything in detail, and then largely as a result of the controversy about who 'founded'

---

[1] 'Schools for the Industrious Classes', anonymous article in the second publication of the Central Society of Education, London, 1838, p. 376. See also G. C. T. Bartley, *The Schools for the People*, London, 1871: '. . . the principal object being to keep the little children from the danger of falling into the Mill stream . . .' (p. 108).

[2] Thomas Pole, *Observations relative to Infant Schools*, Bristol, 1823, p. 8.

[3] Letter addressed by Brougham to Owen, *N.M.W.*, Vol. I, No. 3, p. 21, November 15, 1834.

[4] Pole, *Observations relative to Infant Schools*, p. 6.

infant schools.[1] Owen himself mentions Buchanan and a young woman called Molly Young,[2] and two youths who replaced Buchanan.[3] The teachers of the schools in general were 'carefully selected for the fitness of their qualifications'.[4] Owen was subsequently less than kind to Buchanan's abilities as a teacher, describing with 'surprise and horror' what he saw at the Westminster school.[5] A good deal of the credit for the success for the New Lanark infant school obviously goes to Buchanan, despite Owen's later judgment that Buchanan did not have some of the qualifications to make a good teacher of an infant school, 'who ought . . . to be one of the most intelligent, kind, and accomplished persons'.[6] Owen *must* have appointed Buchanan because he loved children—the whole point of the school was that it emphasised, in an epoch when education was being judged by standards of economy and a modicum of efficiency, the element of affection and kindness. In the New Lanark context, and *because* of it, Buchanan certainly 'succeeded in a task under which all commonplace schoolmasters, wedded to old methods, would have broken down'.[7] It is likely that, transplanted to Westminster, Buchanan found the situation more difficult. The age range was wider, he had fewer helpers, and above all, did not have Owen to set the sights for him. Owen's criticism of the Brewer's Green school, 'governed in the spirit and manner of the old irrational schools',[8] was ultimately a comment on what Brougham and his large, level-headed committee at Westminster required the school to be, the beginning of the process of adapting Owen's creation to other purposes.

[1] See Rusk, *A History of Infant Education*, pp. 135–45. There is a letter to Buchanan from his children in Cape Town in CUL/402 (March 3, 1831) describing their efforts to run infant schools in South Africa.

[2] See *Life*, p. 193.

[3] See *ibid.*, pp. 197 and 210, for a reference to, presumably, one of these brothers, and *N.M.W.*, Vol. III, No. 64, January 16, 1836, p. 94.

[4] James Smith, *Notes*, quoted in *N.M.W.*, Vol. II, No. 80, May 7, 1836. Owen describes them as 'men and women of experience in teaching useful knowledge' (Letter to Brougham, *N.M.W.*, Vol. 1, No. 1, November 1, 1834, p. 12).

[5] See *Life*, p. 210.

[6] *N.M.W.*, Vol. I, No. November 1, 1834, p. 12.

[7] Note on the origin of infant schools in *The Westminster Review*, Vol. XLVI, No. 1, October 1846, p. 220.

[8] *Life*, pp. 210–11. In a controversy about the origin of infant schools in 1836 Owen in fact affirmed that 'poor James Buchanan had to form his children into the old character of society, a little improved: into believers and slaves of a system, founded in falsehood, and supported by deception . . .' (*N.M.W.*, Vol. III, No. 64, January 16, 1836, p. 94).

Owen's identification with working class movements led to the garbling of the early history of these schools. In 1832 *The Westminster Review* was talking about the 'infant schools contrived by Mr Buchanan at New Lanark',[1] and Brougham too, in 1834, was relegating Owen to the background, though by 1848 he had abandoned this view. In that year he told Owen of a meeting at which he had explained 'your being author of Infant Schools, and gave their whole History including J. Buchanan being lent to us by you. It is now a clearly understood point in Education History.'[2] The point here is that Owen was being dismissed increasingly from the end of the 1810's as a *mere* philanthropist or visionary, as the situation required. The *Westminster Review* was in 1847 still insisting that Buchanan was the 'original *founder* in the proper sense of the term' of infant schools, 'inasmuch as it is not so much those who with philanthropic objects establish a school, as he who first introduces the plan which makes a school succeed, to whom the country is chiefly indebted . . .'[3] But Owen was not the distant philanthropist. Buchanan, of course, was the teacher, but Owen was among the children often enough for them to 'cling round him as their common parent'.[4] Owen was planner and provider, but he was also intimately involved in the operation of the schools.

It was from this 'inferior model in Westminster', turning back towards more orthodox concepts of education, and particularly to moral and religious training of a more rigid kind, that Samuel Wilderspin 'derived his first notions of an Infant-School, aided by the frequent hints which he thankfully received from me when he commenced and was organizing the school in Spitalfields'.[5] Wilderspin had met Buchanan and been invited to take charge of the second infant school opened in London, in Spitalfields.'[6] The 'frequent hints', Owen tells us, consisted in giving him 'general and minute instructions how to act with children and to govern them without punishment, by affection and undeviating

[1] Vol. XVII, No. XXXIV, October 1832, p. 407.
[2] Quoted in Podmore, *Robert Owen*, p. 598.
[3] Vol. XLVII, No. XCIII, July 1847, p. 484.
[4] Alexander Ross in *The Working Bee*, Vol. I, No. 34, March 7, 1840 (CUL/ 1250). Ross grew up at New Lanark.
[5] *N.M.W.*, Vol. III, No. 64, January 16, 1836, p. 94.
[6] For a discussion of Wilderspin's claims to have founded infant schools, see Rusk, *A History of Infant Education*, pp. 146–57. For a sympathetic study of Wilderspin see James Leitch, *Practical Educationists and their Systems of Teaching*, Glasgow, 1876, pp. 166–85.

kindness'.[1] Though Wilderspin was later to claim that he 'got no practical instruction either from Mr Owen, or his pupil (Buchanan)',[2] in the first edition of *On the Importance of Educating the Infant Children of the Poor* (1823) he declared:

> 'Having taken the liberty of mentioning the name of Mr Owen, I take this opportunity of returning my sincere thanks to that gentleman for having visited the Spitalfields Infant School several times. He has been pleased to express his approbation of the system there pursued, and during these visits has given many useful hints, for which I beg most humbly to thank him; and here I may observe, that I could not have brought the school to its present state had I not received some assistance.'[3]

It was not just success, as has been suggested, that 'induced him to recant'[4] (Wilderspin omitted this paragraph from later editions); Owen in the 1830's was a dangerous teacher to have to acknowledge. Owen's name was now, to the orthodox, anthema. He had to disappear from the records. His contribution to infant education had already by the 1830's been adapted and absorbed; it was an easy matter to draw a curtain across his name. At Spitalfields, and throughout his subsequent career as organiser of and propagandist for infant schools, Wilderspin's activities represented a deliberate turning away from Owen's concept of education to something much more rigid and theology-centred. Wilderspin can only claim credit for having founded and disseminated *his version* of the infant school.

Giving evidence to the Select Committee on Education in 1835, Wilderspin summarised his views on what education a child should have received before leaving the infant school. A child ought to know:

> '. . . the first four rules of Arithmetic and a good deal of the elements of Geography; it ought to know how to read well enough to read any book in simple language; it would have a tolerable knowledge of the quality of such things as immediately come under its notice; it would have a slight knowledge of the elements of Natural History, of the habits and manners of different animals, taught by pictures; it would have a tolerable knowledge of the leading facts of the New

---

[1] *Life*, Vol. IA, p. 336 (though the page number is missing).
[2] *N.M.W.*, Vol. II, No. 103, October 15, 1836, p. 401.
[3] Quoted in *Life*, Vol. IA, p. 336.
[4] Rusk, *A History of Infant Education*, p. 149.

Testament, which are communicated by pictures in the same way; it would have a knowledge of form; the child would be able to distinguish a triangle from a square, and an octagon pillar from any other pillar.'[1]

But this is not the whole story, because within this framework Wilderspin's emphasis was on words, not things, on books, lessons and apparatus. In the lessons on botany, for instance, the children were supposed to be introduced to words like *monandria, diandria, triandria, pentandria, monogynia*, and so on.[2] Wilderspin's methods were no doubt less terrifyingly linguistic in practice than they appear to be on paper, but principles of love, instruction-plus-amusement and the inculcation of a spirit of inquiry naturally receded when aims of producing a linguistically and arithmetically trained child were associated with them. The Brewer's Green school may have attempted 'to do too much . . . They had lessons, tasks, study . . . they sought prematurely to develop the intellectual powers.'[3] The movement Wilderspin inaugurated certainly did.

The clearest model of what happened in the 1820's to Owen's idea of infant education is a school founded in Walthamstow in 1824, a school described as 'the first Church Infants' School'.[4] Its founder, Rev. William Wilson, brother of the founder of the Spitalfields school, in 1825 published *The System of Infants' Schools*, which shows clearly, on the basis of actual experience, how the idea was being adapted. In Thomas Pole's *Observations relative to Infant Schools*, published two years before Wilson's work, the ambiguities involved in adapting Owen's total concept of infant education had already been made evident. Pole confessed that he was unacquainted with the details of the education given at New Lanark, and 'would confine his recommendations to the mechanical parts' of Owen's plan.[5] Pole, recommending Owen's plan, went on to describe experience at an infant school in Bristol, the master

[1] Quoted in Salmon and Hindshaw, *Infant Schools*, p. 63.
[2] See *ibid.*, pp. 63–4. One of the debts elementary education has owed to Wilderspin, said the Hadow Report on the Primary School, was 'a mistaken zeal for the initiation of children at too early an age to formal instruction' (*Report of the Consultative Committee on the Primary School*, H.M.S.O., 1931, p. 3).
[3] R. D. Owen, *Threading My Way*, p. 91.
[4] The phrase is used in both the Hadow *Report . . . on Infant and Nursery Schools*, H.M.S.O., 1933, p. 3, and Birchenough, *History of Elementary Education in England and Wales*, p. 48.
[5] *Observations*, p. 8.

of which had been trained at Brewer's Green. The situation described was in some respects remote from that at New Lanark (although corporal punishment was not used, the master 'sometimes puts on them a pair of wooden handcuffs, for a few minutes . . . If a child runs away from the school, or plays truant, he puts upon his legs an instrument, not unlike the stocks',[1] an approach similar to Lancaster's). Pole, showing no resistance to such developments, in other ways still stood close to Owen. There is an inter-mingling of the terminology of *A New View* and of phrases mirroring different philosophies. He states, for example, the objects of infant schools:

> '. . . the cultivation of their morals, and the preservation of their health, to which may be added, the promotion of mutual affection, social harmony, personal cleanliness, becoming manners, and due subordination . . . Infant schools, are, in no small degree, made places of amusement and exercise, as well as calculated to render the poor little creatures far more comfortable and happy than they would be at home . . .'[2]

The ambiguities inherent in the uses to which the infant school was beginning to be put can be seen in the very casualness of Pole's approach. Owen's school was the product of a detailed philosophy and careful selection of and instructions to his teachers; Pole, on the other hand, comments that 'to conduct a school in as perfect a manner as possible, requires no talents or acquirements beyond what ordinary persons possess, and the manner of carrying on the school, may be learned in a fortnight or less.'[3]

When we turn to Rev. Wilson's conception of an infant school, we find that the difference from Owen's lies fundamentally in what Wilson conceives its *function* to be. 'It is designed', says Wilson, 'to correct the moral feeling, the passions, and the heart; as well as to store the memory with that which is excellent and useful . . . it gives that preference decidedly rather to the improvement of the moral feeling and the influence of true religion, than to the development of the intellectual powers.'[4] Owen saw infant education as a self-contained period, offering enjoyment and general development within a context of affection and

---

[1] *Ibid.*, pp. 45–6.
[2] *Ibid.*, pp. 22–3 and 38.
[3] *Ibid.*, p. 9.
[4] *The System of Infants' Schools*, second edition, 1825, pp. 6–7.

mutual understanding; Wilson injected into the infant school situation the function of *preparation*, preparation for entry into National Schools:

> 'They will enter these establishments . . . prepared, at least, to think, to feel, and to obey. The ground will have been broken up, many of the obnoxious weeds removed . . .'[1]

Wilson's exposition of the religious content of infant education and of the methods of presentation of religious and other topics was, however, relatively undogmatic. Though pictures round the walls prepared the child 'for that course of thought which will aid his conceptions' when he met the biblical narratives, and though suitable texts for display round the room included:

FEAR GOD, HONOUR THE KING, GOD IS LOVE, LOVE ONE ANOTHER, THOU SHALT NOT STEAL, DRUNKARDS SHALL NOT INHERIT THE KINGDOM OF GOD . . .[2]

Wilson declined 'to be very particular on these topics'.[3] There is, however, in Wilson's *System*, as in Wilderspin's work, an interest in words, particularly in the scriptural context, absent at New Lanark. The infants at Wilson's school committed to memory the names and the order of the books of the Bible, the number of chapters in each book, and the natural history of the animals in the Bible (including lion and camel, but also hart, cameleon, cockatrice, cankerworm, palmerworm . . .).[4] Lessons were delivered, for the most part, to the whole school assembled and were 'learned in the same tone of voice, with one simultaneous clap of the hand—to the same footfall, or the same beat of the tambarine. The consequence of this is, unity, not division.'[5] In this we see concepts of educational purpose and practice related to the practice of the monitorial school; the infant school instrument was being adapted to techniques hitherto reserved for older children. More orthodox views of education were absorbing the new organism.

Wilson stood midway between the New Lanark situation and the infant schools of the thirties; the process at work had not yet been completed. Wilson could still proclaim that fear was 'under no circumstances, a suitable source of authority in an Infants's school,' adding, in block capitals, that 'THE FIRST OBJECT OF THE TEACHER OF AN

---

[1] *Ibid.*, p. 8.
[2] *Ibid.*, p. 110.
[3] *Ibid.*, p. 21.
[4] *Ibid.*, pp. 41 and 111.
[5] *Ibid.*, p. 17.

INFANTS' SCHOOL MUST BE TO CONCILIATE TO HIMSELF THE
FOND ATTACHMENT OF HIS CHARGE'.[1] He advocated 'spacious, freely
aired and lighted' rooms so that children would look forward to school
'as to a scene of real amusement and comfort'.[2] Wilson stressed the
importance of music and 'rhythmical action',[3] opposed the use of
rewards and allowed of punishment only rarely, and allowed for
moments of 'absolute rest and silence' between lessons. A play-ground
or garden was provided, 'and for half an hour during each school-time,
when the weather is suitable, the little flock is turned out for amusement
and play'.[4]

Wilson stated his overall objectives to be threefold:

'... to bring the mind itself into action, and to improve its faculties
... to prepare the child for the discipline of the schools in which he
may be destined to pursue his education ... to improve the tone of
his bodily powers and health'.

This is a far cry from *A New View*, but when it comes to the details of
the classroom situation, Wilson's objectives seem less formidable. The
child should only have to commit to memory what is 'nearest to the
language of infancy, the teacher should move from the present to the
absent, and moral powers should be trained by practice not precept'.[5]
None of this is demonstrably Owenite; it is, however, humane.

Despite opposition to the idea of infant schools, partly because of its
association in the early 1820's with Brougham,[6] Whigs, Radicals and
Dissenters, the infant school movement was growing, and in June 1824
a meeting was held in London at which the speakers included Brougham,
Wilberforce and William Allen, and at which an Infant School Society
was established, with Wilderspin as peripatetic school organiser. A year
later 34 new schools had been opened and 14 others were nearly ready.[7]

[1] *Ibid.*, pp. 13–14.
[2] *Ibid.*, p. 19.   [3] *Ibid.*, p. 21.   [4] *Ibid.*, p. 45.   [5] *Ibid.*, pp. 29–38.
[6] A Banbury clergyman in 1825 told a visitor that the infant school had not
been more widely adopted 'because it was invented by Mr Brougham' (Hawes,
Henry Brougham, p. 109). For a reply to an attack on infant schools in relation
to Brougham, see *The Edinburgh Review*, Vol. XLII, No. LXXXIII, April 1825,
pp. 208–9.
[7] See Salmon and Hindshaw, *Infant Schools*, pp. 53–4. The first secretary
was J. P. Greaves, a disciple of Pestalozzi and founder, in the late 1830's of a
non-Owenite community experiment at Ham Common (see Armytage, *Heavens
Below*, pp. 171–83, *The Educational Circular and Communist Apostle*, particularly
No. 6, May 1842, and Pare MS 578/129—an address to Owen when he visited
Ham Common in 1843).

Other organisers and adapters entered the field. David Stow, above all, creating the Glasgow Infant School Society in 1827, followed the Wilderspin direction, with an extremely individual approach to infant education, involving a careful approach to the concept of training, through understanding and action, and a theory of 'picturing out in words' which operated through a detailed question-and-answer technique and use of analogy.[1] Stow's ideal pupil, it has been said, was 'an infant saint with some knowledge, and Wilderspin's an infant prodigy with some religion'.[2] Despite Stow's bright school buildings, playgrounds, pictures and objects, the emphasis was on facts, training in obedience, and words. The regulations of his Glasgow Model Infant School laid down that 'the only school-book shall be the Bible'. The curriculum read:

'Monday—Bible biography.
Tuesday—Bible history, or illustrations of animal nature.
Wednesday—Moral duties, from Bible examples or precepts.
Thursday—Miracles from the Old and New Testament.
Friday—Bible history, or illustrations of inanimate nature.
Saturday—Parables, Promises, &c.'[3]

The story of the early infant school foundations must be seen, therefore, as a series of fresh starts. That made by the Mayos stemmed not from Owen, but from Pestalozzi, and came to mark the end of any real Owenite dynamic in the formal provision of infant schooling. The Rev. Dr Charles Mayo made his first contact with Yverdun in 1819, and opened a school in 1822 'to be conducted on Pestalozzian principles, for the children of the upper classes' at Epsom.[4] Mayo and his sister were anxious to demonstrate the validity of Pestalozzi's concept of education through object lessons, through the demonstration of simple facts. There is only the most superficial resemblance, however, between these aims and Owen's.

In 1826 Mayo, having turned to the problem of the popular infant

[1] See Fraser, *Memoir of the Life of David Stow*, p. 69 for a comment on Stow in relation to English and European developments in education, and Stow's *The Training System of Education*, Glasgow, 1836, for an explanation of 'picturing out'.
[2] Salmon and Hindshaw, *Infant Schools*, p. 73.
[3] Quoted in 'Schools for the Industrious Classes', second publication of the Central Society of Education, p. 381.
[4] H. Holman, *Pestalozzi. An Account of his Life and Work*, London, 1908, p. 315.

school, made an irrevocable step beyond even Wilson's view of it as preparation. Infant schools must be seen, said Mayo, 'not as insulated institutions, but in their relation and connexion with other establishments. What invaluable preliminaries do they offer to the work of Sabbath-school instruction.'[1] Their *first* aim was 'the development of moral and religious sentiments'. The development of intellectual faculties was 'subordinate to this moral end,' and considerations of health merely followed 'in the train of other advantages'.[2] The Home and Colonial Infant School Society, which came into existence in 1836 as a result of the Mayos' efforts, sought entirely to remodel the infant school as it had been known. The Pestalozzian 'object lesson' became part of the process of making 'the Infant School . . . once more a *sacrifice to the Lord*'.[3] The infants were to be taught 'cheerful, prompt obedience',[4] not to break the Sabbath, and to be industrious (in this most directly attacking previously established infant school practice):

'Habits of industry have been too little cultivated in Infant Schools; they are very important in a moral point of view; they are the outposts of virtue . . .'[5]

A text-book used in these Church infant schools offered the children a Scripture Alphabet:

'*A—is an angel, who praises the Lord;*
B—is for Bible, God's most holy word . . .
U—is for Uzzah, who died for his sin;
V—is for Vashti, the hard-fated queen;
W—is for whale, to Jonah a dread;
Y—is a yoke, 'tis the badge of a slave;
Z—is for Zaccheus whom Jesus did save.'[6]

[1] Rev. Charles Mayo, *Observations on the Establishment and Direction of Infants' Schools; being the Substance of a Lecture delivered at the Royal Institution, May, 1826*, London, 1827, p. 12.

[2] *Ibid.*, p. 15. The deliberateness of this list of priorities is confirmed several times in the lecture.

[3] Dr and Miss Mayo, *Practical Remarks on Infant Education*, p. 6.

[4] *Ibid.*, p. 40.

[5] *Ibid.*, p. 49.

[6] 'Quoted from T. Bilby and R. B. Ridgway, *The Infant Teachers' Assistant* in 'Schools for the Industrious Classes', Central Society of Education, second publication, p. 380. The book advocates the use of the Bible for *all* lessons, and that children should learn all the passages relating to the working of the Holy Spirit . . . the parallels between Moses and Jesus . . . the names of all the

The Mayos had seen the importance of the infant school movement that sprang up at the end of the 1810's, and from 1826 took steps to tame it.

There continued, of course, to be a great variety of practice in the infant schools,[1] though the strong trend by the 1830's was towards the inculcation of piety and direct preparation for monitorial school life. To run an infant school on non-sectarian principles was difficult, as can be judged from a letter written to Owen in 1830 by a sympathiser in Bermondsey. He had 'upwards of two years since' built a large school for infants and premises to accommodate a Mechanics' Institute, 'both of which have failed for want of support, the former in a great measure by it being unconnected with any religious party'.[2] In the same year Owen disowned his progeny. In an *Address to the Infant-school Societies* he acknowledged a dilemma. His infant school at New Lanark had been established 'as the first practical step in a system intended to supersede that which has ever pervaded savage and civilized life', and its purpose conflicted therefore with society as it was. The principles on which either society itself or the infant school were based had to change —'for they are in direct opposition to each other'. Infant schools as they now were in 1830 were, he told their patrons, 'evidences of your good intentions, and also of the vicious circumstances in which you are involved. They are in many instances a mockery or caricature of the original school.'[3] By 1838 this condemnation was categorical. In that year his newspaper, *The New Moral World*, reprinted an item from the *Infant School Melodist*:

'The Bank-Note; or, Divine Promises

Should all the banks in Britain break,
The Bank of England squash;
Bring in your notes to Jesus' bank,
You're sure to get your cash.

Nay, if you have but one small note,
Fear not to bring it in;

---

mountains mentioned in the Scripture . . . sins recorded in Scripture, with examples . . . all that is said of No. 7 in Scripture . . . The offices of angels . . .' (p. 381).

[1] See Hill, *National Education* for the most valuable survey of education in the 1830's (for a description of one of the schools in which some of the original motive force of infant education was retained see pp. 191-2).

[2] MS letter in CUL/256.

[3] *N.M.W.*, Vol. II, No. 66, January 30, 1836.

Come boldly to the bank of grace,
The Banker is within . . .

But, ah! my bank can never break,
My bank can never fail;
The firm's THREE PERSONS IN ONE GOD,
Jehovah, Lord of all . . .'

It was in publishing this that the journal explained that 'a razor is a useful instrument, when used for its customary purpose, but it is by no means so when it cuts a throat', suggesting that, 'were it not that we see the dawning of a better day', it might have been better if 'this additional power of poisoning the springs of mental health had never been discovered, and put into the hands of interested ignorance'.[1]

By this date new working class movements were setting their own educational targets—at infant and other levels. Owen had seen that no battle is definitively won; he found himself, in the field of infant education, defeated not, as in many other things, by his enemies, but by what at least began as his allies. An idea had been asserted, demonstrated, adopted, diverted and all but destroyed.

(iii) Educationists abroad

We saw in the previous chapter the relationship between Owen's views on education, the very language in which he proclaimed them, and the sources of rationalist, libertarian thought that became accessible in the 1790's. Such a relationship makes it possible for us to look briefly, as a final case history in the fate of ideas, at claims for the influence in Britain of other educational reformers, particularly continental ones.

Of claims that Owen took his whole ideology and practice from Bell and Lancaster, little needs to be said.[2] Owen, one must assume, as his son tells us, was 'enthusiastic at first' about the monitorial method, but 'gradually changed it for something more thorough and effective'.[3]

---

[1] *Ibid.*, p. 321.
[2] For such claims, made emphatically, see *The Westminster Review*, Vol. XLVI, No. 1, October 1846, p. 220 (the New Lanark schools were a result of the 'missionary labours' of Lancaster . . .), and Central Society of Education, second publication, p. 376 (the New Lanark schools 'were commenced at the suggestion of Joseph Lancaster . . .').
[3] *Threading My Way*, p. 77.

Certainly by the writing of *A New View* he had abandoned most of his enthusiasm. The basic fact about his schools was not so much how the teachers taught, but that they taught at all. James Smith, impressed in 1820 by the results of Owen's 'providing a sufficient number of masters', proclaimed that at New Lanark 'the Lancasterian system of monitorship is entirely exploded'.[1] The shape of the New Lanark developments was governed, in fact, not by Owen's early and restrained interest in Bell and Lancaster, an interest which contained the very precise points of criticism strongly expressed in *A New View*, but by his overall analysis of character and society.

More important than this theme is the assumption sometimes made that Owen was part of the process by which the continental educational reformers, primarily Pestalozzi and de Fellenberg, extended their influence into Britain.[2] It is often assumed, rather differently, with a not-too-precise idea of the process involved, that the ideas that Owen absorbed during his formative period were primarily those associated with Rousseau, a doctrine 'which so permeated the air of the time that one did not need to imbibe it by reading: the doctrine that mankind is naturally good and that it is only institutions which have perverted it'.[3] What we can accept is that, wherever the focal source of Owen's derived assumptions lay, an ideological currency which included a radical approach to environmental education was accessible, in his period in Manchester, to be 'imbibed'. It was not, however, just a hazy Rousseauism that he imbibed; it was a specifically Godwinian optimism and it spoke the vocabulary of Helvétius.

To assert the possibility of Owen's have been influenced, not by the *philosophes* but by the continental practitioners is a very different matter. It assumes that there were channels open through which their impact could be felt.

Owen made a continental tour at the beginning of 1818, and apart from meeting a very large number of European dignitaries, visited 'the three then most noted schools for the poor in Switzerland'.[4] He described the first as being 'Father Oberlin's, a Catholic school . . . at Friburgh', a

---

[1] *N.M.W.*, Vol. II, No. 80, May 7, 1836.

[2] See, for example, Barnard, *A Short History of English Education*, edition of 1949, p. 69, and Cullen, *Adventures in Socialism*, pp. 62–3.

[3] Wilson, *To the Finland Station*, p. 90. See also Podmore, *Robert Owen*, p. 126.

[4] *Life*, p. 240.

mistake on Owen's part, for the school run by Père Girard.[1] The second was Pestalozzi's at Yverdun, only 'one step in advance of ordinary schools'.[2] Owen was more impressed by the third, de Fellenberg's at Hofwyl. Oberlin was interested in infant education, but the three Owen visited were not. These visits of themselves, however, are of minor consequence in this analysis: the pattern of education at New Lanark was by now well established, his infant school had been in operation for over two years, and actual arrangements in his schools more or less precisely matched the plans and principles enunciated in *A New View*, six years before.

Owen had, in fact, formed a second partnership in 1809 *because of a dispute with his first set of partners over his very precise intentions in the field of education*. The important question, therefore, is the extent to which the work of the continental reformers could have been known to Owen roughly by that date.

There were, of course, aspects of Pestalozzian techniques which might have proved attractive to Owen. Pestalozzi put forward a scheme of instruction for elementary education consisting of three elements:

'The first embraced the intuitive perception of the objects of nature and art by which the child is surrounded, with the acquisition of their names. The second embraced intuitive instruction in number. The third, intuitive instruction with respect to form or dimensions.'[3]

Such a stress on educational methods which enable the child to use his sensory and perceptual experience was not far removed from Owen's insistence on abandoning precept for example and understanding. But outside this doctrine, and some of the techniques stemming from it, there was little in Pestalozzi's overall position to attract Owen. Pestalozzi's purpose (though ultimate effects are rarely the same as purposes) was much closer to the limiting positions we examined in the first chapter, accepting, for example, the undesirability of social change, even through education. Pestalozzian education trained the mechanic and

[1] See Rusk, *A History of Infant Education*, edition of 1951, pp. 119–20. Oberlin's school was at Ban de la Roche, Oberlin was a Protestant, and had run infant schools, unlike the 'Oberlin' described by Owen. Owen's mistake has recently been repeated in Margaret Cole, *Robert Owen of New Lanark* (pp. 88 and 129) and Harvey, *Robert Owen, Social Idealist* (p. 79).

[2] *Life*, p. 244.

[3] *Pestalozzi and his Principles*. Prepared at the Request of the Committee of the Home and Colonial School Society, 1864, p. 46.

labourer to 'pass through life with eyes to see and ears to hear', extended the range of their vocabulary and ideas:

'. . . it is the development of an innate power, the formation of an abiding habit, that constitutes its (education's) true value'.[1]

Although Pestalozzi criticised de Fellenberg for aiming 'to fit the child for his particular position in society', and contended that 'the educator ought to regard the child, not with reference to the artificial institutions of society, but with a view to what he is in himself',[2] he was, in by-passing the problem of social status acquiescing in it. He believed, in fact, that 'to be happy and useful in his own sphere is the particular aim of every man, and the attainment of this aim should be furthered by his education'.[3] Pestalozzi argued that only the improvement of spiritual qualities mattered, because 'man as a whole in his inner nature must be improved if the external circumstances of the poor are to be bettered'.[4] The fundamentals of the Pestalozzian approach were far removed from those of Owen. It was, however, Pestalozzi's practice that attracted attention.

Though the first volume of Pestalozzi's *Léonard et Gertrude* was published in 1781, it was not until 1799, at Stanz, that he ran his first educational venture, an asylum for children. From 1799 to 1804 he was schoolmaster and administrator at Burgdorf, and from 1804 at the most famous of his educational enterprises at Yverdun. Only at Burgdorf did his reputation become substantial,[5] and only at the height of his fame from about 1807, was there an influx of visitors 'from all parts of Europe'.[6] There is no evidence, in fact, of Pestalozzi's methods and aims being really known in the British Isles until 1815, when Mr Synge, of Glanmore Castle, Wicklow, visited Yverdun.[7] Bell visited Yverdun in 1816, but the two men's minds 'did not unite. Bell left without being touched by the Pestalozzian grace.'[8] Owen, as we have seen, visited him

---

[1] *Ibid.*, p. 24.

[2] *Ibid.*, p. 41.

[3] J. A. Green, *The Educational Ideas of Pestalozzi*, London, 1905, edition of 1914, p. 81.

[4] Quoted in *ibid.*, p. 69. See also E. Biber, *Henry Pestalozzi, and his Plan of Education*, London, 1831, edition of 1833, p. 12 ('he did not . . . expect that an amendment of circumstances would better their moral condition').

[5] See *ibid.*, p. 41 and Compayré, *Pestalozzi and Elementary Education*, p. 50.

[6] Green, *The Educational Ideas of Pestalozzi*, pp. 62–3.

[7] See Salmon and Hindshaw, *Infant Schools*, pp. 77–8.

[8] Compayré, *Pestalozzi and Elementary Education*, p. 77.

in 1818, and Rev. Charles Mayo in 1819. Pestalozzi saw Mayo as the agent for implementing the hope he 'had long and ardently cherished, that his system would at length be introduced into England'.[1] Only in the mid-1820's did Pestalozzi's ideas become in any way a force in Britain, largely from Mayo's lecture to the Royal Institution in May 1826. This lecture caused *The Edinburgh Review* to reflect that Pestalozzi's name:

'. . . is known as a familiar household word on the Continent . . . we in this island, from accidental circumstances, are hardly acquainted with its sound'.[2]

Owen, and others interested in education, knew of and visited Pestalozzi of course, long before this date, but not early enough to have had any possible impact on Owen.[3]

Although, on his 1818 visit, Owen was attracted more to de Fellenberg's schools at Hofwyl, and sent two of his sons to be educated there, there was no more possibility of direct influence from Hofwyl to New Lanark than there was from Yverdun. The school of industry at Hofwyl was not founded until 1809, and two other schools, one an 'institut agricole' and the other 'un institut d'éducation pour les classes aisées' were established still later.[4]

Robert Dale Owen, from his intimate experience of Hofwyl, summarised the 'one great idea' of de Fellenberg's life as being 'to seize the extremes of society and carefully to educate both: the one to be intelligent, cultivated workers; the other to be wise and considerate legislators . . . I believe he imagined there would be rich and poor to the end of the world.'[5] The chairman of a meeting at Hofwyl in September 1812 considered that the schools 'changent en citoyens religieux et utiles à la société, des malheureux, qui, sans cette éducation en seroient devenus le fléau'. They would produce 'de bons domestiques de campagne, et fournir des ovriers habiles aux divers atteliers nécessaires à l'agricul-

---

[1] *Pestalozzi and his Principles*, Home and Colonial Society, p. 43. See also Margaret E. M. Jones, *A brief Account of the Home and Colonial Training Institution and of the Pestalozzian System*, London, n.d., p. 3 (incorrectly giving the year of the visit as 1818).
[2] Vol. XLVII, No. XCIII, January 1828, p. 118.
[3] For a letter from Mayo to Owen in 1823, mentioning Pestalozzi, see Appendix B below.
[4] See D. A. Chavannes, *Rapport sur l'Institut d'Education des Pauvres à Hofwyl*, Geneva, 1813, pp. 28–9.
[5] *Threading My Way*, p. 135 (pp. 122–50, tell the story of his years at Hofwyl).

ture'.[1] De Fellenberg himself, in a document published at Hofwyl in 1809, defined his aim as being not 'agiter le peuple' but to show:

> '. . . par le fait, comment il est possible d'apprendre au paysan, à l'artisan, à se trouver plus heureux dans son état qu'aucun monarque ne l'est sur le trône, et à ne rien craindre tant, que de se voir enlevé à la carrière qui lui a été assigné par le suprême ordonnateur des choses'.[2]

De Fellenberg, like any John Mason or Sarah Trimmer, was seeking to confirm the poor in their pre-ordained status, however enlightened the mechanism of achieving it.

The school of industry at Hofwyl did, in fact, give the pupils a most imaginative curriculum, intimately related to the day-to-day experience of the children in the fields and elsewhere. It is important to point out, however, that the 'industrial' training greatly outweighed the education in school:

> '. . . il ne s'agit point ici d'une école d'instruction, mais d'une école de travail. L'instruction proprement dite étant ici l'accessoire, ne prend qu'environ deux heures par jour'.[3]

Such humanitarian advance as this all represented was on a very different scale from that at New Lanark. Neither de Fellenberg nor Pestalozzi, what is more, thought at all in terms of infant education.

These visits, it should be added, were arranged for Owen by Professor Pictet, 'the celebrated *savant* of Geneva',[4] whom, if we are to believe Owen's autobiography, Owen had not met before 1818. Pictet arranged the tour in order to introduce Owen to leading French and Swiss figures in the world of politics, science and letters. There is no reason to believe that Owen was acquainted with the work at Yverdun or Hofwyl before his visit. Although two articles on Hofwyl had appeared in *The Philanthropist* in 1813 and 1815,[5] even at those dates it was too late seriously

---

[1] Chavannes, *Rapport*, p. 7.

[2] *Extrait du second Cahier des Feuilles d'économie rurale d'Hofwyl, publié en 1809.* See also F. L. Gauteron, *Coup d'Oeil sur l'Influence à esperer des Etablissemens d'Hofwyl*, Paris and Geneva, n.d., p. 3.

[3] A. Rengger, *Rapport sur l'Institut d'Education des Pauvres à Hofwyl*, Paris and Geneva, 1815, p. 27. For further details of the curriculum see also *ibid.*, pp. 8 and 11–26, and Chavannes, *Rapport*, pp. 9–15.

[4] *Life*, p. 229.

[5] One in the same issue as a review of *A New View* (Vol. V, 1815). See Bestor, *Backwoods Utopias*, p. 143, note.

to affect the principles Owen had established emphatically for himself, or the plans elaborated certainly since 1809 for the future educational arrangements at New Lanark. No separate works on de Fellenberg and Hofwyl appeared in English until 1820. In December 1818, in fact, *The Edinburgh Review* was saying that Hofwyl 'has just begun to attract notice in this country . . . there is nothing more natural than that the first intimation of Mr Fellenberg's plans should powerfully interest the thinking part of the community'.[1]

A New View and New Lanark trace back to eighteenth century French ideas, not nineteenth century Swiss practice.

It is even less likely that Père Girard's name could have meant anything to Owen before 1818. Oberlin, whom Owen may, of course, have visited, began to build schools at Ban de la Roche from 1767, including, after his marriage a year later, infant schools:

'In this work Madame Oberlin became a valuable helper. Infant schools, adult schools . . . soon followed the establishment of the regular schools.'[2]

Oberlin was not, however, an educational publicist, had his work suspended by the French revolution, and was known on the continent at the beginning of the nineteenth century in religious circles and for his work in improving agriculture.[3] Thomas Pole, writing his *Observations relative to Infant Schools* in 1823, made no reference to Oberlin, and it is difficult to imagine how, until British educators began to look at other continental experience in the late 1810's, the work of Oberlin can have been known at all in this country.[4]

None of this is to suggest that Ban de la Roche was unsuccessful, unimportant or uninfluential. It means that the influence was weak, and emphasises that the impact of the ideas of the rationalist enlightenment in Britain, leading to the kind of work Owen undertook at New Lanark, was of far greater importance, because the channels of communication for them lay open, whereas for the spread of information about the work of educational experiment on the continent, up to and beyond the end of the Napoleonic wars, such channels were closed.

[1] Vol. XXXI, No. LXI, December 1818, pp. 150–1. The article was probably by Brougham (see Leopold, *Robert Dale Owen*, pp. 11–12).

[2] Josephine E. Butler, *The Life of Jean Frédéric Oberlin*, London, 1886, p. 64.

[3] See *ibid.*, p. 174.

[4] See Salmon and Hindshaw, *Infant Schools*, pp. 7 and 33, and Mrs Townshend, *The Case for School Nurseries*, Fabian Tract No. 145, 1909, pp. 12–14.

In *Pioneers of Popular Education*, H. M. Pollard takes as his main thesis the influence of the continental reformers on Britain, and his thesis is the importance of studying:

'... the efforts of a few remarkable reformers who, in the years succeeding Waterloo, pitted themselves against the tide of national insularity and strove not only to acquaint themselves with the work of prominent educationists abroad but also to persuade their compatriots how retrogressive were their ideas on schools and child-training ...'[1]

The reformers singled out include Lady Byron, the Mayos, Kay-Shuttleworth and J. P. Greaves.

These are people who in one way or another did feel the continental influence that Pollard is anxious to investigate, but the implication throughout this quotation and the book (combatting national insularity by importing continental ideas) is that national insularity was monolithic and that continental influence came only in the late 1810's, through direct contact between reformer and reformer. If the period 1789–1815 contains, as Pollard paints it, nothing but Bell and Lancaster, then it is logical to assume, as Pollard does, that the period after 1815, when the road to Yverdun and Hofwyl began to be known, contains nothing but bringers-home of educational souvenirs. What we have seen, in fact, is that there was in the period 1789–1815 a major contact, not between reformer and reformer, but between reformer and *ideas*. What Pollard is examining is only the second-generation contact, when already, as a result of the first-generation contact, new educational assumptions were being broadcast and implemented. Pollard therefore discusses the Mayos and the Home and Colonial Infant School Society, founded in 1836, without telling the story of infant schools at New Lanark in 1816, and in London, Bristol and elsewhere from 1818 on through the 1820's. Wilderspin and the Infant School Society, founded in 1824, are ignored.[2]

Pollard suggests, then, that it was 'in large measure because of such excursions as these and the expansion of ideas that they brought about that Britain eventually realized the extent of her insularity and sought

[1] H. M. Pollard, *Pioneers of Popular Education 1760–1850*, London, 1956, p. 273.

[2] So, to all intents and purposes, are the Mechanics' Institutes, the foundation of University College, London, the adult and other educational work of the co-operative and Chartist movements (as also, for that matter, Shaftesbury and the Ragged Schools). The title, as well as the thesis, is misleading.

ways and means of improving her educational status'. Owen's visit did not have 'any dramatic results as far as the importation of foreign ideas into this country was concerned'.[1] Both of these statements are historically irrelevant. By neglecting the development of educational thought in its more general social setting, Pollard inevitably misleads. His misplaced emphasis in the picture of educational pioneering is the outcome of failing to put movements of ideas into perspective.

This is, again, not a question of belittling the continental reformers, or their ultimate influence, but of showing that ideas as well as schools play their part in educational reform, and of being concerned to understand how.

[1] *Ibid.*, p. 156.

CHAPTER IV

Architects and Builders

(i) *The ripe ones*

WE ARE concerned primarily with the way in which certain types of thinking took on flesh and blood in the British setting, and from the point of Owen's involvement in New Harmony we find ourselves, therefore, less interested in his career than in the impact of the ideas we have already seen set in motion. Education at New Harmony was not, what is more, under Owen's predominant influence. William Maclure, who also played a substantial part in financing the experiment, imported European teachers who had had experience with Pestalozzi.[1]

Owen's activities at New Harmony between 1824 and its collapse as an Owenite community in 1827, and his subsequent search for an even wider sphere of operations in Mexico, illustrate his unbounded confidence in his view of the omnipotent influence of environment over character, and his now confirmed belief that given the right circumstances he could change the face of the earth in a calculable period of time. The failure of New Harmony as a community project did not in any way shake this belief—and for the rest of his life he was to continue to seek the appropriate conditions in which to initiate a fundamental change in society.

In the years 1824–9 Owen spent most of his time, then, out of Britain, and by and large out of touch with the new channels through which his influence had begun to work.

Initially, of the range of Owen's views it was his propaganda for planned communities that found support among artisans looking for a solution to the problem of poverty. Originally Owen had offered the community as a model for governments, to remove the social nightmares

---

[1] For education at New Harmony, see especially Bestor, *Backwoods Utopias*, Bestor (ed.), *Education and Reform at New Harmony*, and R. D. Owen, *Threading My Way*. Of more general interest is Rowland Hill Harvey, *Robert Owen, Social Idealist*, which uses manuscript material of Owen's son, William. In addition to the items in *Bibliography* there are also: Vernon L. Parrington (Jr.), *American Dreams: A Study of American Utopias*, Providence, 1947, and Mark Holloway, *Heavens on Earth. Utopian Communities in America 1680–1880*, London, 1951.

of unemployment and poverty, and their attendant evils of crime and corruption. In the early 1820's, however, the co-operative community was also being adopted by working class co-operators as their own model, as the way to by-pass the intolerable burdens of the society in which they lived. Co-operation, under the impetus of Owen's views, developed in the 1820's either as a form of living and producing co-operatively, or as a means of saving enough initial capital to make it possible to live and produce co-operatively. It is with the early co-operators, therefore, that we see the beginnings of working class or popular Owenism, and of the process whereby many of the targets we have seen Owen raise came to be adopted by working class and popular movements, including ones which were non-Owenite or even anti-Owenite in philosophy. Early working class co-operation was Owenism without Owen.

Although Owen had some contact with the nascent movement on his visits from America,[1] he was unenthusiastic about this form of self-help on the part of the workers. 'When Mr Owen first came over from America,' wrote William Lovett, 'he looked somewhat coolly on these "Trading Associations", and very candidly declared that their mere buying and selling formed no part of his grand co-operative scheme.'[2] Contact between Owen and the fend-for-itself co-operative movement was very restricted until after 1829.[3]

There are two aspects of the early co-operative movement of particular importance: it was a movement of self-consciously 'ripe' (to use a word of William King's) working people, and it was a movement initially concerned with *material* advancement. 'We know', said William King, leader and propagandist of the Brighton co-operative movement in the late 1820's, 'that the working classes generally, are not yet ripe for WORKING UNIONS: but we know, at the same time, that there is a sufficient number of RIPE ONES to make a beginning.'[4] Members of a

[1] He addressed, for example, a meeting at the London Mechanics' Institution in September 1825, and two years later 'gave a series of Sunday morning addresses at breakfasts held at the Co-operative Society's rooms' (Podmore, *Robert Owen*, p. 376).
[2] *The Life and Struggles of William Lovett*, p. 43.
[3] Frank Peel, in *The Risings of the Luddites, Chartists and Plugdrawers*, Brighouse, 1888, gives an enthusiastic but chronologically idiotic picture of working class involvement in controversy around 'the opinions' of the celebrated theorist, Robert Owen' which were 'making some noise in the country' in 1812! He shows a Luddite ringleader rejecting the 'processes of Owen' as 'too slow' (p. 14).
[4] *The Co-operator*, No. 5, September 1, 1828.

co-operative society were 'more enlightened . . . their knowledge is farther advanced', and one of the qualifications laid down for members was that 'they should not be ignorant and prejudiced persons, but as well informed as their rank in life admits of'.[1] The primary aim of such societies was, in the words of the first object listed by the London Co-operative Society in 1825, to 'aid in forming in all countries, particularly in Great Britain, COMMUNITIES OF MUTUAL CO-OPERATION, in the production and distribution of wealth'.[2] This latter society, formed in 1824, aimed at 'removing the difficulties standing in the way of a general acceptance of Owen's views, by means of lectures, discussions, publications of various kinds . . .'[3] There is no mention in the *Rules* of education as such, though the subjects of importance for co-operators, advertised in *The Co-operative Magazine* for public discussion included 'What is the best mode of educating and training children?'[4]

For these early societies the community-objective was, in fact, a powerful encouragement to the acquisition and dissemination of knowledge. Owen was suspicious of their limited trading aims, and it is probably true that where the community-objective was absent, social and educational aims were muted.[5] The very basis of the new societies, however, acted in general as an incentive to the widening of intellectual horizons.

By the 1810's, as a result primarily of what limited education was provided by the monitorial schools and the better dame schools, a wider interest in the acquisition of knowledge, and a growing enthusiasm for education as a means of personal and social progress, a stratum of 'ripe ones' had come into existence, whom it was possible for Owen's message

[1] *Ibid.*, No. 6, October 1, 1828.
[2] *Rules for the Observance of the London Co-operative Society*, London, 1825, p. 3 (GL).
[3] Podmore, *Robert Owen*, p. 374.
[4] *Ibid.*, p. 375.
[5] The Meltham Mills Provident Trading Society, in the West Riding of Yorkshire, for example, founded in 1827, had no such objective. It did not accumulate profits, and forestalled Rochdale in the practice of profit-sharing: 'When we commenced our store co-operation was becoming strong, but on a system of the profits accumulating, which we knew would never answer, so we adopted the plan of paying profits on the amount purchased, and by so doing we stood firm when the others fell' (letter written by the Secretary of the Meltham Mills Society in 1871, quoted in *The Co-operative News*, August 28, 1943, p. 7). There is no evidence from its records that the Society had any interest in education.

to reach. In 1813 *The Edinburgh Review*, in an article on British and National schools, argued the efficacy of the schools and the enthusiasm of the poor for the education they provided. From observation and inquiry, said the article, 'we can ourselves speak decidedly as to the rapid progress which the love of education is making among the lower orders in England'. The article adduced three types of evidence for this progress:

> 'We have met with families in which, for weeks together, not an article of sustenance but potatoes had been used; yet for every child the hard-earned sum was provided to send them to school ... the number of letters which pass through the post-office, and, by the circumstances of their direction and superscription, prove that they are between persons in the lower ranks of life, has increased in a remarkable proportion during the last twenty years. Sunday newspapers are another extraordinary proof of the progress of reading, and the love of political information, among the lower orders of the people ...'[1]

Owen's campaign for communities coincided, therefore, with the awakening among some of the 'lower ranks' of new ideals.

From a simple acceptance of community, the co-operators and Owenite trade unionists moved towards the erection of educational targets. The story of the social and political movements of the 1820's and 1830's cannot be divorced from this growing awareness of the power of knowledge, of the inhibiting power of ignorance. What *The Edinburgh Review* in 1826 called 'the almost expiring controversy between the dark-loving school and the educators'[2] amounted really to a hope that everyone now realised that education was *inevitable*. The review in fact, stressed the need for those who had been instrumental 'in spreading a general taste for knowledge' to help to guide it.[3] The point here is not the *Edinburgh's* search for means of harnessing the new 'general taste for knowledge'—but its recognition that the taste existed. So strong was the impetus towards education among the co-operators in the late 1820's, in fact, that William Thompson, in his work to help to build the co-operative movement in London, had to resist the

---

[1] Vol. XXI, No. XLI, February 1813, p. 216. Halévy (in *The Growth of Philosophic Radicalism*, p. 289) ascribes the article to James Mill.

[2] See p. 20 above.

[3] Vol. XLV, No. LXXXIX, December 1826, p. 196.

suggestion that the co-operators 'should abandon the idea of establishing communities in favour of building a Co-operative school'.[1] By 1832 we find Thomas Arnold suggesting that 'it is vain now to say that questions of religion and politics are above the understanding of the poorer classes —so they may be, but they are not above their *misunderstanding*, and they will think and talk about them, so that they had best be taught to think and talk rightly'. He recommends a glance at 'Owen's paper, "The Crisis", or at the "Midland Representative", the great paper of the Birmingham operatives. The most abstract points are discussed in them, and the very foundations of all things are daily being probed.'[2] The growth of an independent working class state of mind now made it essential, in the eyes of observers like Thomas Arnold, to ensure that the workers 'be taught to think and talk rightly'.[3] Since the educational patrons of the working class, however, were not agreed on the extent and nature of the education to be provided, and since what *was* provided was so clearly inadequate for 'the ripe ones', it was in and through movements like that of the early co-operators that the educational ideals publicised by Owen ultimately had their strongest impact.

In January 1825 *The Edinburgh Review* did not find that 'the extravagances of Mr Owen are making much way in the world',[4] and it is true that the attempts to set up a model community by various committees of dignitaries and through subscriptions had come to nothing.[5] What *The Edinburgh* did not realise was that Owen's 'extravagances' were indeed making a way at a different level. The same *Edinburgh* article also expressed 'an entire unbelief in all projects for regenerating mankind, and giving a new character to future generations, by certain trite or fantastic schemes of education'. It denied that any permanent effect

---

[1] R. K. P. Pankhurst, *William Thompson (1775–1833) Britain's Pioneer Socialist, Feminist, and Co-operator*, London, 1954, p. 140.

[2] A. P. Stanley, *The Life and Correspondence of Thomas Arnold, D.D.*, 1844, edition of 1858, Vol. I, p. 263.

[3] Arnold was expressing here the answer to one of the main by-problems of his central task, that of effectively welding, on behalf of the new middle class, 'the spirit of the traditional humanism with the complex demands of business and politics and administration and professional services in an industrialized nation which had now also to govern an Empire' (Clarke, *Education and Social Change*, London, 1940, pp. 23–4). It was not just an empire, but an increasingly self-assertive working class, that the middle class was being called on to govern.

[4] Vol. XLI, No. LXXXII, p. 316.

[5] See *Proceedings of the First General Meeting of the British and Foreign Philanthropic Society*, London, 1822, p. 14, for one such subscription list.

would result from the precepts or practice of schools—'the year after the boy has left the school, he will be precisely in the same state . . . as if he had been all the time at home'.[1] The only conceivable 'material improvements' in education would be the saving of money, time and suffering through an extension of the use of 'the more advanced and intelligent children to teach the rest'.[2] The role of Owenism was in this period to arm popular movements with a diametrically opposite philosophy, and to assert educational values which opposed such restricting and sterile modes of thought.

For some twelve months, from January 1821, George Mudie, a printer and journalist, had published *The Economist* in an attempt to disseminate Owen's principles among working men.[3] At the same time he persuaded the London printers to launch a co-operative scheme, beginning with what Max Beer describes as 'co-operative householding' and aimed at the establishment of a community. The Constitution of this short-lived Economical and Co-operative Society described the *immediate* object of the Society as being 'to form a fund for the purchase of food, clothing, and other necessaries at wholesale prices; and . . . to form arrangements for co-operating in the care of their dwellings, the superintendence, training, and education of their children'.[4] Mudie believed that Owen's principles and plans would both produce abundance and 'disseminate knowledge . . . saturating the public mind with intelligence'.[5]

An original contribution to the discussion of education in the journal was contained in plans it put forward for education in the co-operative venture launched by the Economical Society. The Society, which was to consist of 250 families, was to have its own educational facilities and its own teachers.[6] Mudie proposed that no teacher should be with the children for more than about three hours a day, thus enabling the

[1] No. LXXXII, pp. 316–18.

[2] *Ibid.*, p. 321.

[3] The title included the words: 'explanatory of the New System of Society projected by Robert Owen, Esq.' Helene Simon, in *Robert Owen. Sein Leben und Seine Bedeutung für die Gegenwart* (p. 154), and Frances M. Page in Hearnshaw (ed.), *The Social and Political Ideas of some Representative Thinkers of the Age of Reaction and Reconstruction* (p. 108), make the mistake of believing *The Economist* to have been run by Owen himself. Owen's contact with the paper was of the most tenuous.

[4] Quoted in Beer, *A History of British Socialism*, p. 205.

[5] *The Economist*, No. 1, January 27, 1821, p. 5.

[6] See *ibid.*, No. 1, pp. 11–12.

teachers to 'devote their whole attention to the business of instruction during the time they are with the children', and avoid 'lassitude and irritation'.[1] The children would thus 'never be withdrawn, for a single instant, from kind, intelligent, vigilant observance, training, and instruction'. As co-operative living would make the work of the women much lighter, it was likely that many of them 'would be both qualified and disposed to undertake what may easily be rendered the "delightful task of teaching the young idea how to shoot" '.

Mudie had looked at the accounts available of de Fellenberg's schools at Hofwyl, and compared them with New Lanark. He believed that, as at Hofwyl, a community would provide a total education, the children being educated all the time, in school, at table, in the gardens, in field and country. He outlined the system at New Lanark, largely on the basis of the report by the Leeds deputation in 1819. He had also seen the private journal of one of the members of that deputation, John Cawood, and admitted that he had never been more moved than on seeing the delight with which Cawood 'suffers the feelings of a benevolent heart to run over, as it were, in expressions of affectionate love and admiration of the children, and of blessings on their innocent and endearing deportment'.[2] But, Mudie pointed out, he had described the education at Hofwyl and New Lanark in detail, because 'excellent as they are, they fall far short of the perfection which is proposed to be introduced into the system of the villages of Unity and Co-operation'. The difference Mudie postulates between Hofwyl and one of the proposed communities amounts to one of the earliest radical criticisms of de Fellenberg or any of the continental educational reformers, whose reputation was now growing in Britain:

'Mr Fellenberg,' says Mudie, 'avowedly restricts the extent and quality of the instruction to be given to the pupils in his School of Industry, to such branches of education only as are *necessary* for them as husbandmen and as shall induce them to prefer the condition of labourers in which they are to be placed rather than aspire to higher stations in society; and, though the institution at New Lanark is not deformed by this contracted principle—yet the practical results are nearly similar; for as the children must at an early age necessarily go to some employment, either in the works, or into the world, their

[1] *Ibid.*, No. 6, March 3, 1821, p. 95.
[2] *Ibid.*, No. 9, March 24, 1821, pp. 132–3. See No. 8, March 17, 1821, for his comments on Hofwyl.

education from that period must proceed less regularly, or be entirely interrupted.'

In the projected Owenite communities 'the regular acquisition of knowledge, and progress in intelligence, will go on, without interruption, for many years', and in fact throughout life.

Mudie was concerned essentially with the definition of practicable methods for the Economical Society's project. A concern with education in the wider world, as part of the process of reshaping that world, and *preparing it for community life*, appeared to any significant extent only later in the 1820's.

Other moves besides that of the Economical Society in London were being made in the direction of community experiments, notably at Orbiston in Scotland. The leading spirit in the Orbiston venture was Abram Combe, who was wildly enthusiastic about Owen's views on character formation,[1] and who stressed, like *A New View of Society*, that he regarded such social evils as the want of personal liberty 'to be caused solely by the *Ignorance* of the people'.[2] It was men like Mudie and Combe who in the early 1820's reinvigorated Owen's message and helped to win working class support for the complex of ideals embedded in it.

The idea of co-operation was spreading, and community was its keystone. When in 1827 the Brighton Co-operative Benevolent Fund Association was created, it set for itself two objectives, 'to raise by a small weekly contribution a fund for the purpose of enabling proper persons (who have not themselves the means) to join Co-operative Communities', and 'to spread a knowledge of the Co-operative system'.[3] One of the men to whom this knowledge was spread was Dr William King.[4] King, associated in his work for education in Brighton with people like William Allen and Lady Noel Byron, accepted Owenite co-operation, but not Owen. He did not approve of Owen's views on character formation, and wrote three months before his death that we

---

[1] See Combe's prefatory letter to Robert Owen in the former's *Metaphorical Sketches of the Old and New Systems, with Opinions on Interesting Subjects*, Edinburgh, 1823.

[2] *Ibid.*, p. 8.

[3] Brown, *Brighton's Co-operative Advance*, Manchester, n.d., p. 28.

[4] For an excellent commentary on King, see Sidney Pollard, *Dr William King of Ipswich: A Co-operative Pioneer*, Co-operative College Papers No. 6, Loughborough, 1959. See also Chapters II–IV of Brown, *Brighton's Co-operative Advance*.

should 'not remodel society according to the original idea of Owen'.[1] Owen's name was never, in fact, mentioned in King's *The Co-operator*. King was already a supporter of de Fellenberg's views on the combination of work and education, and was an enthusiastic convert to the idea of co-operation; he started to publish *The Co-operator* at a crucial moment in the history of the movement. At the time of the first issue, on May 1, 1828, King knew of the existence of four co-operative societies. On February 1, 1829 (No. 10), he announced that there were 14 in existence and 11 forming; on August 1 (No. 16) there were 'upwards of seventy', and on December 1 (No. 20) there were 'about one hundred and thirty'.[2] Throughout 1829 *The Birmingham Co-operative Herald* also reported rapid progress in co-operative trading and production throughout the Midland Counties. In April there was one Society in Birmingham; by August there were three. The first half dozen issues of the *Herald*, from April 1, 1829, give enthusiastic details of co-operative activity in Leicestershire and Derbyshire, Loughborough and Walsall, Worcester and many other areas. How firmly the growing movement held to Owen's view of co-operative effort towards the objective of community-organisation can be seen from the *Herald* of August 1829, when, after advancing a series of propositions about society, it asserted:

'That the establishment of Communities on the principles advocated by Mr Owen, of New Lanark, having for their object "Mutual Co-operation in the production—and, equality in the distribution of all the necessaries and comforts of life", would be the means of avoiding all the evils, and of attaining all the good, noticed in the preceding propositions.'[3]

The principles and rules for a co-operative society or 'working union' published in No. 6 of *The Co-operator* (October 1, 1828) show to what extent the explicit aims of the co-operators were widening. The rules suggest that 'members who have leisure, should meet at the room and form themselves into classes for mutual instruction . . . labour must be directed by KNOWLEDGE'. But adult education was only one proposal. Members 'will begin to pay particular attention to the education of their children. They should select the best school the neighbourhood

---

[1] Quoted in Brown, *Brighton's Co-operative Advance*, p. 60.
[2] *The Quarterly Review*, Vol. XLI, No. LXXXII, November 1829, p. 372, echoes these figures.
[3] No. 5, August 1, 1829.

affords; and agree to send their children to the same . . . But a still more desirable plan would be, to have a school of their own, and employ a master, at a salary'. This school 'should combine learning with industry, that the children should not acquire either pride or laziness, but habits of active carefulness'.

King stressed very strongly (No. 16, August 1, 1829) that the co-operators should set up schools for their children 'in order to prepare them for communities at an early age'. King, however, like Owen, though not like the working class Owenites in the Brighton Society, inclined towards an acceptance of the structure of existing society (though in the later numbers of *The Co-operator* he stated this acceptance much more emphatically than Owen).[1] Although King took up the basic community-plus-education theme from Owen, his view of an acceptably structured society kept him closer to de Fellenberg's more restricted position when it came to defining the form of education desirable for the sons of workmen; King had a much stronger sense of vocationalism, and a more limited total vision of education than Owen. He offered a very down-to-earth analysis of the value of the education:

'We *must* go to a shop every day to buy food and necessaries—why then should we not go to our own shop? We *must* send our children to school—why should we not have a school of our own, where we could bring up our children to useful trades, and make them good workmen and sober lads?'[2]

This was to some extent a retreat towards 'rescue' positions. King sought to produce immediately applicable proposals which, like de Fellenberg's school of industry, did not tamper with wider social problems. In the last issue of *The Co-operator* King obviously accepted the implications of de Fellenberg's system. At Hofwyl, he explained, the children of the poor 'have not been brought up above their station, for

[1] The Owenites 'were later to advise their members to read the first 17 numbers of the *Co-operator*, but not the later issues' (Pollard, *William King of Ipswich*, p. 30). King thought that 'the noblest spectacle upon earth, is a wise and good king, reigning over a great and happy people' (*The Co-operator*, No. 21, January 1, 1830). Owen treated royalty and aristocracy as one of the facts of life, and tried to recruit their assistance. He never attempted to *justify* them.

[2] *The Co-operator*, No. 1, May 1, 1828. See also No. 10, February 1, 1829, in which Mr Carson of Birmingham, is reported as speaking 'of the education of the children of the workman. He does not talk in high flown language of the great lengths to which education might be carried.' He wanted the children to turn out to 'be good workmen instead of bad ones'.

their habits of living and clothing have been those of the workman . . . but they stand a better chance in the race of life than those who have been less usefully educated'.[1] This, said King, was how co-operators should proceed. A piece of land should be purchased, upon which moderate accommodation should be erected. A master should be obtained from Fellenberg . . .' Pressing limited proposals for, largely, an education for vocation and sobriety, and insisting that co-operation and its educational schemes did not represent an attack on the upper classes 'in a spirit of hostility and spoliation', King argued confusedly. 'Knowledge is the only parent of plenty', he had previously asserted, 'and ignorance is the only parent of poverty.'[2] The rich, therefore, had amassed their capital 'by superior knowledge alone—the poor have given this capital to the rich instead of saving it for themselves, from ignorance alone. Had all mankind remained always ignorant, not one would have ever been rich . . . The world was first deluged with ignorance, in order to prove, to the end of time, that knowledge, and knowledge alone, is the true benevolent and omnipotent parent of virtue, religion, happiness, and plenty.' In King's reasonable picture there is an element of unreality, an ambiguity caused by a process of subtraction from Owen. There were others in the working class movement who, as we shall see, were to try to overcome Owen's own ambiguities by a process of addition.

Co-operation, with the objective of community-building in one form or another, had become by the end of the 1820's a movement dedicated to the application of Owen's ideas by working people themselves. Ventures in co-operative trading, production and housekeeping were on a very limited scale, but those engaged in the movement saw it as one which would expand to the point of reshaping the whole of society to accord with Owen's views. When Owen in 1829 returned conclusively from his various adventures on the continent of America, William Pare, who was to play a prominent part in the Owenite movement,[3] wrote to him on behalf of the Birmingham co-operators:

'During your absence from this Kingdom the last twelve months, I trust the grand principle of Co-operation have made sufficient

[1] *Ibid.*, No. 28, August 1, 1830.

[2] *Ibid.*, No. 20, December 1, 1829.

[3] Holyoake gives an enthusiastic picture of Pare in *Sixty Years of an Agitator's Life:* 'He had an assuring voice, the genius of enthusiasm, which won others to unity, and made no enemies . . . the best representative of the philosophical principles of Robert Owen of all his disciples' (edition of 1902, Vol. I, pp. 40–1).

progress to induce you to stay, at least for some time to assist, or rather I should have said to take the lead in a still further development for them . . . it is my conviction that the time for the inception and adoption of the New Views is peculiarly auspicious.'[1]

Owen, engaged in schemes by which he hoped to transform the face of continents, had, as we have seen, viewed the co-operative trading movement as a very weakling version of his schemes; it was, however, a version which had been growing for nearly a decade, and which had begun to provide a vehicle for working men for whom schemes of social betterment had to include some salient provision for working class education.

(ii) Perturbed spirits

At no stage in his career did Owen directly advocate *political* action to improve the position of the working class. His rationalist philosophy kept him bound in the belief that the question was one of ordered social reorganisation plus education. He never abandoned his belief that agitation for political reforms went both too far and not far enough: too far in that it inflamed passions and led to social disharmony, which, to his tidy rationalist outlook, was anathema; not far enough in that political reforms merely touched the fringe of the problem. He advocated the co-operative community in the 1810's precisely in order to by-pass all the unnecessary, dangerous and misleading paraphernalia of political action.

Out of the working class response to Owen, however, came politics and a concern for social betterment expressed in a different form and a different terminology, but nevertheless a child of Owen's.

Many of the early working class Owenites found themselves driven by the growing pressure for parliamentary reform to combine their directly Owenite objectives with more explicitly political ones. Between 1829 and 1831 such working class Owenites organised a succession of bodies, including the London Co-operative Trading Association, the British Association for Promoting Co-operative Knowledge and the National Union of the Working Classes—which mark the transition from 'pure' Owenism to radical working class politics.[2] There was a

---

[1] For a MS copy of the letter, dated September 26, 1829, see Pare MS 578/6.

[2] For a discussion of these organisations see *The Life and Struggles of William Lovett*, pp. 40–89. See also Podmore, *Robert Owen*, pp. 424–6, Wallas, *The Life of Francis Place*, 1925, edition, p. 271, and Mark Hovell, *The Chartist Movement*, Manchester, 1918, pp. 50–1.

considerable overlap of personnel from the British Association for Promoting Co-operative Knowledge, which came to an end in 1831, to the National Union of the Working Classes, which was founded in that year. William Lovett, John Cleave, James Watson, Henry Hetherington, and many others who were to be prominent in the Chartist movement, became active in the National Union of the Working Classes after being involved in one way or another in the earlier co-operative organisations and movement of ideas. Lovett, for example, was secretary of the British Association.

The British Association was a propagandist organisation for the dissemination of Owenite co-operative views. William Lovett, describing its inception, tells how, during Owen's absence in America, 'the leaders of the working men who were in favour of Owenism and also of political Radicalism, met together and opened co-operative shops'. They finally 'founded the British Union,[1] for enquiries reached London from all sides for information concerning co-operative matters . . . Our work was both practical and theoretical and we extracted from Owenism as much as we had in common and discarded all points of difference. All the leading men were workmen . . .'[2] In 1829 and 1830 Owenite ideas were still the common denominator and of predominant importance, just as they had been earlier, in 1825, for example, when John Stuart Mill and some of his friends held a three-month-long debate with the London co-operators, which, in Mills's words, 'was a *lutte à corps* between Owenites and political economists, whom the Owenites regarded as their most inveterate opponents'.[3] By 1831, however, in the charged atmosphere of reform agitation, independent working class action for political rights had assumed new proportions. Podmore describes the shift taking place about 1830 as being brought about by 'a number of working men and others who were more democratic than Owen and his middle-class followers'. These men had 'listened sympathetically to Owen's teachings . . . But reforms were in the air, and the

---

[1] It was referred to variously as the British Union for the Diffusion of Co-operative Knowledge, the British Association for the Promotion of Co-operative Knowledge and the British Association for the Spread of Co-operative Knowledge.

[2] Quoted from the Place MSS. in Beer, *A History of British Socialism*, 1948 edition, Vol. I, pp. 299–300. Lovett describes the leaders of the British Association as being 'in favour of Owenism and also of political Radicalism'.

[3] *Autobiography*, World's Classics 1925, edition, p. 105. For 'Two Speeches on Population' delivered by Mill in this debate see *The Journal of Adult Education*, Vol. IV, No. 1, October 1929.

working class element in Owen's London audiences were naturally drawn off into political propaganda.'[1]

The main forum for the new political struggle was the National Union of the Working Classes, and its main publicity organ was Henry Hetherington's *The Poor Man's Guardian*. Hetherington, publisher and campaigner for a free press, was a convinced follower of Owen throughout his life, to the point of expressing in his *Last Will and Testament* his gratitude 'to Mr Owen for the happiness I have experienced in contemplating the superiority of his system'. He 'could not die happy without recommending my fellow-countrymen to study its principles and earnestly strive to establish them in practice'.[2] *The Poor Man's Guardian*, however, particularly under the editorship of Bronterre O'Brien from 1832, had frequent occasion to attack 'pure' Owenite opposition to the cause of parliamentary reform and political rights. At a National Union meeting on November 28, 1831, a speaker declared that 'the plan of Mr Owen could not be followed out until a proper foundation was cleared away. (Hear.) ... it would not do for (people) to be so good as Mr Owen required. (Laughter.)'[3] On July 23, 1832, another speaker referred to 'such political imposters as Burdett, Hume, and Robt. Owen' and singled out, to cheers, Owen as 'one of the greatest political imposters of the day'.[4] Tempers, it must be remembered, were running high on the subject of parliamentary reform. These debates in the National Union and the discussions in the pages of *The Poor Man's Guardian* show the complexity of the divergence between the 'pure' Owenites, the co-operators, on the one hand, and the new political radicalism, which was not so much anti-Owen as adapted Owenism, on the other hand. One feels, reading the reports, the redirection of working class Owenite energies into new channels, in a period of new enthusiasms and opportunities. There are at this point in time no hard-and-fast allegiances and demarcation lines between alternative working-class radical attitudes.[5] William Lovett, for example, only recently Secretary of the British Association for Promoting Co-operative Knowledge, and

---

[1] *Robert Owen*, pp. 424–5.

[2] Reprinted in Ambrose G. Barker, *Henry Hetherington 1792–1849. A Pioneer in the Freethought and Working Class Struggles of a Hundred Years ago for the Freedom of the Press*, London, n.d., pp. 59–60.

[3] *The Poor Man's Guardian*, Vol. I, No. 24, December 3, 1831, p. 188.

[4] *Ibid.*, Vol. I, No. 59, July 28, 1832, p. 475.

[5] Throughout the thirties and forties, as Cecil Driver points out, 'many a northern operative professed to be a trade unionist, a radical, an Owenite co-operator, and Ten Hours man all at the same time ...' (*Tory Radical*, p. 261).

later to be attacked by the left wing of the Chartist movement for his lack of militancy, was proclaiming in November 1831 that 'he thought the crisis was coming when the aristocracy would be hurled from its seat of tyranny and plunder. The question was whether the people would die for want of bread or fight for it; he for one would rather fight for bread than die for want of it. (Cheers.) If the time was not come for them to arm, the time was come for them to talk about it. He then read Colonel Macerone's letter on arming the people, as published in the *Morning Chronicle*, and reprinted as a penny pamphlet.'[1]

In the new situation of emphatic, independent working class agitation for political reform, energies were beginning to be redirected, and objectives being redefined. In this context the position of *The Poor Man's Guardian* and of Bronterre O'Brien, its editor from the end of 1831 or the beginning of 1832,[2] was of particular importance. O'Brien, in the early thirties the outstanding spokesman for independent working class political agitation, and extremely critical of the Owenite position on parliamentary reform, nonetheless remained sympathetic to Owenism. At a tea organised by the 2nd Co-operative Congress, in October 1831, for example, O'Brien was invited to speak. He expressed surprise that anyone should have doubted his commitment to the co-operative movement, and concluded what the report of the Congress described as 'an able and luminous address, which was interrupted with frequent applause, by assuring his audience that the sacred and benevolent cause of Co-operation should ever command his services'.[3] His speech was devoted to a justification of the movement for parliamentary reform, in terms intended to demonstrate to the co-operative movement that they were both striving for the same end though placing different emphases. *The Poor Man's Guardian* shows extremely clearly both this redirection of former Owenite energies, and an extraordinarily patient attempt to keep open channels of communication between the co-operative and politically radical organisations.

An intensive discussion of the relations between Owenism and the political reform movement took place in the *Guardian* between September and November 1832. On September 1, an editorial made a lengthy analysis of the Owenite position. 'Every thing emanating from Mr Owen', it considered, 'is entitled to impartial consideration, and if possible, to

---

[1] *The Poor Man's Guardian*, Vol. I, No. 23, November 26, 1831, p. 181.
[2] See Beer, *A History of British Socialism*, 1948 edition, Vol. I, p. 285.
[3] *Proceedings of the Second Co-operative Congress*, 1831, pp. 18 and 21.

a fair trial, because we believe his PRINCIPLES are, in the main, true.'
Having accepted his principles, however, the editorial expressed its
suspicion of:

> 'the various schemes of the leading co-operators, who are avowedly
> indisposed to confer upon the industrious classes their POLITICAL
> RIGHTS, and who, indeed seek every opportunity to speak sneeringly
> and contemptuously of their possession, as a consideration of no
> value. We, on the contrary, contend that till the industrious classes
> become possessed of political power . . . no permanent improvement
> will or can take place in their condition . . . The co-operators and the
> radical reformers are obnoxious to the aristocracy in nearly the same
> degree, except that the drivelling of the former is less alarming to the
> evil doers than the honest and fearless political avowals of the
> latter.'[1]

Three weeks later the paper had abandoned the irritation that 'drivelling'
indicates, and made a plea for working class unity. 'Our enemies, the
Aristocracy,' it said, 'have heretofore mastered us solely because we
have been disunited.' In the following extremely important passage it
made the precise appeal:

> 'Let us all unite against the common enemy, and turn against him
> his own weapons. Above all, let the RADICAL take the OWENITE by
> the hand, and the OWENITE do the same by the RADICAL, for both
> parties are the *real*, and only *real friends* of the working people . . .
> The disciples of Mr Owen may differ from us as to the *means*, or
> "*modus operandi*", but they have precisely the same eventual object
> in view, namely, to *establish for the workman dominion over the fruits
> of his own industry* . . . if we cannot agree to march together, let us
> at least throw no obstruction in each other's way.'[2]

A meeting 'to discuss a point of difference which appears to exist
between the National Union of the Working Classes and Mr Owen,
relative to the importance of conferring political Rights upon the
Working Classes' was held at Owen's Institution of the Industrious
Classes, which would hold 2,000 people. It was 'crowded almost to
suffocation . . . whilst there were several hundred persons in the street
unable to obtain admittance'. Robert Dale Owen 'wished Co-operation

---

[1] *The Poor Man's Guardian*, Vol. I, No. 64, September 1, 1832, p. 513.
[2] *Ibid.*, No. 67, September 22, 1832, p. 538.

and Radical Reform to go hand in hand . . . the surest means of obtaining . . . the amelioration of the condition of the working classes'.[1]

The editorial in the issue of September 29 returned to the theme of unity, announcing that 'numerous are the letters we have since received thanking us for our advice, and applauding our liberality towards the Owenites'. This liberality, however, 'we regret to say, has not been met by a corresponding spirit on the part of our suspicious and supercilious co-adjutors'. At a further meeting at the Institution, Owen had taken the occasion 'to revert to his favourite theme—the *"violence of the Radical party"*; and to designate us a set of men "possessing little or no knowledge of the affairs of government", and wholly incapable (did we even obtain all we wanted from government) to make any beneficial use of it'. The editorial considered Owen 'incapable of *knowingly* doing or saying anything injurious to the cause of justice' since he had 'for forty years laboured incessantly for the good of mankind'. Never before, perhaps, it asserted, 'did a human being pursue a public career with motives so remote from personal, with objects so purely disinterested and philanthropic'. But, it concluded:

'He has been so long elevated above the atmosphere of human passions, that he hardly knows what is going on in this nether world . . .'[2]

Owen had, earlier in the year, been trying to define 'the most useful knowledge that can now be given to the public'. His first answer was 'undeniable general facts' which will calm the 'perturbed spirits, engendered by the erroneous notions transmitted to us through the less experienced ages of human existence'.[3]

'These perturbed spirits,' he explained, 'under the present system of error . . . are forced to become the firebrands of society; whereas . . . they might be rendered highly valuable to their fellow-men, not as we find them now, the leaders of factions, parties, and sects, but the guides of the human race to permanent happiness and well-being.'[4]

[1] *Ibid.*, pp. 541–2.
[2] *Ibid.*, Vol. I, No. 68, September 29, 1832, pp. 545–6. For further contributions to this discussion see also *ibid.*, pp. 548–9, No. 69, p. 557, and No. 73, p. 588 (the date of the last, November 3, 1832, mistakenly appears as 1831).
[3] *The Crisis*, Vol. I, No. 1, April, 14, 1832.
[4] *Ibid.*, No. 2, April 21, 1832.

For him, the political reformers were also 'perturbed spirits'.

Though the impact of Owen on the working class had now produced diverging responses, there was a strong element in working class thinking in general of the identity of the working class as a class, and of generally-held independent working class objectives. The role of Bronterre O'Brien as editor of *The Poor Man's Guardian* was of inestimable importance in this process. Owen, in spite of himself, had helped to give the working class this self-awareness, this conviction that better things were attainable, that *it* could attain them. Working class political radicalism did not seek to replace Owenism, but to add another dimension to it.

Since the accent of the new radicalism was on the acquisition of political rights as the prerequisite to obtaining social justice in general, education, as one might expect, was a less explicit and immediate concern of the new movement than in the Owenite organisations and publications. Explicit references to education in *The Poor Man's Guardian* are, in fact, rare. On the other hand, the very publication of the paper and the fight for the repeal of the 'taxes on knowledge' were a conscious educative act. The new movement understood that without liberty of the press the fight for political rights could not be won. *The Poor Man's Guardian* announced weekly beneath its title that it was 'published in defiance of "law", to try the power of "might" against "right".' Its permanent motto was 'Knowledge is Power'.

Education, for the working class political reformers, meant *political* education; the fight for education meant the fight for a free press and for parliamentary representation; the fight against ignorance meant the fight against the newspaper stamp. The educator-in-chief of the movement was not Owen the social reformer and philosopher, but Hetherington, the publisher. The problem, for them, was not infant schools but the right to publish. Conversely, every meeting convened under the banner of the fight against the 'taxes on knowledge' was in fact about education. A 'Meeting of Friends to the FREE CIRCULATION OF KNOWLEDGE' held in Birmingham on August 9, 1831, for instance, adopted a number of resolutions, the first of which declared 'that the duties and other restrictions on newspapers and cheap publications . . . tend to perpetuate ignorance . . . to restrain the working classes from acquiring political knowledge', and called for the abolition of the taxes on knowledge. The second deplored the prosecutions against cheap publications, and the third stated:

'That we witness with regret, not unmixed with indignation, the readiness of Government in granting an enormous annuity for educating a Princess . . . whilst it postpones the consideration of a question on the result of which must mainly depend the confirmed ignorance or knowledge of a whole people.'[1]

The fight for a free press assumed the attainment of a reasonable standard of elementary literacy among the working class. It asserted the lack of cheap newspapers, not the lack of schools, to be the first obstacle to the removal of ignorance. The consequences of the lack of cheap publications, and the ignorance attendant upon it, were 'but too apparent in the impoverishment of the manufacturing classes, and in the gross ignorance of the agricultural classes'. The aim, therefore, was 'to get rid of that greatest of all national evils, POLITICAL IGNORANCE'.[2] For the moment, the radical reform wing of the working class movement had no specific objectives in the field of formal education. Political ignorance, not ignorance, was its target.

(iii) Obtain this knowledge

The independent working class movement for political rights was not to flourish into Chartism until the later years of the 1830's. The Owenite co-operative movement was already approaching its climacteric when the National Union of the Working Classes was coming into existence. The period 1831–4 was one of enormous Owenite activity, with, in essence, three currents running through it—the independent activity of Owen and the 'pure' Owenite movement, the association of Owen with the growing working-class co-operative movement, and the meteoric phase of Owenite trade union activity.

By 1830 the co-operatives were a national movement. Individual co-operatives were beginning to think in terms of broader developments than they had been able to do in the early days, and such developments almost invariably included some provision for education. When the First Liverpool Co-operative Society took a shop in that year, the accommodation included 'a room for the members to meet in, and

[1] *Ibid.*, Vol. I, No. 7, August 20, 1831, p. 56. One contributor to the discussion at this meeting 'highly approved of the idea of the Working Classes taking the education of their children into their own hands, instead of having it retailed to them by the "great" . . .' (*ibid.*, p. 52).
[2] *The Poor Man's Guardian*, Vol. I, No. 56, July 7, 1832, p. 450 (report of meetings of 'the Friends of the Working Classes and a Free Press' in London).

another for a library. There were also facilities for the provision of a school. The early Liverpool co-operators . . . regarded education as an essential phase of their work.'[1] One of them devised plans for making the Liverpool Society wholesale agents for other co-operative stores, and devoting some of the profit to establishing:

'a school or college in or near Liverpool, that would in a few years be sufficient with a little assistance from the labour of the children three or four hours a day, to pay for the board, lodging, clothing, and a superior education of some hundreds of the children of co-operators, none other to be admitted, and each co-operative society to have the privilege of sending one, two, three or more pupils according to the amount of the commission upon their purchases . . . co-operative knowledge would, above all others, be the first instilled knowledge into the minds of the rising generation.'[2]

Such proposals also appeared elsewhere and were extensively discussed in *The Birmingham Co-operative Herald*. Owen's infant education system was spreading, affirmed the journal, but life itself undid their work. The co-operators needed to look to later education. The answer lay in the proposed co-operative colleges, and the establishment of preparatory schools for them 'in every town where there is one or more Co-operative Society, similar to our present infant schools, but with some improvements'. From here the children would go to the Colleges, to be built in 'healthful situations in the country'.[3] These were to remain only proposals, but on a less grandiose scale the co-operators in most towns were enthusiastically using the co-operative movement as the base for the organisation of their own educational schemes.[4] The astonishing difference between the issues of *The Economist* in 1821–2 and those of *The Birmingham Co-operative Herald* and the *Lancashire Co-operator*[5] less than ten years later lies in the comprehensiveness of

[1] W. H. Brown, *A Century of Liverpool Co-operation*, Liverpool, n.d. p. 20.
[2] *Ibid.*, p. 22. The proposals were almost certainly by John Finch.
[3] *The Birmingham Co-operative Herald*, No. 17, August 1, 1830.
[4] For a detailed plan to establish a northern co-operative 'school for 500 children from 4 years old to 14 years', see MS letter to Owen from William Carson, March 1832, CUL/522, in Appendix B below.
[5] From September 3, 1831, it became *The Lancashire and Yorkshire Co-operator; or, Useful Classes' Advocate*. Its motto was: 'NUMBERS without UNION are POWERLESS—And UNION without KNOWLEDGE is USELESS.' It is difficult to refer to issues of this journal, as there are three sets of numbering beginning with No. 1, without a volume reference, and the New Series begun

the social programme discussed in the latter journals, under the impetus of the confidence generated by the spread of the movement at the end of the twenties. In particular, there is in these later journals a commitment to education as an ideal and as a practical contribution to renovating present society, which is barely discernible in the tentative days of *The Economist*.

The Lancashire Co-operator in August 1831 issued an appeal:

'Let every co-operative society adopt a plan of educating the children of the members, by establishing a school for their instruction; or, if this cannot be effected by single societies, let several join. Where neither of these can be effected, I would suggest, that some member or members should receive the children for five or six hours on the Sunday, in order to enable them to read and write.'

The person doing this would inevitably develop a personal interest in the children, would 'observe their peculiar disposition . . . (and) the employments to which they would be best adapted' and would help them to develop their personalities.[1] The journal's concern with the practicalities of co-operative education emerged clearly in its excitement over developments in Salford. 'The First Salford' had succeeded in January 1832 in obtaining 'very eligible rooms' for a Co-operative Sunday school, and the writer of the leading article in the paper had been to look at it on the second Sunday on which it was opened. 'We witnessed with feelings of unutterable delight', he said, '104 male and female adults and children, zealously prosecuting their studies in an as attentive, quiet, and orderly manner as though the school had been in existence as many years.' The school taught 'really useful knowledge' on Sunday mornings and afternoons, and was preparing accommodation for a total of 200 students. It was also intended that the school would open three nights a week, 'for the teaching of Reading, Writing, Arithmetic, and Grammar, and as soon as arrangements can be made we are informed they propose opening classes for the teaching of Geometry, Mathematics, Drawing, Political Economy, &c. to the senior scholars'.[2] That at least some of these proposals were implemented can be seen from the fact that the name of the school changed to the Salford Co-operative Night and

in February or March 1832 bears no dates. For educational, as most other, developments this is probably the most informative and useful of the co-operative journals.

[1] *The Lancashire Co-operator*, No. 5, August, 6, 1831.
[2] *The Lancashire and Yorkshire Co-operator*, No. 12, February 4, 1832.

Sunday School, the teachers of which issued a Declaration later in the year, urging that Manchester and Salford co-operators should meet together frequently to discuss their principles, and putting forward a scheme for Sunday evening meetings, at which lectures on co-operation would be given or extracts from relevant works read. The teachers would meet quarterly to appoint readers and lecturers, who would give their services voluntarily. The issue which reported this also contained a further appeal for help with books and apparatus, and an expression of gratitude to Lady Noel Byron for her assistance.[1]

The journal was preoccupied also with the possibility of establishing Co-operative Industry Schools, a co-operative version of infant schools.[2] In February 1832 it announced that the Benevolent Co-operative Society at Worsley (north of Manchester) intended opening such a school in less than a month.

By this time some 400–500 societies were in existence, and all of them, recognising that 'they owed their existence to Owen's teaching', and looking up to him as their 'founder and prophet'.[3] Education was now a prominent feature of their activities. By 1830 Owen was aware that the working class, on whose behalf he had expended so much energy, now possessed a movement which was a force to be reckoned with, but he was still prepared only to fraternise with the movement that spoke in his name. Ultimately he chose, as William Pare had begged him, to lead, but for the moment he was prepared only to lecture, and the central message of his lecture was the acquisition of knowledge. In January 1830 he issued an *Address to the Operative Manufacturers and Agricultural Labourers in Great Britain and Ireland*, in which he told them that, as producers, their labour was badly directed and they were being deliberately kept in poverty:

'. . . to direct your skill and industry aright, you require knowledge of a superior description to any that has yet been given to you; and, above all things, you should endeavour to obtain this knowledge'.[4]

---

[1] *Ibid.*, New Series, No. 8 (probably September 1832). Issue No. 12 (February 4, 1832) had referred to the intention of the First Salford of asking Lady Shelley to become a patroness. See also the *Address* of the Salford Co-operative Institution in 1836, in Appendix B below.

[2] George R. Skene, in *The Lancashire and Yorkshire Co-operator* (No. 6, November 12, 1832) proposed this name as being preferable to that of infant school.

[3] *Robert Owen*, p. 397.

[4] Pare MS 578/13.

That Owen was now lecturing the co-operators in these terms is borne out by Lady Noel Byron, who in 1830 sent two friends to a co-operative meeting to hear Owen speak. They reported to her that Owen had fulminated, telling the Society that its members were too ignorant, and that without knowledge the movement was nonsense'.[1] In January of that year he told the quarterly meeting of the British Association for promoting Co-operative Knowledge that they had the power to create 'more wealth than any rational being will desire to consume. Employ, therefore, my friends, all the time you have to spare in acquiring real knowledge.'[2]

Between the busy lecturing and publishing activity of 1830 and the inauguration of his Association of the Industrious Classes in February 1832, Owen saw with increasing conviction that his most important work was propaganda among the working class. In 1831 he attended the first two Co-operative Congresses, taking his turn in the chair, moving resolutions, and urging courses of action. After the first Congress he was reported as saying that 'he had been present at meetings of persons of every rank in life, on a great number of occasions, but that he had never before seen a greater display of real talent, sound good sense, and genuine eloquence'.[3] But he was not yet enmeshed in the movement with complete conviction.

His own new organisation, entitled the Association of the Intelligent and well disposed of the Industrious Classes, for removing the Causes of Ignorance and Poverty, by Education and Employment, was probably established during 1831,[4] though it did not begin activities in its own premises until February 1832. *The Poor Man's Guardian* reported the opening:

'On Sunday last Mr Owen delivered two opening Lectures at his institution in Gray's Inn Road, upon the objects of the institution, to upwards of 1,500 persons, among whom were a large portion of ladies. The proceedings commenced and concluded with music and singing.'[5]

[1] Ethel Colburn Mayne, *The Life and Letters of Anne Isabella, Lady Noel Byron*, London, 1929, p. 329.
[2] Quoted in *The Birmingham Co-operative Herald*, No. 12, March 1, 1830.
[3] John Finch in *Liverpool Chronicle*, June 8, 1831. There is a copy in *Co-operative Congresses*.
[4] See *The Crisis*, Vol. II, No. 20, May 25, 1833.
[5] *The Poor Man's Guardian*, Vol. I, No. 38, March 3, 1832.

Before very long this institution was to become closely bound up with Owen's activities in the co-operative movement, and to see the establishment of a scheme for the co-operative exchange of goods; apart from any co-operative activities that came to be conducted on its premises, however, it continued throughout this period to exist as an institution in its own right, housing the Association, conducting educational activities and providing a basis for Owenite propaganda. The aims of the Association included lectures, the establishment of 'Seminaries for young persons of all ages and both sexes, to form a useful and superior character from infancy to maturity', the establishment of Schools of Industry, and the provision of a library and reading room.[1] In May 1833 Owen again detailed a plan 'to ensure the advantages proposed in the objects of the Association to its members', These included:

> 'First. By the regular delivery of Lectures on every Sunday at eleven in the morning, and seven in the evening, on the Science of Society, with the view of forming a public opinion based on TRUTH.
>
> Second. By holding the Social Festivals . . . once in each fortnight for the purpose of affording a rational, economical, and beneficial recreation for the members of the Association . . .
>
> Fourth. By establishing Adult Evening Schools for instructing those who are desirous of forming a correct method of estimating the advantages of the co-operative system over the competitive, and enabling artisans to acquire an intimate knowledge of those sciences which are peculiarly applicable to their particular trades.'[2]

The difficulties caused by the use of the premises as an exchange market, and a move to other premises in Charlotte Street in May 1833, however, were enormous. The first reference to a school on the Association's premises occurred in *The Crisis* in May 1832.[3] The Association for Removing the Causes of Ignorance had in January issued an *Address to All Classes* declaring its intention of making educational provision a central part of the work of the new Institution. Owen had by now come to believe that the prevailing ignorance was an *enforced* ignorance, used, together with unemployment, as a mechanism for preserving injustice, and the *Address* pin-pointed the causes of 'wretchedness, misery and

[1] *The Resolution intended to be proposed at the* PUBLIC MEETING *to be held on the 12th instant, at the* ROYAL LONDON BAZAAR, 1832, in Pare MS 578/40.
[2] *The Crisis* Vol. II No. 20 May 25, 1833, p. 155.
[3] *Ibid.*, Vol. I, No. 5, May 5, 1832, p. 18. A speaker had announced that 'several children registered for education in the school'.

degradation' in Britain as, firstly, 'the *ignorance* by which, through artificial arrangement, the mass of the population are retained and held in mental bondage', and secondly, 'the *compulsory idleness* of a large part of the population'.[1] The education to be provided fell into three categories: regular lectures to explain 'in a familiar manner, *the science of society*', arrangements for 'rational, economical, and beneficial recreation', and schools established on 'principles in accordance with human nature'.[2] The major thread that runs through the details is attention to the individual personality of the child. 'Every child', says the first principle, 'shall gradually be made acquainted with his *own nature*.' The instruction given would not only be in line with the general laws of human nature, but would be 'adapted also to the *peculiar organization* of each child.' Means would be found to create '*entire confidence* and *sympathy* between the instructor and the instructed'.

In April Owen had announced that schools would be opened at the Institution in a fortnight. There were to be three, taking children at the ages of fourteen months, five or six, and eleven. Day scholars were to be admitted, but the grand design was to remove children entirely from unfavourable circumstances and prejudices. Boarders, would, therefore, be admitted, at the charge of two guineas a month.'[3] The fees would cover food, lodging and clothes, and was the lowest possible if the children were to have a 'good and attractive appearance' and make a favourable impression. A *Prospectus* for the proposed schools announced that for lack of funds only the first of the three schools would be opened for the moment, and it was to take boarders only. An infant day-school was to be established 'as soon as arrangements for the purpose can be found'.[4] The principles outlined for the school again stressed the importance of the individual personality of the child, and of presenting material to the children which 'according to the age and capacity of the children, they will be able fully to comprehend'. The most striking sentence in the document announced that 'familiar conversation will be the common medium of instruction, whether intellectual or moral'.[5]

Whatever may have been achieved at Gray's Inn Road, however,

[1] *Address to All Classes in the State from the Governor, Directors and Committee of the Association*, January 14, 1832, p. 3.

[2] *Ibid.*, pp. 3–4.

[3] *Proceedings of the Third Co-operative Congress*, p. 41.

[4] *Prospectus of the System of Education to be pursued in the Schools attached to the Institution*, n.d., p. 3.

[5] *Ibid.*, p. 2.

collapsed in the difficulties of early 1833, and a new start in October 1833 was attended by immense physical and other problems.[1] That the spirit, if not the actual organisation, behind the school was Owen's is clear from the rules and regulations, and, to show how alive the spirit of New Lanark was in the new institution, they are worth quoting in full:

'*Constitution.*—1. Every pupil shall be encouraged to express his or her opinion.

2. No creed or dogma shall be imposed upon any.

3. Admitted facts alone shall be placed before the pupils, from which they shall be allowed to draw their own conclusions.

4. No distinction whatever shall exist; but all be treated with equal kindness.

5. Neither praise nor blame, merit nor demerit, rewards nor punishments, shall be awarded to any: kindness and love to be the only ruling powers.

6. Both sexes shall have equal opportunities of acquiring useful knowledge.

Routine.—Gymnastic exercises, spelling, reading, writing, grammar, geography, Latin, French, arithmetic, geometry, algebra, and the other branches of mathematics; and, as soon as possible, music and dancing.

Teachers.—1. To observe that the strictest order prevails.

2. To maintain among the pupils the best social feelings.

3. To create the best possible circumstances for the formation of the best moral, intellectual, and physical characters.

4. To visit on alternate weeks the parents of absentees.

Hours.—Morning, from nine until twelve. Afternoon, from two until four.'[2]

In addition to attempts to found schools by the Institution, private ventures by sympathisers individually or in groups also took place in London, as advertisements in *The Crisis* indicate.[3]

[1] See *The Crisis*, Vol. III, No. 20, January 4, 1834, for a 'Report of a Meeting of the Friends and Patrons of the School (lately commenced in the Institution of the Industrious Classes, 14, Charlotte Street . . .)'.

[2] *Ibid.*, p. 150.

[3] See Vol. III, No. 20, January 11, 1834, for the Prospectus of the 'Westminster Rational School, and General Scientific Institution, Grosvenor-street, Millbank. Founded 1833', and Vol. III, No. 29, March 15, 1834, for an advertisement for 'Portbury's School Rooms, 31 Crown Street, Oxford St' (Portbury had previously helped to run the Institution's school).

For the first time, Owen was able, with convinced and eloquent allies and disciples (including his son, Robert Dale),[1] to conduct continuous, large-scale publicity activities. This was the Institution's primary educational function, and the central feature of the Institution's activities were the lectures and discussions. The debate with the radical reformers took place in September 1832 at the Institution, and throughout 1832 *The Crisis* gives evidence of constant lectures on a wide variety of topics, discussions of moral and other issues, and social evenings with lectures.[2] A report of one of the regular Thursday evening meetings at the Institution (probably written by Owen himself) described the attendance as 'numerous', the speakers as 'various', the interest as 'considerable' the feeling as 'harmonious' and the duration as 'long', and drew conclusions from the scene:

> 'What a different and superior method this, of the productive classes spending increasingly long nights at our discussions, than at the public-house, or spirit shops, whose noisy senseless mirth, swells upon the gale of evening. Institutions for rational discussion on useful and important subjects, ought to be much more numerous and splendid than gin shops.'[3]

It is clear from this description that a substantial part of the audience came from 'the productive classes'. Some writers have suggested that the Association was essentially a middle class organisation. The annual subscription to the Institution in the Gray's Inn Road, a guinea and upwards, was beyond the pockets of working men. Tickets for the monthly, later weekly, festivals were 3s. (1s. 6d.) to members)—'clearly suited to the pockets of the comparatively well-to-do.'[4] The *membership* of the Association, and audiences at some of the *social* events in the

[1] He took over the editorship of *The Crisis* from his father as from November 3, 1832 (Leopold, *Robert Dale Owen*, p. 115). He was editor until April 20, 1833. He was also president of an off-shoot of the Institution—the Social Missionary and Tract Society for Promoting Human Happiness, designed to publicise the Institution, communities and the principles behind them, including by 'public lecturing in the open air and otherwise' (*The Crisis*, Vol. I, No. 33, October 20, 1832).

[2] A typical 'social festival' is described in *The Poor Man's Guardian*, No. 64, September 1, 1832, p. 523. It consisted of a concert, a lecture by Owen, and dancing 'kept up with much spirit and vivacity until a late hour . . . upwards of five hundred persons present . . .'

[3] *The Crisis*, Vol. I, No. 33, October 20, 1832.

[4] Podmore, *Robert Owen*, p. 426.

early days, probably did consist largely of middle-class sympathisers.[1] Entrance to lectures, however, was 1d. or 2d., or free.[2] The Institution, what is more, shared premises with the National Equitable Labour Exchange, and its activities were becoming increasingly bound up with the co-operative and trade union movements. It existed, in fact, to carry the Owenite message into the working class.

Lecturing activities at the Institution ranged from' the management of children'[3] to a 'familiar and practical course' on chemistry and geology', a series by Robert Dale Owen on geography and lectures on astronomy.[4] One issue of *The Crisis* alone advertised for the coming week lectures on geography and 'the Change of Society' (by Owen), a public meeting, and lectures on geology and astronomy; it also contained a report of a lecture by Owen on the employment of children in manufactures.[5] Part of the importance of this kind of activity lies in the fact that it coexisted with intensive and difficult activity in connection with the enormous co-operative labour exchange scheme.

Owen was in 1832 becoming organisationally involved almost exclusively with working class activities, not only as a leader in the accepted sense of the term, but as a teacher. He lectured them on the Science of Society, hectored them to acquire knowledge and to behave rationally. His message was unchanged, and he was accepted as leader not only because he had proposals to make about co-operation and the reorganisation of society into planned communities, but because he had something to say about human nature, about the possibility of controlling circumstances, and of altering the basis of human life. He continued to affirm and reaffirm that 'children are, without exception, passive, yet wonderfully constituted compounds which are capable of receiving individually and collectively, any character whatever. The same child might be rendered, by different treatment, a savage or civilized human being, intelligent or ignorant, virtuous or vicious'.[6] It was this message of man's imprisonment in circumstances not of his own choosing which bound the working class movement to Owen. It was a principle on the

[1] Most of the Owenite trading organisations probably raised funds by similar means (see *The Poor Man's Guardian*, Vol. I, No. 79, December 8, 1832, for example, for a 'social ball' advertised by the Equitable Labour Exchange, Poland St.). See *ibid.*, No. 78, December 1, 1832 for a criticism of these high prices.
[2] For an advertisement for free lectures see *ibid.*, Vol. I, No. 54, June 23, 1832.
[3] *The Crisis*, Vol. I, No. 36, November 10, 1832.
[4] *Ibid.*, No. 41, December 15, 1832.
[5] *Ibid.*, Vol. II, No. 2, January 19, 1833.
[6] *Ibid.*, Vol. I, No. 2, April 21, 1832.

basis of which the working class could begin to believe in the possibility of escape from the imprisonment.[1] Owen's philosophy of education, re-expressed in the *Outline of the Rational System of Society*, reprinted in *The Crisis* in May 1832, was of critical importance to the working class reader. From the starting point of the effect of external circumstances on character, he was led to propose that 'all shall be educated from infancy to maturity, in the best manner known at the time', that 'all shall pass through the same general routine of education, domestic teaching and employment' and that 'both sexes shall have equal rights, privileges, and personal liberty'.[2] The enormous working class support for Owen in the years 1832–4 was to a very large extent stimulated by this awareness of Owen as a spokesman for social justice, of which popular education, now the subject of practical experiment, widespread debate, and the concern of influential social movements, formed an important ingredient.

(iv) Equitable exchange

The first Co-operative Congress was held in Manchester on May 26 and 27, 1831.[3] The congresses mirrored the co-operators' desire to further the nationwide co-ordination of the co-operative movement, through the establishment of wholesale and production schemes and to accumulate enough profits to establish co-operative communities. Owen was present at the congresses from the start, but was unenthusiastic about their community schemes, being unconvinced that their, by his standards, small efforts could be fruitful.[4] The third congress, however, was held at the Institution in Gray's Inn Road in May 1832, which now became the nerve-centre of the movement, and *The Crisis* the bearer of its message. The third congress, outlining practical arrangements for a 'healthy and sound state of existence', clearly indicated the extent of Owen's impact on the co-operators:

[1] Owen was aware of objections being made to his reasoning, and in an editorial (*The Crisis*, May 26, 1832) entitled 'Formation of Human Character', he stated and tried to answer such objections. See also *ibid.*, Vol. II, No. 29, July 27, 1833.

[2] *Ibid.*, Vol. I, No. 10, May 26, 1832.

[3] For a review of the congresses held between 1831 and 1835 see Holyoake, *The History of Co-operation*, 1908 edition, pp. 120–5, although his details and dates, here as elsewhere, should be treated prudently. The fullest documentation is in *Co-operative Congresses*.

[4] See Holyoake, *The History of Co-operation*, p. 177, and the report of the first two congresses.

'Amongst such practical arrangements, we would particularly call your attention to the following:— That equal education, and *that* too, the best which human knowledge can now devise, should be imparted to every human being, male and female . . .'[1]

Owen's commitment to the movement had produced his enthusiastic support for the idea of the Labour Exchange or Exchange Bazaar. Such Exchanges were a feature of the British co-operative movement from about 1830. One of the earliest was opened by the British Association for Promoting Co-operative Knowledge early in 1830, to which some forty co-operative societies in London probably sent their surplus produce for sale.[2] The First Western Co-operative Union, in London ('the most significant early Labour Exchange'[3]) added a labour bank to its shop in 1831-2. The Gothic Hall Labour Bank, in London, first advertised by William King,[4] its founder, in 1831, and started in 1832, aimed to show:

'. . . that the interest of all classes would be promoted by introducing measures for supplying each others wants, by Mutual Exchanges, effected through the agency of General Deposit Banks, for goods of all kinds and descriptions, each and every depositor having a claim on the general stock, to the extent of their respective deposits'.

Each depositor valued the articles brought, and if the valuation was approved by the Council, 'the amount is immediately paid to the Depositor in the Exchange Notes of the Institution, with which Notes, the Depositor purchases any suitable article that may be contained in the Bazaar'.[5] King issued in 1831 a series of leaflets explaining briefly *The Workings of Money*, *The Workings of Money Capital*, and similar themes, as a kind of ideological substratum on which to erect his proposed Exchanges.[6] It is clear from the leaflets how deeply Owenite his

---

[1] *An Address to the Governments of Europe and America*, in *The Crisis*, Vol. I, No. 3, April 21, 1832. A supplement contains a resolution of the Congress urging the government to remove 'all impediments to the cheap diffusion of knowledge . . .'

[2] Podmore, *Robert Owen*, p. 402.

[3] W. H. Oliver, 'The Labour Exchange Phase of the Co-operative Movement', in *Oxford Economic Papers*, Vol. 10, No. 3, October 1958, p. 357.

[4] This is not Dr William King of Brighton, as some writers have thought (including Podmore, *Robert Owen*, p. 405).

[5] W. King, *Gothic Hall Labour Bank*, London, n.d., pp. 1-2.

[6] King claims that 80,000 of these leaflets were issued in 1831 (*ibid.*, p. 4 GL).

assumptions were, and the Gothic Hall exchange also contemplated establishing 'a reading Room and Self-Supporting Agricultural and Horticultural School.'[1] The idea of an inter-change of surplus produce appealed to Owen, as did that of a new standard of value, based on labour.[2] Owen's adoption of the exchange bank idea was given a major public airing in July 1832, and the report in *The Poor Man's Guardian* of the meeting at which he did so[3] is one of the clearest expositions of the way the new scheme fitted into the general Owenite philosophy. The resolution put forward by Owen stated that 'the present system of society had proved inadequate to produce the prosperity that ought to exist'. The monetary system was the chief cause of existing evils and gold, silver, and bank notes, were inadequate 'to exchange the wealth that may be produced by the industry of the United Kingdom'. The time had come, therefore, 'for the introduction of a natural medium of exchange, by means of notes representing the average labour or time necessary to produce the wealth which each note should be made to represent'. He went on to propose that a Preliminary National or Parochial Bank be established, and that the funds accruing from such banks should be devoted, among other things, to feeding and educating the poor. No power could now prevent the principles he had enunciated in his *Report to the County of Lanark* from being put into practice. Preliminary banks were already in operation, 'and the contributors to them were astonished at the ease with which exchanges in them were effected. The success of such plans would provide the poor with the means of maintaining and educating themselves.' The new Exchange Banks, he wrote in August, together with the Infant Schools, 'when conducted according to the original principles which the founder developed when he first publicly recommended their adoption, will, in their effect, prove to be the two greatest discoveries which have been made in modern times; but these are but small benefits, and mere preliminary measures'.[4]

The Exchange was opened on September 17, 1832, and lasted until June 1834. Other exchanges were opened in London and elsewhere. The object of the Birmingham Exchange was 'to enable all persons who

[1] *Ibid.*, p. 1.
[2] For Owen's ideas in this connection, and the National Equitable Labour Exchange, see Podmore, *Robert Owen*, pp. 408–20.
[3] Vol. I, No. 58, pp. 470–1 (incorrectly numbered 491).
[4] *The Crisis*, Vol. I, No. 22, August 4, 1832.

possess, or can produce, any kind of useful wealth, *to exchange it* for that which is produced by others'. The justification for this aim was the theme that King and Owen had accepted, and that all the early socialists elaborated—that labour was 'the real and only source of all wealth'.[1]

Three aspects of this Labour Exchange enthusiasm need to be emphasised. Firstly, the exchanges, as Owen himself stressed, were a means to an end; beyond them lay the possibility of community developments and the reorganisation of society—labour exchanges, like infant schools, were a gateway to a new society. Secondly, alongside the exchanges and in some cases in direct association with them, the educational work of lecture, discussion and school continued prominently. Owen and his followers continued, throughout this period of intensive work and difficulties over the National Equitable Exchange, to publicise the principles that were to lead to the renovation of society. On May 1, 1833, for example, the Exchange and the New Lecture Rooms opened at their new Charlotte Street premises, which *The Crisis* described as being 'admirably adapted for lectures, Public meetings, Festivals, and the business of an Equitable Labour Exchange . . . Nearly 12,000 persons can stand in this place under cover, and hear a speaker with an ordinary voice; 3,700 may be seated.'[2] The same evening a 'Great Public Meeting' was held at the Exchange, 'denouncing the Old System of the World, and announcing the Commencement of the New'.

On May 12, Owen lectured at Charlotte Street to explain in greater detail some of the points he had made on May 1, and the core of his lecture was his answer to the question: Why do I wish so much to remove ignorance?[3] The following night a *Manifesto of the Productive Classes* was adopted at another 'Great Public Meeting' held at the Exchange, proclaiming it to be the duty of governments 'to adopt national measures to train and place all the population of their respective dominions within such arrangements as shall make them physically, intellectually, and morally, useful members of society'.[4]

The third point to emphasise is that in organising Exchange Bazaars, as in co-operative trading and production associations in general, self-

---

[1] *The Birmingham Labour Exchange Gazette*, No. 1, January 16, 1833. The five issues of the *Gazette*, in January and February, 1833, referred frequently to the difficulties Owen was encountering with his London premises.

[2] *The Crisis*, Vol. II, No. 17, May 4, 1833.

[3] *Ibid.*, Vol. II, No. 20, May 25, 1833.

[4] Pare MS 578/44.

confident co-operators were making education a prominent feature of their activities.

A lucid glimpse of such educational activities was given to the Co-operative and Trades' Union Congress held in London in October 1833.[1] James Rigby, a stalwart of Owenite activities from the 1830's, was reporting from Manchester. It appeared to them, he said, that 'the best means of removing the evil of life is to create intelligence . . . Hence the formation of the schools which he represented.' They taught 250–300 pupils three nights a week, 'and it is not an uncommon thing in our school to see little ragged boys learning geometry and algebra, and acquiring considerable knowledge of the elementary principles of some of the sciences'. They had also established Sunday schools for the same purpose, and the teachers taught gratis. The scholars subscribed some of the money. Owen, from the chair, asked 'what kind of feeling was manifested between master and pupil?' Rigby replied:

'. . . we teach the children that no individual can love or hate at pleasure; that his character is created for him by organization and surrounding circumstances; and neither rod nor stick, nor any instrument of punishment has been used in our school since its commencement . . . our rod is a rod of love . . . Our first or most advanced class has a vote in all the transactions of the school; the other classes have a right to send a petition to the teachers for any thing they want . . .'

They had had difficulties in arranging the classes, being reluctant to place younger and more advanced pupils above older pupils, including adults. The latter had agreed to this necessity, however, and 'we put them through the sieve by a strict examination, and the result was that in the lowest class of all we had several adult married men'. In August of that year the House of Commons had for the first time voted a sum of money (£20,000) for educational purposes, and the committee of the Manchester school 'had resolved to petition government for part of the money which had been voted in Parliament for the promotion of education amongst the people; but the scholars hearing of this intention, petitioned the masters to abandon their resolution, as it might subject the school to some tyrannical restraint . . . now we carry on successfully without any pecuniary assistance'. The pupils had also established a

[1] *The Crisis*, Vol. III, No. 7/8, October 19, 1833.

'sort of scientific school' amongst themselves, 'for the purpose of initiating themselves into the practice of teaching, as the masters would not always be with them; and they wished to qualify themselves for supplying their places as the school should happen to be deprived of their services'.

The co-operative movement itself and the nation-wide educational work of lecturing, debate and the organisation of schools for children and adults, were now the embodiment of the principles which Owen had held, propagated and worked for since the 1790's. How strong Owen's personal influence now was can be judged from a letter written in September 1832 by Rev. J. E. ('Shepherd) Smith, shortly himself to become temporarily a prominent figure in the Owenite movement. 'I may mention', he wrote to a correspondent, 'what, perhaps you won't hear from the newspapers, that Mr Owen's co-operative system was set agoing here on Monday last; it is a very large establishment. I was quite surprised when I saw it.' In the hall ('a superb room') Owen, he says, lectures two or three times a week, 'and sometimes collects 1,300 people . . . the system is much more popular among the working classes than I had any idea of before I came here, and likely to be accepted to a considerable extent'.[1]

(v) Demos

The way in which Owen's 'system' came to be accepted, in fact, by the trade union movement, the way in which a tremendous, though short-lived, national trade union movement came into being in Britain for the first time on any major scale, under the impact of Owen's views, is a familiar story. Owen spent a great deal of time in 1833 travelling, and lecturing to working class audiences on the merits of co-operation and community, making a particular point of lecturing to trade union audiences, 'to explain to them his new system, and to indicate to them the true use of their organisation and how they could make it the instrument of a real economic freedom'.[2] It is less clearly recognised, however, that in 1833 Owen was only intensifying a process that the Owenites had already begun. Between 1831 and 1833 the trade unions had been under pressure from local co-operative movements to participate in the new process of changing society. William Pare had lectured Doherty and the

[1] W. Anderson Smith, *'Shepherd' Smith the Universalist. The Story of a Mind. Being the Life of the Rev. James E. Smith, M.A.*, London, 1892, p. 81.
[2] R. W. Postgate, The Builders' History, London, n.d., p. 75.

cotton spinners in 1830 to 'form yourselves into co-operative societies',[1] and from *The Birmingham Labour Exchange Gazette* it is obvious that by January 1833 a wide range of trade unions were succumbing to the co-operative pressure. The labour exchange, in fact, was the main instrument which brought trade unionists into contact with new co-operative emphases in the analysis of society. The *Gazette* reported at the end of January that 'the members of Trade Unions seem to be laying hold of the subject of "Equitable Labour Exchanges" in right earnest'. Many of the trade unionists who had attended lectures and meetings of Owen's in Birmingham in November 1832, 'have since promoted Meetings in their various trades . . . deputations from the Committee of the Birmingham Branch Exchange have attended to give any explanations required or reply to any objections urged.'[2] Meetings to discuss the equitable exchange system were held in January and February in Birmingham by unions in an astonishingly wide variety of trades, including carpenters, stone masons, gun makers, jewellers, tailors, boot and shoe makers, bricklayers, platers, brassfounders, locksmiths, silk hatters and hair dressers.[3] The aim of the meetings was to discuss means of raising money to help the Birmingham Exchange by buying shares. No. 3 of the *Gazette* announced that 'most of these bodies have already commenced raising a number of Quarter Shares of £5 each' and No. 5 (February 9, 1833) published some *Draft Rules adopted by various bodies of Trades to raise money for purchase of £5 shares in Birmingham Branch Exchange*.[4]

The outstanding trade union support Owen came to command was among the builders and potters, and the developments in the builders' union in particular provided the basis for Owen's creation, the Grand National Consolidated Trades Union. It is in relation to developments in these three directions that one can see at its most sharply focused the way in which Owen caused the acquisition of knowledge and an ideal of education to be written into the programme of the working class movement.

The Operative Builders' Union came into existence in 1831, and by July 1833, when supporters of Owen in the Union invited him to come to Manchester, it was engaged in a frontal conflict with the masters.

[1] *Newspaper Cuttings*, No. 33.
[2] *The Birmingham Labour Exchange Gazette*, No. 3, January 26, 1833.
[3] See *ibid.*, Nos. 3–5.
[4] No. 5 was the last issue; it recommended that its readers should read *The Crisis* instead.

Owen's informant wrote to him on July 6, 1833, saying that the unions received more than £1,000 per week and that 'the Joiners, Masons, Bricklayers, and indeed all connected with building are now out of work . . . these parties are anxious to hear further on Labour exchange'.[1] Owen was firmly opposed to any kind of class opposition to the masters, and considered strikes futile and misguided. After all, his doctrine told him, and he told the builders, that if circumstances govern character, 'the middle and upper classes have been formed, like yourselves by the progress of events or circumstances . . . they could not have thought, felt, and acted otherwise . . . they are now . . . real objects for sympathy and compassion, and not for punishment'. The whole of society, not just the working class, needed to be emancipated from the slavery of error. Preaching a message of *understanding* and co-operative endeavour, Owen was received with adulation by the building workers, who were bewildered by the worsening of their conditions, resulting partly from new large-scale organisation and systems of contracting. The London carpenters in November 1833 addressed their 'General Body', calling on it to 'study to ascertain, we beseech you the cause of our impoverishment, and prosecute your inquiries till you have discovered the remedy for the evils that afflict us'.[2] Understandably, as Postgate points out, 'for men struggling in such darkness, Owen's teaching came as a great light. Problems that had puzzled them were solved: inexplicable facts fell into their place in a general scheme: the way out was clear.' Postgate also justifiably points out that such an acceptance of Owen's programme demonstrated the immaturity of the British workers. 'They swallowed it whole. Some of the leaders may have had a clearer conception of it, but for the rank and file it was a "system" devised for them by a "benevolent Mr Owen".'[3]

None the less, Owen's views brought new considerations into relief among wide sections of the working class, and helped in 1833 and 1834 to strengthen their self-confidence. The Operative Builders' Union, with its headquarters in Birmingham, rapidly swung to Owenism. Owen toured the country speaking to Union lodges, and in September addressed the 'Builders' Parliament', a delegate meeting representing the union as a whole.[4] Owen put forward simple proposals for a 'Grand

[1] Quoted in Postgate, *The Builders' History*, pp. 75–6.
[2] *Ibid.*, p. 82.   [3] *Ibid.*, p. 112.
[4] The 'Parliament' lasted six days, and was attended by 270 delegates. The King was alarmed and pressed the Cabinet to take strong measures (see Webb, *The History of Trade Unionism*, pp. 130 and 142).

National Guild of Builders', organised regionally, so that the workers could build without the unnecessary luxury of masters. Owen's plans were accepted, the Union was reorganised and the Grand National Guild of Builders was in existence by the end of September 1833, immediately offering direct labour and organising its own projects, including the building of its own Guildhall in Birmingham.[1]

The Objects of the Guild, as defined in Owen's 1833 *Proposals*, began with the following four points:

'1. The general improvement of all the individuals forming the building class; ensuring regular employment for all.
2. To ensure fair remuneration for their services.
3. To fix a reasonable time for labour.
4. To educate both adults and children.'[2]

Object No. 8 stated the more comprehensive aim: 'To obtain good and comfortable dwellings for every member of the Union; extensive and well-arranged workshops; places of depôt for building materials; halls for the meetings of the Lodges and Central Committees; schools and academies for the instruction of adults and children in morals and the useful sciences.' The 'Parliament' adopted a Manifesto which spoke in the language of Owen: 'the real interests of all parties are sacrificed to the errors of those who do not understand the resources of our country'. The industrious classes had 'been made the victims' of these errors. The Manifesto elaborated on the aims given in the earlier *Proposals*. Two intentions, relating to education, were given in detail, and there can be no doubt that the phraseology, if not the pen that wrote them, was Owen's:

'6th.—We shall be enabled to form arrangements in all parts of the British dominions to re-educate all our adult Brethren that they may enjoy a superior mode of existence, by acquiring new and better dispositions, habits, manners, language and conduct, in order that

---

[1] 'It included, on paper, a lecture-hall and various schoolrooms for the children of members' (*ibid.*, pp. 130-1). The Union contained many 'men who would work as masters when they could get a contract, and seek work as hands under another master when they could not . . . the Owenite recipe appealed to craftsmen of an independent mind' (W. H. Oliver, 'Robert Owen and the English Working-Class Movements', *History Today*, November 1958, p. 793).
[2] *Proposals for the Establishment of a National Association for Building, to be called 'The Grand National Guild of Builders'* . . . in Cole, *Robert Owen*, pp. 245-6.

they may become such examples for their children as are requisite to do justice to all young persons whose characters are to be formed to become good practical members of society.

7th.—We shall form arrangements, as soon as circumstances admit, to place all the children of the Brethren, under such instruction of persons and influences of external objects as shall train or educate the *will, inclination* and *powers* within each to induce and enable them to become *Architects and Builders* of the human character.'[1]

Owenism, to his supporters among the Staffordshire potters, also meant co-operative production, directed by the Union.[2] By September 1833, supporters in the National Union of Operative Potters were writing to tell them that 'there is no section of the country where the march of intellect is making more rapid strides than this and I beg you will make public this first solid proof of the disposition and ability of the people to look after their own interests'.[3] Owenism won over the leaders of the Union, but his conquests lay in the committee-room; he never captured the potters at their benches, but Owenism almost did'.[4] There was opposition, particularly from the Methodists, and the Union leaders had to camouflage their intentions. The scheme for a co-operative factory for the production of pottery was not launched until June 1834, under the auspices of the Union but kept separate from its other affairs. A member of the Union's Board of Management wrote to Owen in November 1833, to relate the progress of events. 'You my Dear Sir', he told Owen, 'have it now in your power to work out our complete emancipation . . . we must have you—your advice, your practical experience, the materials are truly to hand but the design is wanting.'[5]

Out of Owen's commitment to working class organisation, and such increasing support for his views among the working class, sprang the trade union fervour of 1834. The Grand National Consolidated Trades

[1] *Friendly Declaration of the delegates of the Building Branches*, in Postgate, *The Builders' History*, p. 463. The only record of a second 'Builders' Parliament in April 1834 was 'the decision to found Schools for the education of the members' children and also to establish lectures for teaching the principles of Science to any of their body who wanted to learn them (quoted in *ibid.*, p. 107).
[2] See W. H. Warburton, *The History of Trade Union Organisation in the North Staffordshire Potteries*, London, 1931, Chapter IV and Appendix C, reproducing letters to Owen in the CUL.
[3] Quoted in *ibid.*, p. 256.
[4] *Ibid.*, p. 70.
[5] *Ibid.*, pp. 258–9.

Union of Great Britain and Ireland, which recruited between a half a million and a million members in 1834, was under Owen's absolute influence and leadership. It was *his* organisation.[1] He outlined his scheme for such a national body in October, 1833, lecturing at Charlotte Street. 'There is no other alternative', he said, 'but national companies for every trade . . . All trades shall first form associations of lodges', which would send delegates to county lodges; these in turn would form some ten provincial lodges. At the head of the structure for each industry there would be a grand national congress. A 'grand national establishment' in London would act as central co-ordinator.[2]

Owen captured the leadership of the trade union movement in this way with a bold plan for concerted national trade union activity, at a time when the seeds of national trade unionism had already been sown. John Doherty's efforts from 1829, culminating in the National Association for the Protection of Labour, had shown by 1831 that the basis for nation-wide organisation existed, with the Association covering unions in Lancashire, Cheshire, Derby, Nottingham and Leicester, mainly in the textile trades, but also bringing in various societies of mechanics, blacksmiths, coalminers, agricultural labourers and others. The Glasgow *Herald to the Trades' Advocate* in October 1830 reported that it was said to have 'upwards of 80,000 members'.[3] There can be no doubt that Doherty, his *Voice of the People* and the National Association for the Protection of Labour laid the foundations, particularly in Lancashire, on which the Grand National Consolidated was built. Doherty, an Owenite, and a gifted organiser and leader, in 1831 quarrelled with the Manchester committee behind the *Voice*, and published a statement explaining what the philosophy had been behind his work on behalf of the working classes:

'. . . my only object has been, to raise them in the scale of society. . . to give them power and consequence, by uniting their exertions, and

---

[1] For details see G. D. H. Cole, *Attempts at General Union—A Study in British Trade Union History 1818–1834*, London, 1953, (Chapter XV) and Podmore, *Robert Owen*, pp. 445–51. The Webbs' *The History of Trade Unionism* contains (Chapter III) a useful but not very well documented account.

[2] See *The Crisis*, Vol. III, No. 6, October 12, 1833, pp. 42–3.

[3] *Herald to the Trades' Advocate and Co-operative Journal*, No. 3, October 9, 1830, p. 47. The news item is headed 'National Trades' Union' and reports that 'the Duke of Wellington has his eye upon this association'. The Webbs give the possible membership of the Association as a hundred thousand, and the circulation of *The Voice of the People* as thirty thousand (*The History of Trade Unionism*, 1950 edition, pp. 120–4). The latter figure is extremely unlikely.

directing their energies to a common object, the attainment of which would confer a common good. The ground-work of such a union has, at all events, been laid . . .'[1]

The Association helped to make the attainment of power and consequence through a united movement a readily graspable aim, and for many textile trade unionists, in particular, the Grand National merely meant a resumption of the efforts of two or three years before. Doherty's efforts unquestionably prepared the way for the widespread acceptance of Owenism. Early in 1830, in fact, William Pare had addressed his open letter to Doherty; Pare had seen an address of Doherty's 'advising an active union . . . among, not only the workmen of one particular trade, but of all trades, to assist in supporting men in case of a turn-out'. Pare thought that this would be difficult to accomplish and, 'if accomplished, would fail to produce the desired effect'. His advice, therefore, was 'to form yourselves into co-operative societies of from 50 to 300 members each'.[2]

From these ripples grew the tide of the Grand National Consolidated Trades Union, beginning in November and December of 1833, though the organisation was not officially formed until February 1834. The first real attempt to set up a national inter-trade union organisation had been the Philanthropic Hercules in 1818, and it is interesting to compare the Constitution of the Grand National with the Articles of the earlier organisation. The nearest to an item on education in the 1818 Articles read:

'That at any time the committee may think proper, for the purpose of keeping the bond of Friendship and Union, and giving an opportunity to the several members to see, converse, and associate with each other, they may call a general meeting of all the members, at such time and such place, as may be determined upon . . .'[3]

What had been a casual provision in 1818 became, in the Owenite fervour of 1834, a systematised necessity. Article XXXVII of the *Rules*

[1] *A letter to the Members of the National Association for the Protection of Labour*, n.d., p. 21. The *Letter* was published in late 1831 or early 1832. The quarrel was occasioned by Doherty's decision to remove the publication of the *Voice* to London. He mentions that on arrival in London he was given sympathetic support by Owen and the co-operators.

[2] See also pp. 190-1 above. The letter, in *Newspaper Cuttings*, No. 333, addressed to 'Mr John Doherty and the Manchester Cotton Spinners', is undated, but the references in it fix the date as early in 1830.

[3] Reprinted in Cole, *Attempts at General Union*, p. 169.

and Regulations of the Grand National is most directly comparable with the above:

> 'Each Lodge shall, as soon as possible, make arrangements for furnishing the means of instituting Libraries or Reading-Rooms, or any other arrangements, affording them every facility for meeting together for friendly conversation, mutual instruction, and rational amusement or recreation.'[1]

The crucial statement of philosophy, however, is in Article XLVI. The initial aim of the Union, it began, was to raise or prevent any further reduction in wages, and obtain shorter working hours, but:

> '... the great and ultimate object of it must be to establish the paramount rights of Industry and Humanity, by instituting such measures as shall effectually prevent the ignorant, idle, and useless part of Society, from having that undue control over the fruits of our toil, which, through the agency of a vicious money system, they at present possess; and that, consequently, the Unionists should lose no opportunity of mutually encouraging and assisting each other in bringing about A DIFFERENT ORDER OF THINGS, in which the really useful and intelligent part of society only shall have the direction of its affairs, and in which well-directed industry and virtue shall meet their just distinction and reward, and vicious idleness its merited contempt and destitution.'[2]

A comparison of this statement with *A New View* or Owen's 1817 addresses, for example, shows that Owen, or at any rate Owenism with Owen's acquiescence, had come in the course of trade union agitation from 1833 to place a new emphasis. Owen had already come to stress the role of money in maintaining an inequitable society, and labour notes, as the medium of exchange, were designed, to restore to the producers 'control over the fruits of our toil'. There is nevertheless in the condemnation of vicious idleness to its 'merited contempt and destitution' an anger which Owen had previously not expressed or acceded to.

During these trade union developments in late 1833 and early 1834, education played a central part in all formulations of policy. In February

---

[1] *Rules and Regulations of the Grand National Consolidated Trades Union of Great Britain and Ireland*, in Webb, *The History of Trade Unionism*, 1950 edition, p. 731.
[2] *Ibid.*, p. 732–3.

1834, in a memorial entitled *Progress of Civilisation. National Objects of the Productive Classes*, Owen included among the objects—universal education, 'scientific, physical, intellectual and moral'.[1] James Morrison, editor of *The Pioneer*, now the official organ of the Grand National, was announcing in the same month that 'the Union has also made another advance, in the establishment of depots for goods, the erection of or renting of workshops, and, above all, the means of education'.[2] In May 1834, a correspondent in Sutton-on-Ashfield, near Mansfield, wrote to Owen eager to know whether the Grand National Consolidated, 'of which we are members is about to be placed under other arrangements, viz., your projected System of Co-operation—if so we shall Hail the Glad Day as the First of the Glorious Age when Delusion and misery shall give place to Truth and Happiness'. In the meantime, the experience of the local stocking-frame workers had been 'that strikes amongst us will not Insure any Permanent advantage', and as they had £100 left in a Local Union Fund, 'we . . . have resolved to appropriate it to a different purpose, and we have taken a commodious Building on a Lease for 5 years at Rent of £10 per Annum, and Believing that knowledge is power, shall appropriate the upper room, 13 yards by 6, to the purposes of a school, lecture-room, etc., the lower part the same Dimensions as a warehouse, etc., with a house adjoining to commence Trading on the Co-operative and Equitable exchange principle'.[3]

Throughout these early months of 1834, at the height of the dove-tailing co-operative and trade union activity, the Institution in Charlotte Street was obviously a hive of educational planning and activity. *The Crisis* inserted an advertisement in February which read:

'It is proposed to establish a Library, Museum, Laboratory, &c., with Apparatus for Lectures for the Diffusion of Useful Knowledge among the Working Classes.—Subscriptions and Donations received by the Secretary . . .'[4]

Owen himself found time in May and June to lecture three times at the Institution on education,[5] and on April 19 *The Crisis* found it necessary to publish an Editorial (presumably by Smith), in answer to a correspondent who had complained of an attempt to 'force the principles of

---

[1] Quoted in Cole, *Attempts at General Union*, pp. 124–5.
[2] Quoted in *ibid.*, p. 25.
[3] Quoted in Podmore, *Robert Owen*, pp. 449–50.
[4] *The Crisis*, Vol. III, No. 25, February 15, 1834.
[5] On May 18 and 25 and June 28. See *ibid.*, Vol. III, Nos. 7, 8 and 13.

the social system on adults . . . and leaving our children to take their chance'.[1]

The National Equitable Labour Exchange went out of existence in June and the Grand National Consolidated to all intents and purposes during the summer of 1834. Owen had throughout behaved with a great deal of heavy-handed paternalism (and had indeed been induced to do so by the kind of adulatory treatment he received);[2] by the middle of 1834 he had quarrelled with Smith, closed down *The Crisis*, and parted company with James Morrison.[3] After the collapse of mid-1834, in the first issue of *The New Moral World*[4] (published to replace *The Crisis*) on November 1, 1834, Owen was quoted as saying that the time had arrived 'for new measures to be adopted, because the mania of Radicalism has ceased, the excitement of the Trades' Unions to force up or even maintain, the monied value of labour, in opposition to the overwhelming power of individual competition, is dying a natural death'. This is scarcely a statement of contrition, but is an apologia of sorts. Owen had viewed the working class both as an agglomeration of under-privileged individuals in need of his guidance and as newly-offered instruments to help to change society and introduce Owen's social system. It had been incidental to Owen that equitable exchange or trades unionism would be beneficial to the working class—they were for him the first stages in benefiting the *whole* of society. For three or four years the two processes had coincided, and now, after the conviction of the Dorchester labourers in March 1834, and after the failure of movements for co-operative exchange and production, Owen looked at the situation and saw not defeat, but, characteristically, the end of a phase doomed to die.

Whatever happened to Owen and Owenism, 1831–4 did not leave the working class as it had been before. Exchange banks and Owenite unionism left barely a tangible trace behind, but they had played their

---

[1] *Ibid.*, Vol. IV, No. 2, April 19, 1834.

[2] Postgate, in *The Builders' History*, quotes an astonishing letter from James Morrison, 'one of the most level-headed leaders of this time,' to Owen, in 1833: 'Your doctrines have made me a *better* and a *happier* being . . . since my personal intercourse with *you* I have become better . . . Be, then, my Physician . . . your practice inspires my perfect confidence . . . I shall look upon you as a Father and try to become a faithful Son . . .' (pp. 83–4).

[3] See *Ibid.*, p. 109, and G. D. H. Cole, *Robert Owen*, pp. 215–19.

[4] Published from Charlotte Street, now the home of the Grand National's successor—the Association of All Classes of All Nations.

part in intensifying the process of self-awareness we have previously seen growing among the working class. Other educational forces were now at work, but Owen's contribution to the definition and cause of popular education had been, and remained, of an extremely distinctive kind. The people were being educated, says one biographer of Owen, discussing the Grand National, 'in spite of Church and Government. Even hundreds of thousands of them who could not read were in a very real sense educated by the struggles of the preceding six years. Demos was not quite the same person as he had been in Owen's younger days.'[1]

[1] McCabe, *Robert Owen*, p. 76.

CHAPTER V

On Higher Ground

(i) *The power to control*

THE TRANSITION we have witnessed taking place in Britain was basically from the predominant acceptance among all classes of the kind of ordered, structured society expressed typically by John Mason, to the conviction, among the newly cohering working class, of the possibility of *acting* and *educating* against the status quo. Previous debates about education had been conducted largely in terms of the extent of popular education desirable in order to preserve and eliminate dangers to the existing framework of society. Under Owen's impetus a mass movement had come to see the possibility of using education to change that society. Idealistic this may have been to a degree, but the effect of this conviction on working class self-confidence in this period is difficult to exaggerate.

The overall economic and experiential causes of intensified working class feelings of identity and solidarity through this period are not of detailed concern to us here. The Hammonds offer the view that 'what came about during this period was the alienation of the working classes, due not to the positive influence of ideas or enthusiasms, but to the effect of experience on ways of thinking and looking at life', though they go on to add that this does not 'detract from the superb and essential services to the development of working-class thinking of such men as Paine, Cobbett, and Place . . .'[1] One man involved in the events of 1834, 'Shepherd' Smith, who basically had little sympathy with the materialistic implications of Owenism, and looked upon the workers, in his biographer's words, as 'partially-developed animals to be enlightened',[2] described the effects of working class experience in this period in very similar terms. The trade unions, he wrote, whatever one might think of them, were going to change the pattern of government and trade, but 'children must creep before they walk; the people must learn by experience, and by reading and thinking. They are evidently improving

[1] *The Town Labourer*, 1949 Guild Books edition, Vol. II, p. 110.
[2] Smith, *'Shepherd' Smith the Universalist*, p. 102.

every day . . . Every strike, every failure is teaching them wisdom . . .'[1] Although it is, of course, true that the identity of the working class was forged very much by the economic conditions of the 1820's and the realities of social conflict before and after the 1832 Reform Bill, it is important not to underestimate the role of ideas in this process.

In the 1820's and 1830's there was, as we have seen in the case of the builders, a determined, precise eagerness for ideas, ideas which offered the possibility of sustained thought and action. This emergence of what H. L. Beales called 'a distinctively working class movement' was not merely a 'struggle against insecurity: it was a reaching out for the power to control'.[2] Owen did not approve of all the forms which the yearning to control was to take, but one of the most immediate and lasting effects of his ideas on the working class was to persuade it that it held such power, and had, among other things, the absolute power and right to educate and be educated.

The equipment of working class movements with educational aims did not, of itself, mark an advance on the objectives of the Philanthropic Hercules in 1818. It might be argued that the reverse was the case. Engels came close to doing so when he criticised the English Socialists (i.e. Owenites) for being 'too intellectual and too metaphysical, with the result that their practical achievements have been negligible'.[3] It is true that over Chartism the Owenites were too intellectual and metaphysical and needed, as Engels went on to say, 'to come down to earth, if only for a short time, and support the Charter as a practical objective'.[4] To suggest, however, that before 1844 the practical achievements of Owenism had been negligible is indicative of a confusion. Engels had previously acknowledged that the worker's 'efforts to cultivate his mind have a direct connection with his fight against the bourgeoisie',[5] but when it comes to an actual case history Engels tends to discount the role of the not-immediately-practicable ideas as negligible. The Owenite activity of the twenties and early thirties was not negligible, even on Engels's own terms. The kind of Owenite ideas we have seen circulating,

[1] Letter of May 30, 1834, in *ibid.*, p. 104.
[2] H. L. Beales, *The Early English Socialists*, London, 1933, p. 52. Julius West described Owen's activities as 'a clue to the future of working-class movements at a time when such a clue was badly needed' (*A History of the Chartist Movement*, London, 1920, p. 41).
[3] *The Condition of the Working Class in England*, translated by W. O. Henderson and W. H. Chaloner, Oxford, 1958, p. 269.
[4] *Ibid.*, p. 270.
[5] *Ibid.*, p. 242.

in providing a stimulus for working class movements during this period, mark, not a diversion from purer political and industrial aims, but the infusion of a sense of purpose and meaning into the whole. The advent of Chartism may have increasingly consigned Owenite organisation to the background; the effect of Owen's ideas in the twenties and thirties represents nothing less, however, than an act of liberation.[1]

In an extremely valuable commentary on the history of English educational institutions and their relationship to social developments, Sir Fred Clarke pointed out that 'the mass of the English people have never yet evolved genuine schools of their own. Schools have always been provided for them from above, in a form and with a content of studies that suited the ruling interests. It is not surprising, then, that the avowed purpose of such schools until quite recently (he was writing in 1939) 'was to induce usefulness rather than culture . . . The Charity Schools of the 17th and 18th centuries and the elementary schools of the 19th century were all alike devoted to the same end'.[2] The only time when the popular movement came near to shaping educational provisions from below in the emergence of mass education in the nineteenth century was between the years 1832 and 1834, and in the period of the efflorescence of Chartism in the later thirties and early forties. By this period the working class had become aware not merely of their own ignorance and the poverty of the traditional types of education available, but of the precise possibilities and nature of a real, in Owenite terms a rational, education. The Owenite movement proper, and the wider movements with which it became for a period identified, established schools and ran lecture courses on political, social and scientific subjects; they gave rise to private ventures in education, and wrote educational aims into the constitutions of trade unions and co-operative societies; they planned infant and adult education; they issued cheap publications and taught masses of people to analyse economic and social issues; they made ideas a real tool in the work of social reformation. All this was in a real sense education from below. On the other hand, Owen in particular advocated such education from below only as a substitute; popular

---

[1] J. F. C. Harrison has expressed the view that 'the Owenism of the early thirties . . . collapsed with the Grand National Consolidated Trades Union in 1834, and had not produced very much in the way of educational effort' (*Learning and Living, 1790–1960*, London, 1961, p. 110). This view fails to take into account the educational impetus that was part of all Owenite activity in this period.

[2] *Education and Social Change*, p. 30.

education, for him, was a function of proper government. At the second Co-operative Congress, in 1831, for example, he described the first duty of government as being 'the best mode of distribution', and the second as being to make 'arrangements by which every child shall have all his physical and moral powers developed in the best manner'. He had waited for more than twenty years for the right moment, and 'the time has now arrived to compel Government to believe, that we do know how poverty shall be put an end to, and how every child, in future, shall be made a good, a virtuous, and a charitable being'. The co-operative movement, he advised, 'should adopt such measures, as shall compel the Government to do good both to us and to themselves'.[1]

There was, as we have seen, however, a tension in the Owenite and working class movements between the demand for government action and the desire to provide independently. By the 1830's, however strongly the popular movements had pursued the educational ideal, it is unlikely that they could have succeeded in 'capturing' education. By the 1830's, however firmly entrenched in their anti-educational positions some diehards may have been, the question was no longer, among the 'educational patrons of the lower classes' how to prevent education, or even of embarking 'in the ship of knowledge in order to delay the voyage', but of directing it.

(ii) Schools or prisons

Many of the attitudes towards education prevalent in the 1830's were, of course, parallel to ones we saw in existence or taking shape in the 1790's. The later range of views could be examined by taking such a case history as education in relation to work and industry, though we have omitted from our story two of the themes relevant to it—Owen's role in the 1810's as a pioneer of industrial legislation, and the widespread establishment of schools of industry and the range of attitudes embodied in them. Owen's contribution to the humanisation of industry had been, in fact, part of the credentials by which he came to be accepted by the working class movement.[2] This discussion would involve an examination of industrial conditions from the 1790's to the 1830's, the problem

[1] *Proceedings of the Second Congress*, p. 16.
[2] See *Life*, pp. 155–68, R. D. Owen, *Threading My Way*, pp. 102–3, and Podmore, *Robert Owen*, Chapter IX, for Owen's investigation of mill conditions and activity for parliamentary legislation. The best account of the events leading up to the 1819 Act is in M. W. Thomas, *The Early Factory Legislation*, London, 1948, Chapter II.

of the education of factory children, and the existence in the 1830's of a small number of mills which took pains to evolve relatively advanced educational provisions.[1] A survey of the schools of industry would be a consideration for the most part of the extent of the vocational content of such schools, and above all of the motives behind them. It would involve, again, a consideration of what was involved in the transition from the 1790's concept of the school of industry as a rescue operation to teach children 'their duties to God, their neighbours, and themselves', to the acceptance by the co-operative and other popular movements of the school of industry as an integral part of their programmes.[2] Whatever shifts in emphasis may have occurred in this process, it should not be imagined that Clara Reeve's was no longer present in the 1830's.[3]

The Mechanics' Institutes, and their sister-organisation, the Society for the Diffusion of Useful Knowledge, provide a more useful case history however, because they not only demonstrate the existence of a wide range of attitudes, but offer a series of important comparisons with the educational thinking and practice of the Owenite and Owen-stimulated movements of the 1820's and 1830's. There are, however, several general points of reference it would be helpful to establish first.

Public education in the 1830's consisted to all intents and purposes of the limited networks of National schools and nonconformist British schools. Although the British Society, in particular, had begun by this period to respond to some of the pressures towards a more humane concept of education and to broaden its curriculum, the basic content of education in the bulk of both societies' schools was not significantly different from at the turn of the century. There is an amusing description of the annual examination of the children at the National Society's Central Model School, in 1838, in the presence of the Archbishop of Canterbury and about 200 visitors.[4] A class of girls 'read some portion

---

[1] See A. H. Robson, *The Education of Children Engaged in Industry in England, 1833–76*, London, 1931, pp. 22–5, and Dobbs, *Education and Social Movements*, p. 165.

[2] For an illustration of the early co-operative movement's commitment to the idea of schools of industry, see Resolution 19 of the second Co-operative Congress (*Co-operative Congresses*) asking 'that the Societies be urged to establish Schools of Industry . . .'

[3] For an early compilation of material on the schools of industry see William Davis, *Hints of Philanthropists*, Bath, 1821. A useful survey of such schools in the 1830's is contained in Frederic Hill, *National Education*.

[4] *N.M.W.*, Vol. IV, No. 169, January 20, 1838, p. 98 (reprinted from the *Morning Chronicle*).

of Scripture history, were interrogated thereupon, and repeated the Catechism and the Collects; they did not, however, appear thoroughly to understand the meaning of the words asscending and descending, for several of the girls, in answer to the question, 'What did Christ do after his Crucifixion?' replied, "He descended into heaven".' Some pains had been taken with the children's reading, but, the report continued, 'we much object to the practice of compelling the children to make a genuflection every time they pronounce the name of Jesus. As this word occurred some thirty or forty times in the course of reading one chapter, the effect of a large class of girls making a curtsey at every ten or twentieth syllable had rather a risible effect.' The complete curriculum of the school was reading, writing, arithmetic ('very imperfectly taught'), the Creed, the Collects, and Scripture history. There was no mental arithmetic, geography or natural science. 'No books were introduced relating to general history, or natural history, to the heavens above, or the earth beneath.' The report, while not looking at the British Society's rival establishment in the Borough Road 'with a too friendly eye . . . for the people of this country have a right to a much more efficient system of education than can be conferred by the plans of either Bell or Lancaster', points out that at the Borough Road geography, natural history, geometry, outline drawing, astronomy and the elements of several other sciences were taught ('however imperfectly').

> 'Let it be borne in mind', it stressed, 'that the national school we have been describing is the central, model, and normal school of a society which professes to educate 516,000 children of the poorer classes . . . there is no reason to conclude that the offspring is better than the parent.'

Frederic Hill, describing the same school, commented on the extremely strict discipline, 'the harsh language and angry tones in which the boys were constantly addressed; and . . . the cuffs and blows that were inflicted from time to time'. The monotonous tones of the readers showed 'that the sense had not reached their heads, still less penetrated to their hearts'.[1]

Opposition to the education of the children of the poor had not,

---

[1] *National Education*, pp. 97–8. In 1842, the British Society's schools in the Metropolitan district were the subject of what the Hammonds call 'a shattering report' from the inspector delegated to examine them. Even in the inculcation of a knowledge of the Scriptures, the inspector found a 'great and lamentable' ignorance (*The Age of the Chartists 1832–1854*, London, 1930, pp. 190–1).

however, completely disappeared. In 1835 a school of industry was founded in a village near Windsor, combining school subjects with the cultivation of two acres of land, basket-making, etc. Subscribers included the King, the Queen, some of the nobility and prominent Tories. It was found that:

'In general the poor people are anxious to avail themselves of the advantages of such a school, and the only opposition that has been manifested is by the farmers, some of whom don't like it . . .'[1]

Mary Howitt tells how, probably in the late 1820's, she arrived in Esher, and found that the only school in the neighbourhood, in 'the distant and obscure hamlet of Oxshott', founded in 1820 with royal support, was no longer in use. 'The windows were broken, and the whole premises in a state of dilapidation. The farmers were glad that so it should be, as the peasants, if educated, would no longer be beasts of burden.'[2] By the 1830's, however, this particular wing of the 'don't-like-it' school was no longer a force capable of shaping educational history.[3]

By the 1830's the spectrum of educational ideas begins on the right, in its most significant form, with men like the Lord Chief Justice, who told the Grand Jury at Chelmsford in 1832 that:

' "It was no longer a question now whether the poor are to learn or not, because, by the rapid diffusion of knowledge in every direction, that was set at rest; but it was a very important question whether the knowledge so given would be a blessing or a curse to the country." He recommended great attention to the morals, comforts, and employment, as well as to the education of the poor.'[4]

This was to be the dominant, if not always the most explicit, theme in British educational discussion from now on. The churches and governing circles could not agree on what form the attention to the education of the poor, and its control, should take, but in the need to pay such attention they concurred.

There were men like the Rev. Hugh Stowell, virulent anti-Owenite

[1] *N.M.W.*, Vol. III, No. 107, November 12, 1836, p. 20 (reprinted from the *Morning Chronicle*).

[2] *An Autobiography*, Vol. I, p. 281.

[3] Even in 1853, Bertrand Russell tells us, when 'my grandfather established a school in the village of Petersham (where he lived), the gentry complained that "he had destroyed the hitherto aristocratic character of the neighbourhood" ' (*Freedom and Organization*, p. 136).

[4] Reported in *The Hull Advertiser*, Vol. XXXVII, No. 1981, March 16, 1832.

and Manchester champion of what *The New Moral World* labelled 'the stand-still system',[1] who resisted the movement towards a national education system on the grounds that, though ignorance still existed, this was not for lack of educational facilities, but 'the absence of leisure or inclination to learn'. The Church's guardianship was enough.[2] But there were few engaged in the voluntary-versus-state debate who were so self-satisfied; the representative stand-point of the mid- and late-19th century debate was the declaration of the need, by action of one sort of another, more firmly to insure society through education. That education was a form of protection against rick-burning, rioting and other like unpleasantnesses was one of the burdens of evidence quoted extensively by Frederick Hill in 1836.[3] *The Edinburgh Review* in 1847 was arguing that education was 'the only effectual preventive of crime'. To reclaim the masses from 'gross ignorance' and 'temptations to vice', and 'bring them under the influence of a wholesome intellectual and moral training, is the great, the paramount duty of the people of England'.[4] A comprehensive summary of the mid-century rescue position is provided by Sir James Kay-Shuttleworth. In an address delivered after the 1867 Act enfranchising the urban workers, he reviewed the millions of pounds swallowed up annually in theft, the protection of property, the punishment of crime, pauperism, beer, spirits and tobacco.

> 'Property', he concluded, 'would be more secure, indigence more rare, and the whole people more provident and contented, if they were better educated. The old-fashioned alarm of the tyranny of the mob, if they learned to read and write, has changed into a dread of the ignorance, brutality, and misery of an untaught people.'[5]

All this is not to decry the educational activities of men like Kay-Shuttleworth, since the rescue motive in education has to be looked at in the light of other considerations. In nineteenth century educational circles it is common to find elaborations on the theme of whether 'the

[1] Vol. IV, No. 157, November 4, 1837, p. 13. See also Vol. IV, No. 183, April 28, 1838, p. 209. Stowell opposed the Manchester movement for education in a frenzy of indignation at this subversion of the church's authority. See No. 1 (1840) in Rev. Thomas Spencer's famous series of tracts; it is entitled *The Pillars of the Church of England*.
[2] Rev. Hugh Stowell, *A Second Letter to the Inhabitants of Manchester on the Proposed System of National Education*, Manchester, 1837, p. 11.
[3] *National Education* (particularly pp. 97–116).
[4] Vol. LXXXVI, No. CLXXIV, October 1847, p. 521.
[5] 'Popular Education and its Relation to the Religious Denominations,' *Thoughts and Suggestions on certain Social Problems*, London, 1873, p. 183.

schoolmaster be not as essential a protector of life and property as the constable and the policeman',[1] and on the choice with which society was faced:

> '. . . it comes then to this—we must build more schools or more prisons.'[2]

It is refreshing and rare, however, outside the educational statements of working class bodies, to find education for the poor conceived of as a right, and not hedged round with provisos and qualifications. As the Rev. R. W. Hamilton, Minister of Belgrave Chapel, Leeds, put it in a remarkably humane book published in 1845:

> 'However we may congratulate ourselves that the desirableness of Education is universally allowed, because it is not openly impugned, there are many symptoms of dissent. It is held by not a few, if held at all, with many qualifications. They yield, but with no small doubt and reluctance. They know that they are left behind in the progress of opinion, and shame seals their lips. They would, at heart, that the day of ignorance had not passed away.'[3]

Hamilton deplored the fact that in education the religious content, of which in principle he approved, 'has been frequently recommended, not for its high purpose and proper end, but as the source of "peace, order, and social happiness". This . . . seems to imply that an unenquiring and compliant people is all that is desired'. Knowledge, it was true, might be abused, but 'ignorance can never be turned to good . . . Give any knowledge, worthy of the name, without, if you cannot give it with, religion.'[4] There were other writers who, like Hamilton, urged an abandonment to one extent or another of caution and rescue. There was, for example, Richard Whately, Christian Socialist and Archbishop of Dublin, who, while asserting a form of the rescue principle,[5] did so with the same generous spirit as Hamilton:

[1] *The Edinburgh Review*, Vol. LXX, No. CXLI, October 1839, p. 155.

[2] The Bishop of Winchester, Dr Sumner, quoted in *A Memoir of the Right Hon. The Earl of Shaftesbury, K.G.*, compiled under the direction of the Editor of the 'Record', London, 1855, p. 40.

[3] Richard Winter Hamilton, *The Institutions of Popular Education*, London and Leeds, 1845, 2nd edition, 1846, p. 92.

[4] *Ibid.*, pp. 66–7.

[5] 'Who ever heard of an *educated* rabble . . . The more widely . . . you diffuse intellectual culture, the greater is your chance of a peaceable and well ordered community . . .' ('On the Supposed Dangers of a Little Learning,' *Miscellaneous Lectures and Reviews*, London, 1861, p. 208).

'We have no right to force upon any person religious or moral instruction . . . all we can do to provide against the danger of neglecting the moral and religious cultivation of the mind, is, to warn man of the danger of such neglect; and when we have done that, we have done all we can do . . .'[1]

There was J. C. Dyer, who, in a pamphlet published in 1850, in support of secular education, that education would be the 'surest and *cheapest* means of rearing and sustaining good principles, and of preventing the rise and spread of immoral and vicious habits in the lower ranks of life.'[2] Abandoning the argument from expediency, however, he was able to state with rare clarity:

'. . . the indigent and helpless have a clear *right* to be *educated* . . . I have also shown that expediency, or the material good of society, alike require the education of *all* of its members; but it may not be amiss to place the *right* of the poor man on higher ground, whereon it is more firmly based'.[3]

Among the men prepared to place the right to education 'on higher ground' were those like Rev. Thomas Spencer who, as middle-class supporters of working class suffrage, were prepared to state categorically: 'If we cannot give the people knowledge, liberty, commerce, good institutions, and good law, without endangering the Establishment, let the Establishment perish!'[4]

Of this sample of the range of attitudes in the 1830's and after, from the don't-like-it to the right-to-be-educated extremes, it was the education-as-insurance, rescuing-from-revolution, schools-rather-than-prisons trend that was the most representative. Only among the organised popular movements, the co-operative, trade union and Chartist movements most outstandingly, was there a major stress on the need to place popular education, as a right, on higher, firmer ground.

(iii) Beware of Mechanics' Institutions

The Mechanics' Institute movement came to life from 1823 for 'the diffusion of science among the working classes'.[5] The Society for the

---

[1] *Ibid.*, p. 201.
[2] *Remarks on Education*, Manchester, 1850, p. 6.   [3] *Ibid.*, p. 10.
[4] Tract No. 1 (1840), *The Pillars of the Church of England*, p. 11.
[5] Brougham, *Practical Observations*, p. 31. There were similar organisations before this date, but the foundation of the London Institute marks the real beginning of the movement.

Diffusion of Useful Knowledge was instituted in January 1827, its object being 'the imparting useful information to all classes of the community, particularly to such as are unable to avail themselves of experienced teachers, or may prefer learning by themselves'.[1] The Chairman of the S.D.U.K. was Henry Brougham, and the Vice Chairman, Lord John Russell. The Committee included William Allen and James Mill. The S.D.U.K. and to a very large extent the Mechanics' Institutes were governed, as we shall see, by the ideology of middle-class utilitarianism. The point from which we must begin, however, is not their ideology, but the mere fact that they were designed *for working men*. It will be useful, therefore, to look briefly at the opposition to which this new provision gave rise, before looking at the intentions of the organisations themselves, and the response to them of the working class.

In 1828 Charles Knight found some of the Liverpool clergy 'opposed to the educational influence of mechanics' institutes'.[2] The Rev. J. Acworth, when inaugurated as President of the Bradford Mechanics' Institute in 1837, found it necessary to answer those who prophesied that such Institutes would give rise to a populace 'dissatisfied, refractory, ungovernable', and who maintained that 'the different ranks of society will be commingled and annihilated—power will take the place of right, and all will be confusion and anarchy'. The *St James's Chronicle* described the scheme as being 'completely adapted for the destruction of this Empire'.[3] In 1838, the *Coventry Standard*, a High Church Tory paper, published an article entitled 'Beware of Mechanics' Institutions'. They were, the writer was happy to say, 'falling into rapid desuetude. They have done more mischief in their day, as far as this country is concerned, than Voltaire and the whole tribe of Encyclopaedists in their's.' After ascribing their parentage to Brougham, godparentage to the Unitarians and patronage to the Quakers, it told how, in the Coventry Institution, 'books decidedly deistical . . . have found their way into their library; there must have been strange neglect or desperate winking somewhere. The mischief, however, is done.'[4] The writer went on to relate how *The New Moral World* and the Owenite Institutions were reaping the fruits.

These were latter-day manifestations of the fear that the Institutions

[1] *Prospectus*, 1829, p. 17.

[2] Brown, *A Century of Liverpool Co-operation*, p. 15.

[3] Both of these are quoted in Mabel Tylecote, *The Mechanics' Institutes of Lancashire and Yorkshire before 1851*, Manchester, 1957, p. 43.

[4] *N.M.W.*, Vol. IV, No. 186, May 19, 1838, p. 239.

could be productive of nothing but revolution. An earlier and more revealing expression of this recoil from the idea of Mechanics' Institutes occurred in *Blackwood's Magazine* in a review of Brougham's *Practical Observations*, in May 1825. The article began with a series of reminders:

> 'We cannot be ignorant that the educating of the working *adults* of a great nation is a thing without precedent, and on which experience throws no light, save what is abundantly discouraging. We cannot be ignorant that hitherto, whenever the lower orders of any great state have obtained a smattering of knowledge, they have generally used it to produce national ruin. We cannot be ignorant, when we look at our factions, that the lower orders will be surrounded with pernicious as well as beneficial instructors; and when we look at human nature, we cannot be ignorant that they will generally prefer the former.'[1]

Men like Brougham, 'all party-leaders—all violent party men—all innovators—all teachers of things that tend to revolution—all who assail our constitution and general system—should be scrupulously prevented from interfering in any shape with the "education of the people" '. *Blackwood's* was saying in effect—let *no-one* meddle. It went on, in fact, while talking about political faction, to declare that 'the opinions and schemes of these persons are things to be *judged of by the educated*, but not to be *taught to the uneducated*'. The sheer fact that Brougham ('without question, the most fanatical and outrageous party-man in the three kingdoms'), Place and Burdett ('next Mr Brougham, the most fanatical . . .') were associated with the scheme meant that it was designed to 'fill the people with their party opinions'.

The article complained at length that the plans for Mechanics' Institutes catered only for the minority élite of the working classes (which, of course, was largely true), and ignored the bulk of the working men; the education provided by the London Institute was 'as ill adapted as possible to the needs and comprehension of the labourer'. The mechanics who belonged to the Institution probably earned £80–200 per annum, the writer estimated, had better incomes than clergymen, and most of them became masters. Why, he asked, did Brougham, Birkbeck and Co. 'pass by the tens of thousands of coal-heavers, carmen, dustmen, bricklayers, labourers, porters, and servants and labourers of all descriptions, tailors, shoemakers, etc. etc. in order to educate the better mechanics—men who, in comparison, are educated

---

[1] *Blackwood's Edinburgh Magazine*, Vol. XVI, No. C, May 1825, pp. 534–5.

already?' This is merely a debating point here, because the *Blackwood's* writer was not in the slightest degree interested in the provision of such education, and would have been the more indignant if Brougham had been, in fact, attempting this task. Tory publications, complained the article, had no circulation among the working classes. Instead of being educated in general political principle the working man, therefore would inevitably be served with an unbalanced diet:

'... party-politics, that is, the ignorance and profligacy, the scurrility and untruth, the dangerous schemes and doctrines of our factious writers, are to be crammed down the throats of our ignorant working classes as *education*; to *educate* the working man, we must put into his hands the writings of such people as Leigh Hunt, Cobbett and Carlisle, Brougham, Bentham, and Bowring'.

The dissemination of such publications (among 'our ploughmen, weavers, tailors, shoemakers, &c.'—precisely the ones, the writer had previously argued, who would *not* be reached through such schemes) would mean that working men themselves would decide 'upon the changes necessary to be made in the principles of the constitution. If these changes do not mean revolution, they can have no meaning.'[1]

A long footnote to the article saw the same danger in the scheme recently put forward for forming a University of London, and it expressed the hope that 'every friend to his country, and the sound and proper education of his countrymen, will array himself' against it. 'If new Universities be wanted,' it urged, 'let them be formed ... in places remote from the din and frenzy of party-politics. In this political country, the students of a London University would be eternally assailed by the seductions of party-prints and party-leaders ... If the Aristocracy be blind to the object of the education-men, woe to it'![2] The whole Mechanics' Institute scheme was, in fact:

'calculated to take the working classes from the guidance of their superiors ... to give a stimulus to those abominable publications which have so long abounded, and fill the hands of the mechanics with them; to make these mechanics the corrupters and petty demagogues of the working orders generally; to dissolve the bonds between the poor and the rich, create insubordination, and foment

[1] *Ibid.*, pp. 538–41.
[2] *Ibid.*, pp. 545–6. The students would be exposed also to 'the gaming, beautiful women, costly entertainments, &c. of the metropolis ...'

197

those animosities which unfortunately prevail so much already between servants and masters . . .'[1]

In 1831 Thomas Love Peacock levelled a classic piece of irony against the S.D.U.K. (the Steam Intellect Society, as he nicknamed it). The cook in *Crotchet Castle* had set fire to the curtains while reading a sixpenny tract on hydrostatics published by the Society.[2] Peacock's irony was justified, in that much of the material put out by the Society was irrelevant to the actual needs of even the audience it sought to reach, and Peacock was echoing criticism made of the Society and the Institutes by many working men themselves. The *Blackwood's* attack was more than irony. In London lectures had been delivered on 'Chemistry, Geometry, Hydrostatics, the application of Chemistry to the Arts, Astronomy, and the French Language . . . An English labourer not only a statesman, but a chemist, a geometrician, an amateur in mechanics, an astronomer, a linguist, and we know not what beside! . . .'[3] This was a defence of aristocratic England against the challenge of an enlightened populace. Brougham, a Mechanics' Institute, political knowledge or hydrostatics, ultimately for the *Blackwood's* writer meant insubordination and a dissolution of the bonds between the poor and the rich.

When one looks at the actual activities of the Mechanics' Institutes and the ideology behind the publications of the S.D.U.K., it requires an effort to understand such fears. Their sponsors were determined to ensure they remained under the influence of Radical-Whig ideas, if not personalities. Hodgskin and Robertson, the original sponsors of the London Mechanics' Institute, lost control of it almost as soon as they had brought it into existence, thanks to the efforts of Francis Place, who disliked Hodgskin's militant anti-capitalism. Place, against the wishes of the members, made approaches for donations and loans to the Institute, pleading to the reluctant Lord Grosvenor, for example, that 'although teaching them would not remove their discontent, it would make them less disposed to turbulence'.[4] Place, unlike Brougham, was against control of the Institutes by the working men themselves, since 'they cannot be in a condition to take the charge'.[5] When Hodgskin obtained

[1] *Ibid.*, p. 549.
[2] *The Novels of Thomas Love Peacock*, one-volume edition of 1948, pp. 655–6.
[3] *Blackwood's* May 1825, p. 543.
[4] Wallas, *The Life of Francis Place*, 1925 edition, p. 71.
[5] See T. Kelly, *George Birkbeck: Pioneer of Adult Education*, Liverpool, 1957, p. 220.

permission to lecture at the Institute in 1825, Place, 'influential as ever, protested and the experiment was not repeated'.[1] Owen himself was also engaged on one occasion to give a course of lectures at the London Institute, but the course was closed down by the Director after the first lecture.[2] The middle-class patrons and organisers of the Institutes worked hard (not always successfully) to steer them clear of political discussion, of religious controversy and of association with suspect movements like Chartism and Owenism.

The Hull Mechanics' Institute, for example, was anxious to establish itself locally as a respectable organisation. The Report presented to its Annual General Meeting in 1832 announced that 'many who had regarded the Institution with aversion, now considered it not only harmless but useful. To this alteration of sentiment, arising from the good conduct of the Society, was partly attributed the large addition of Honorary Members from the higher classes made during the year.'[3] During the year in which this progress was noted, two lectures had been delivered at the Institute 'On the Causes of the frequent failure of Philanthropic Projects', in which Owen and Owenism were frequent points of reference. At the close of the second lecture, the lecturer 'again referred to the Owenite system, which was certainly incompatible with existing habits, and subversive of many of our affections and kindliest associations'. He felt, however, that Owen's recently founded Association for Removing the Causes of Ignorance and Poverty ... represented a turning-away from the Owenite *system* to a more practicable project which was 'likely to obtain eminent and extensive patronage'.[4]

The reality is that the Institutes were intended to enlist, and enlisted, the support of the 'superior working man' and they confined themselves for the most part to lectures on branches of knowledge which could be considered as having some utility value to the more literate mechanic, and the libraries established in connection with the Institutes, or independently, provided the same kind of service. The members, it was hoped, would be permeated with the values of their patrons.

One of the outstanding features of the Mechanics' Institutes and the S.D.U.K., however, was their reluctance to consider social and political issues. 'Religion and politics', said Holyoake, were 'the terrors of

[1] E. Halévy, *Thomas Hodgskin*, London, 1956, p. 91.
[2] See *Temple of Free Enquiry*, p. 22.
[3] *The Hull Advertiser*, Vol. XXXVII, No. 1993, June 8, 1832.
[4] *Ibid.*, No. 1975, February 3, 1832.

Mechanics' Institutions'.[1] At the beginning, it was intended that the S.D.U.K. should publish works intended to teach the truths of moral and political science, as seen by Brougham and the *Edinburgh* and *Westminster* reviews. It fought shy of doing so, however, for a long time, confining itself largely to the publication of treatises in such fields as astronomy, dynamics, chemistry, mineralogy, brewing, botany and mathematics, together with biographies of men like Newton, Blake and Galileo. The working men 'addressed by this Society found experimentally that their own Harry Brougham, as well as other Liberal leaders, had not faith enough in them to entrust them with political knowledge, but preferred putting out, in the most critical period of the nation's history, treatises on physical science, as a tub to the whale ...'[2] Brougham was led to realise that the omission had been a mistake, and finally the Society published Brougham's *Outlines of Lectures on Politics and Political Philosophy* in 1839 and his *Political Philosophy* in 1840. The content of these publications gives the clearest possible indication of the social ideology implicit in the operations of the Society, and now made explicit. *Political Philosophy*, for example, issued a warning against the 'hazards to which the people is exposed that hastily, and prematurely, and without the greatest circumspection, and the utmost deliberation, changes its institutions'. Careful political study would not only teach the student 'to be cautious and distrustful of theories, and of visionaries as well as imposters', it would also make him 'sensible of the safety and fitness of listening respectfully to the opinions of the good and the wise; of men whose knowledge is greater, whose experience is larger, whose reason is more powerful than his own ... in political, as in all other sciences, it is useful and safe to take the benefit of skilful men's ability and learning'.[3]

Just as, in the 1790's, we saw that apparently conflicting viewpoints on education were in fact segments of the same pattern of the rescue motive, so now at mid-nineteenth century we see the point at which both Brougham and *Blackwood's* were, in the depths of their disagree-

---

[1] G. J. Holyoake, *The History of the Rochdale Pioneers 1844–1892*, London, 1893, p. 23.

[2] Harriet Martineau, *Biographical Sketches 1852–1868*, London, 1870, pp. 159–60.

[3] Henry Lord Brougham, *Political Philosophy*, London, 1840, 3rd edition, 1853, Vol. I, p. 80. For the story of these uncertainties see F. A. Cavenagh, 'Lord Brougham and the Society for the Diffusion of Useful Knowledge', *The Journal of Adult Education*, Vol. IV, No. 1, October 1929, p. 11.

ment, saying more or less the same thing. *Blackwood's* opposed Brougham because his plans led to insubordination and the dissolution of the bonds between the poor and the rich. Brougham prepared his plans precisely in order to prevent insubordination and the dissolution of such bonds. By following the course he had been suggesting, Brougham declared, 'a deference to authority will thus be inculcated'. A people educated in accordance with his principles would be 'disciplined as well as instructed . . . Caution and moderation become familiar to them.'[1] *Blackwood's*, and Tory opinion, saw the protection of the fabric of society in the preservation of the status quo, in resistance to educational forces which might build up to a tempest of change. Brougham, the Whigs and utilitarian Radicals, *The Edinburgh Review*[2] and the S.D.U.K. saw the protection of that fabric in terms of governing, leading and directing the new forces at work, lest they build up *of their own accord* to the tempest.

The Mechanics' Institutes were instruments for the attainment of the same objectives among strategic sections of the working class. Such aims, however, though paramount, were not the only ones. The Mechanics' Institute patrons were also half-aware of a more specific function: they were concerned with the problem of skill.

The question of a skilled labour force assumed increasingly serious proportions throughout the nineteenth century; it was a question productive of strong tensions, since the education of a skilled labour force would, in the eyes of many, also mean the education of precisely those elements of the working class most aware of their disenfranchised status. What middle class Radical opinion, and particularly *The Westminster Review*, its major theoretical spokesman, saw in adult education along Mechanics' Institute lines, was the possibility of providing a scientific or technical training of sorts, superimposed on the elementary system, still hopelessly inadequate, but for which no apparent full-scale extension and improvement was yet in sight.

There were men early in the nineteenth century who were aware that a limited form of education would not only fit the poor to discharge 'the duties of their humble condition,' but encourage *some* to 'press on toward perfection':

[1] *Political Philosophy*, p. 81.
[2] *The Edinburgh Review*, as Brougham saw it, had dedicated itself 'to the promotion of sound and liberal opinions upon all questions in Church and State . . . and assuming the duty of submission to the constitution as fixed and permanent, the frame of our government only being subject to decorous and temperate discussion' (quoted in Clive, *Scotch Reviewers*, p. 55).

'The number of useful artificers will be increased; by whose skilful exertions the resources of our national prosperity will be extended, and Britain's superiority over other nations maintained upon the most noble and commanding ground.'[1]

By the 1830's it was being felt among many employers that the Mechanics' Institutes in particular, and a limited amount of education in general, not only protected them against rick-burning and machinery-breaking, not only improved the general moral tone and intelligence of workmen, but also improved their *work*. Frederic Hill quotes a number of replies from Poor Law Commissioners in, for example, the northern counties, to the question 'Is the industry of the labourers in your neighbourhood supposed to be increasing or diminishing; that is, are your labourers supposed to be better or worse workmen than they formerly were?' Two typical comments are from Northumberland:

'It is thought that the labourers are more skilful workmen in consequence of being better educated' (Bothall).

and:

'Increasing, and better workmen, because more intelligent...' (Whelpington).[2]

There are numerous cases quoted in Hill's book of Mechanics' Institute members not participating in combinations and strikes. It was in a review of the Library of Useful Knowledge that *The Westminster Review* stated the need for skilled workmen most clearly. It gave an account of a number of important crafts, including the manufacture of mathematical instruments, for which considerable skill was required:

'Would any man who possesses the merest school-boy knowledge of such subjects, suppose that workmanship of this nature could be executed without education? or do they imagine that these things grow out of the ground? And if education is necessary, why is it denied? Why are we not, on the contrary, anxious to impart it? There is no answer: and there cannot be.

And the consequence of the present defective system, if system it can be called, is obvious. There is a deficiency of workmen ... there is a consequent and unavoidable deficiency of instruments'.[3]

[1] Irvine, *Reflections on the Education of the Poor*, pp. 14–18.
[2] *National Education*, p. 243.
[3] Vol. VII, No. XIV, April 1827, p. 281.

That the people were already being educated, although imperfectly, was obvious—if they were not, 'the operations of the country could not go on at all'. Why not, therefore, provide education earlier in life, more completely, and more cheaply, 'since that is not a cheap education which costs nothing, if it is to be paid for by the neglect of work, imperfect performance, or destruction of property?' The present system was 'bad in every manner; deficient, tedious, expensive, wasteful, vexatious to the people themselves, and injurious to every body'.[1] The *Westminster* saw the relevance of 'useful knowledge' to the provision of skilled labour, considerably before the problem assumed the proportions it did from the middle of the century.

One outstandingly clear example of the social philosophy behind the popularising work of the Society was the publication in 1830, under the auspices of the Library of Entertaining Knowledge, of a 419-page book on *The Pursuit of Knowledge under Difficulties*.[2] This book is a compilation of biographies and anecdotes of scholars, men of science and the arts, who triumphed over poverty and adversity to achieve distinction in their chosen field. Professor Heyne, a classical scholar at Göttingen, was the son of a poor weaver, and 'had spent the first thirty-two or thirty-three years of his life, not only in obscurity, but in an almost incessant struggle with the most depressing poverty'.[3] Aesop, Terence and Epictetus were originally slaves. Progatoras 'had been a common porter before he applied to study'.[4] The Italian writer, Gelli, what is more, after being elected consul of the Florentine Academy, 'still continued to work at his original profession of tailor, which he had inherited from his father.'[5] But the writer is anxious not to be misconstrued:

'If some of the individuals we have mentioned have risen to great wealth or high civil dignities, it is not for this that we have mentioned them. We bring them forward to show that neither knowledge, nor any of the advantages which naturally flow from it, are the exclusive inheritance of those who have been enabled to devote themselves entirely to its acquisition from their youth upwards.'[6]

[1] *Ibid.*, p. 298.
[2] The Library, published under the auspices of the S.D.U.K., was intended 'to give as much useful information as can be conveyed in an amusing form'. *The Pursuit of Knowledge* was by G. L. Craik (see Cavenagh, 'Lord Brougham and the Society for the Diffusion of Useful Knowledge', p. 28).
[3] *The Pursuit of Knowledge*, p. 25.
[4] *Ibid.*, pp. 31–2.   [5] *Ibid.*, pp. 40–1.   [6] *Ibid.*, p. 53.

Knowledge is available to all who care to pursue it, and is its own reward. But what about the obstacles which beset the poor? The writer's examples 'shew how the most unpropitious circumstances have been unable to conquer an ardent desire for the acquisition of knowledge'. Everyone has difficulties; everyone wishes to know, therefore, how others have overcome theirs. This is the crux. When the writer lists the kind of obstacles he has in mind—'want of leisure, want of instructors, want of books, poverty, ill health, imprisonment, uncongenial or distracting occupations, the force of opposing example, the discouragement of friends or relations, the depressing consideration that the better part of life was already spent and gone'—and shows how they have all exerted their influence in vain, he is never aware of these obstacles as needing to be *removed*, only to be *surmounted*. One should be pleased, he wishes to make the reader feel, not to have had the disadvantage of being born *without* such obstacles to face. 'He who is left to educate himself in every thing, may have many difficulties to struggle with; but he who is saved every struggle is perhaps still more unfortunate.'[1] Even the lack of teachers is not really a disadvantage. Adversity teaches a man 'to learn and practise, to an extraordinary extent, the duties of steadiness, diligence, husbanding of time, concentration of attention . . . In learning these virtues he learns what is more precious than any knowledge . . .'[2]

What *The Pursuit of Knowledge under Difficulties* tried to do was to persuade the workman to be contented with his poverty, his liability to imprisonment, his lack of teachers, leisure and health. It, or at least its ideology, was, of course, the ancestor of Samuel Smiles' *Self-Help*,[3] which, like *The Pursuit of Knowledge*, builds up a mass of evidence of men who triumphed over poverty, adversity and every other form of *disadvantage*, and should be grateful to have had the *advantage* of such a struggle:

> 'An easy and luxurious existence does not train men to effort or encounter with difficulty . . . Indeed, so far from poverty being a misfortune, it may, by vigorous self-help, be converted even into a blessing . . .'[4]

Real education is 'self-culture'. That 'which is put into us by others is

[1] *Ibid.*, pp. 16–17.
[2] *Ibid.*, p. 419.
[3] First published in 1859. Smiles traced the origins of the book to an address he had delivered 'some fifteen years since' (*Self-Help*, 1908 edition, p. ix).
[4] *Ibid.*, p. 22.

always far less ours than that which we acquire by our own diligent and persevering effort'.[1] This is laissez-faire education, accepting the stratification of society, and justifying the system by the few who could fight their way through to honourable poverty-plus-culture, and even, in some cases, moderate wealth.[2]

The S.D.U.K. and Smiles, advocating *individual* self-help, in education and in social action generally, endorsed the status quo. Owen, the co-operators and the Chartists advocated *collective* self-help plus, to one extent or another, state help, precisely in order to challenge and change the status quo.

The 'useful knowledge' movements had some working class support, largely and increasingly among the higher ranks of artisans and even clerical and lower professional workers. There was a good deal of grudging support, of the kind that came from *The New Moral World* when it criticised the Institutes for their lack of democracy, but adding that they had been 'productive of much good. They have awakened dormant intellects . . .'[3] In 1827, Abram Combe's *Register* at the Owenite community of Orbiston had announced the opening of a Mechanics' Institute at Falkirk, affirming that 'nothing is perhaps at present more conducive to the universal diffusion of knowledge, than the establishment of Mechanics' Institutions'. Every new one 'must be considered an additional instrument for the promotion of universal happiness'.[4] Even William Cobbett, inveterate opponent of Brougham and the whole idea of useless 'useful knowledge', 'gave my five pounds as a mark of my regard for and my attachment to *the working classes of the community*', adjuring them 'not to be *humbugged*, which you most certainly will be, if you suffer any body but REAL MECHANICS to have anything to do in managing the concern'.[5]

[1] *Ibid.*, p. 369.
[2] Although 'the great things which have been done for the world have not been accomplished by rich men . . . but by men generally of small pecuniary means . . .' (*ibid.*, p. 365). For an indirect answer to the S.D.U.K.-Smiles position see Kay-Shuttleworth, 'Popular Education and its Relations to the Religious Denominations', in *Social Problems*, p. 180 (there had been men whose 'intellectual life' had triumphed over neglect and privation, but 'I would not have it so in the future. For one strong swimmer who has been enabled to reach the shore, how many have perished unknown?')
[3] Vol. IV, No. 201, September 1, 1838, pp. 363–4.
[4] *The Register for the First Society of Adherents to Divine Revelation at Orbiston in Lanarkshire*, No. 33, July 11, 1827.
[5] Quoted in G. D. H. and Margaret Cole, *The Opinions of William Cobbett*, p. 289.

Many Co-operators and Socialists, Radicals and Chartists, joined the Institutes, eager to take advantage of their facilities, and to use them as centres for propaganda. When the Brighton co-operators first began to hold meetings, they met in the Mechanics' Institute. It was here that Dr William King, Vice President of the Institute, encountered the incipient co-operative movement, some of the co-operators being in his mathematics class.[1] Reference is also ocasionally made to Owenite lectures at Institutes, particularly at the beginning of the thirties.[2] But wherever there was an alternative, more radical and democratic centre, usually in the late thirties and early forties an Owenite Hall of Science, the Mechanics' Institutes were treated more critically. By the end of the thirties the Institutes had lost a great deal of their working class support because in the period of the growing momentum of working class political agitation most of the Institutes banned political discussion.

The very constitutions of the Institutes explain why, in the 1830's and 1840's, when agitation for political and social reform was central to the preoccupations of working men, they lost much of their existing working class support. Not all the Institutes stated as explicitly as Deptford that 'the object proposed to be obtained is the instruction of the Members in the principles of the Arts they practice, and in the various branches of science and useful Knowledge, with the exception of Religion and Politics',[3] but most adopted the principle. Most of them insisted that a minimum percentage of their management committee should be working men (two-thirds at Deptford and Darlington,[4] for example), but opened the door so wide to patronage and middle class influence that the more independent working men were antagonised. Darlington's *Rules and Regulations* stated that the officers 'shall consist of Patrons, a President, Vice-President, a Treasurer, Honorary Secretary, two acting Secretaries, and a Committee of eighteen members . . .' and its first list of officers included four Patrons (the Bishop of Durham, the Earl of Darlington, and two M.P.s) and a President (Lieutenant General Aylmer). The eight Vice-Presidents included one Colonel, one Captain (R.N.) and the Resident Curate of Darlington. The Hon.

---

[1] See Brown, *Brighton's Co-operative Advance*, p. 33.

[2] See, for example, *The Birmingham Co-operative Herald*, Nos. 14–15 (May 1 and June 1, 1830), for reports of two lectures on co-operation at Bolton.

[3] *Rules and Orders of the Mechanics' Institution, for Deptford and its Vicinity . . . Established Michaelmas, 1825.*

[4] *Rules and Regulations of the Mechanics' Institution, of Darlington and its Vicinity. Established the 13th Day of May, 1825.*

Secretary was also a clergyman. Hull made elaborate provisions to 'obtain the support of Opulent and favourably disposed Individuals, and thereby to lighten the pressure upon the operative Mechanic'. It arranged for two classes of members, Proprietary (mechanics) and Honorary (donors). There was to be a 21-member Committee of Management. The President, two Vice-Presidents, Treasurer, two Secretaries and three of the 15 Directors '*may* be chosen out of either Class of Members; but the remaining Twelve Directors *shall* be chosen out of the Class of Proprietary Members only'.[1]

Opposition to the Institutes did not arise, of course, purely because of their structure, but the structure reflected the middle class utilitarian ideology behind them. Opposition on the grounds of the inadequacy of the utilitarian analysis of society was expressed very sharply in an outspoken article in the Glasgow *Herald to the Trades' Advocate* in November 1830. The paper announced that 'the season for commencing Lectures is arrived, and we are again requested by advertisements, handbills, and personal applications to be students, and to support the *Institution*'. Support would be forthcoming, continued the article, for all 'seminaries of learning, particularly those Institutions which teach the great principles of the universe as applicable to the improvement of the human race'. When such principles are distorted, however:

'... we must pause, and recommend to the managers of such Institutions to direct the energies of the professors to the most important subject, viz. That the scientific and mechanical power now brought into existence in Britain ... *be distributed* for the benefit of the working classes; and unless this is done, however much we may admire the analysis of a chemical compound, while in the lecture room; yet we cannot help ... regret that the steam-engine and the chemical compound deprives the labourer of his employment ...'[2]

To working class Owenites and Radicals, the Institutes were, in the words of *The New Moral World* in 1840, merely 'halfway houses to the attainment of sound knowledge'.[3] But if they treated the Institutes with some coolness, for the S.D.U.K. they had nothing but the most down-

[1] *Rules for the Management of the Literary and Scientific Mechanics' Institute, established in Hull, June 1, 1825.*

[2] No. 17, November 6, 1830, pp. 111–12.

[3] Quoted in A. Black, 'Education before Rochdale (2—The Owenites and the Halls of Science)', *The Co-operative Review*, Vol. XXIX, No. 2, February 1955, p. 42.

right contempt. In 1828 Charles Knight one of the sponsors of the Society, and publisher of its works, visited Liverpool seeking support for it. 'He found the working people unresponsive . . .'[1] From 1831, the co-operative congresses showed that unresponsiveness had become confirmed hostility. At the third congress, for example, at least four delegates delivered strong attacks. William Lovett observed that 'the Society for the Promotion (sic) of Useful Knowledge had declared that the results of machinery were cheap production and increased employment. He admitted that it cheapened production, but let them inquire what the bulk of the people gained by it (hear hear!)'[2] James Watson declaimed 'against the Useful Knowledge Society for installing into the people antiquarian and zoological knowledge, instead of making them acquainted with their rights. They patronised Mechanics' Institutions also, but it was only in order to instruct them to create wealth—they cared not, though the creators were starving.'[3] Mr Wigg made fun of the Society's tracts, which 'contain a large number of facts, or parts of facts (laughter)'.[4] The most sustained attack came from William Pare, discussing the notorious publication alluded to by Lovett, *The Results of Machinery*. This work, said Pare, was designed to show that machinery had been beneficial to the working classes. It admitted, however, that machinery occasionally injured the workmen by . . . causing the wages of labour to fall' The book's answer was—savings. Pare quoted:

'There is a glut of labourers in the market. If you (the labourers) continue in the market of labour during this glut, your wages must fall. What is the remedy? To go out of the market (Loud laughter.) . . . Endeavour to acquire the same power: become capitalists. (Laughter.)'

'A greater insult', commented Pare, 'could not have been offered to the working classes of this great empire; and from the part he came, it was esteemed as such. (Loud applause).'[5]

In the same year, Brougham and the S.D.U.K. were major targets for

[1] Brown, *A Century of Liverpool Co-operation*, p. 15.
[2] *The Crisis*, Vol. I, No. 3, April 28, 1832.
[3] *Ibid.*, Supplement. This was said to 'mingled cheers and disapprobation'. There were middle-class sympathisers present, and 'Mr HUME retired when Mr Watson commenced his political allusions'.
[4] *Proceedings of the Third Congress*, p. 22.
[5] *Ibid.*, p. 30. See *The Working Man's Companion. The Results of Machinery, namely, Cheap Production and Increased Employment*, London, 1831 (Chapter XIX, pp. 197–9 in particular).

the wrath of *The Poor Man's Guardian*. In an editorial in June, announcing that 'these *reforming* "Whigs" ' had just passed '*the Bill*' and had 'determined to SUPPRESS THE PENNY PAPERS,' it included in its indictment of the Whigs the fact that they:

> '. . . pretend to teach the people "*Useful Knowledge*"—at the same time that the Lord High Chancellor of England is the chairman of the Society for the *profession* of "*Useful Knowledge*."—And may the curse of Judas blast and sweep the odious hypocrites from the earth they have so long disgraced.'[1]

Driven by the anger of the reform betrayal by the Whigs, and the new administration's failure to repeal the legislation under which the unstamped press was prosecuted, the paper turned in particular on Brougham, who had 'proved himself the same mean-spirited, fawning, sycophantic, slavish ARISTOCRAT, that all his predecessors had been'. The article turned from Brougham to the S.D.U.K., 'the disgusting society at which he is the head', which, 'under the mask of a liberal diffusion of really useful information, has spread abroad more canting, lying, mischievous trash, than, perhaps, any other society that ever existed'.[2]

A strong source of anger among radicals and Owenites was the fact that the S.D.U.K.'s paper, the *Penny Magazine* (which appeared in 1832), lived under a special dispensation which prevented it from being prosecuted, while the radical penny papers were.[3] *The Poor Man's Guardian* made a particularly vicious onslaught on it in August 1832 for publishing a poem by Barry Cornwall entitled 'The Weaver's Song' the refrain of which went:

[1] *The Poor Man's Guardian*, Vol. I, No. 52, June 9, 1832, p. 418.
[2] *Ibid.*, Vol. I, No. 70, October 13, 1832, p. 565.
[3] See C. D. Collet, *History of the Taxes on Knowledge*, London, 1899, Thinker's Library edition of 1933, p. 16, for a discussion of the paper's evasion of stamp tax. For an indication of Owenite opinion in this connection, see a poem entitled 'Diffusion of Knowledge under Difficulties' in *The Crisis* (Vol. III, No. 6, October 12, 1833), telling the tale of a child seeing a boy arrested for selling a radical unstamped paper. The child remembers having:

> '. . . *bought a* Penny Magazine;
> *And one of those blue police-men*
> *Stood near and saw me buy it then,*
> *But did not take the man to jail*
> *For selling me that servile tale,*
> *Which, after reading, Father burn'd,*
> *Lest I its meanness should have learn'd* . . .'

'Sing,—sing, brothers! weave and sing!
'Tis good both to sing and to weave:
'Tis better to work than live idle:
'Tis better to sing than grieve.'

and which ended with the lines:

'There is not a creature, from England's King,
To the peasant that delves the soil,
That knows half the pleasures the seasons bring,
If he have not his share of toil!'

The *Guardian* described this as 'pure and undisguised humbug . . . Pray what is the share of toil allotted to our *patriot* king?' It went on to attack the magazine more broadly because, 'week after week, the work is published containing a pack of nonsensical tittle tattle about forks and spoons, and smock frocks, bridges, waterfalls, and a thousand other things, no doubt entertaining enough, but to the poor and ignorant, utterly useless'.[1] It is not surprising, as the Hammonds report, that some of the working class leaders wanted to organise a rival propaganda.[2]

The range of attitudes displayed towards the Society and the Institutes makes it easier to assess the educational activities of the Owenites and Chartists, who, standing aside from this highly-organised rescue operation, continued to assert the working class's right to education on a wider educational basis. Owen, the Owenites, the Chartists and working class movements in general, were, of course, capable of pressing the education-as-insurance argument in favour of education, but there is a world of difference between their demand for education as part of a programme to rescue from destitution and prepare the ground for a more permanently equitable society, and the view of education as a protective device or manipulative tool that we have seen in the ideology of the S.D.U.K.

(iv) Education by collision

We have seen how, in the early thirties, political radicalism in the National Union of the Working Classes was the legatee of a good deal of Owenite energy and vision. So, in the late thirties, was Chartism, though the story of the Chartist movement after 1837, the pressures at work in

[1] *The Poor Man's Guardian*, Vol. I, No. 60, August 4, 1832, pp. 486–7.
[2] *The Town Labourer*, 1949 Guild Books edition, Vol. II, p. 39.

210

it, and its educational experiments, ideals and impact, are too complex
for us to try to break down here. Owenism itself, in the late 1830's, in
spite of its remoteness from the urgencies of the broader popular
movement, was continuing to establish and keep alive popular traditions
of educational activity and ideals.

For Owen himself, after 1834, in the reassertion of rationalist principles
there was an even stronger concern for human *rights*, for the rational
organisation of society, not just because it was rational, but in order to
alleviate and remove human suffering and injustice. Scientific knowledge
had progressed to the point at which it could give man, 'by a right
direction of it, *the power over the production of wealth and the formation
of character*'.[1] His experience of popular movements turned him away
from class action, but towards a stronger affirmation of a belief that:

> 'Every individual of the human race has a full equal right to the
> earth . . . No man has a right to require another man to do for him,
> what he will not do for that man; or, in other words, all men, by
> nature, have equal rights.'[2]

It is paradoxical that Owenism, at the point of losing its trade union
base, recognisably became socialism.[3] Owen, elaborating schemes for
democratic education and government (largely through the division of
populations into age groups, each with its appropriate mode of education, work and participation in social administration), remained held,
however, in the ambiguous position of a democrat in all save politics,
projecting into his analysis of the social situation his own predilection for
paternalism.[4] Education remained the motive power for all developments, never isolated from social processes and needs. In 1851 he
addressed the teachers. 'You have been engaged', he told them, 'in
teaching the few to sow divisions among the many, that the few . . . may

[1] *Six Lectures delivered in Manchester*, Manchester, 1837, p. 70.
[2] *Ibid.*, pp. 61 and 69.
[3] The word was coined in the late 1820's and as a label for the Owenites was
adopted during the mid-1830's (see H. S. Foxwell, Introduction to Menger,
The Right to the Whole Produce of Labour, p. lxxxii, and Beer, *A History of British
Socialism*, 1948 edition, Vol. I, pp. 186–7).
[4] For examples of Owen's detailed schemes see *The Book of the New Moral
World* (1836), *Six Lectures delivered in Manchester* (1837) and *Robert Owen's
Millennial Gazette*, No. 10A, January 1, 1857. For a statement of his paternalist
democracy see *Letters on Government as it is and as it ought to be*, London, 1851,
pp. 9–14. See also Ralph Milliband, 'The Politics of Robert Owen', *Journal of
the History of Ideas*, Vol. XV, No. 2, April 1954.

tyrannically govern the many.' Teachers had been engaged in 'measures to misform the human character, to perpetuate ignorance and poverty, and to oppose man to man and nation to nation'. It was in 'new moulds', i.e. communities, that the human race could be 'well-fed, well-clothed, well-lodged, well-employed, well-taught, well-governed, and cordially united'. Educating the human race, he told the teachers, 'is the highest and most important task that man can perform for man'.[1]

But Owenism was not just Owen. In his wake came not only the organisers of co-operatives but propagandists and re-thinkers. William Thompson, a more patient, consistent thinker than Owen, worked nevertheless within boundaries he delineated.[2] Thompson (who died in 1833) was an important figure in the co-operative movement, and one of the most influential of the early socialist analysts of capitalism;[3] his contributions to the discussion of education and social reorganisation[4] spell out in detail, though somewhat ponderously, the message of *A New View of Society*. There were men like John Gray, John Minter Morgan and John Francis Bray, who came to accept and publicise Owen's theses in their different ways, producing the text-books of Owenism and co-operation,[5] re-expressing the basic Owenite vision of society and human character, and the tangible possibility of social change, re-asserting, in Owen's very vocabulary, his analysis and his ideal.[6] There were also men like William Pare who, in addition to their practical work of co-operative organisation, carried Owen's doctrines into the lecture and adult school rooms, and those who, like Rowland

[1] *Letters on Education, as it is and as it ought to be*, London, 1851 (incorrectly ascribed to 1849 in *Bibliography*), pp. 1–6.

[2] R. K. P. Pankhurst, in *William Thompson*, makes exaggerated claims for Thompson, under whom, he maintains, many of the Chartist leaders 'served their apprenticeship' (p. 207). Foxwell believed it was Thompson who made Godwin's influence felt (Menger, *The Right to the Whole Produce of Labour*, p. xxxi).

[3] For a survey of these writers, see Beales, *The Early English Socialists*, Chapter V, Beer, *A History of British Socialism*, 1948 edition, Vol. I, Part II, Chapter VII, and G. D. H. Cole, *Socialist Thought: the Forerunners 1789–1850*, London, 1953, Chapters X and XII.

[4] See, for example, his chapter on 'the acquisition and diffusion of knowledge' in *An Inquiry into the Principles of the Distribution of Wealth*, London, 1824.

[5] Morgan's *The Revolt of the Bees* was a standard text in the Owenite educational work of the 1830's.

[6] See, for example, J. F. Bray, *Labour's Wrongs and Labour's Remedy*, 1839, edition of 1931, ('character, whether good or bad, is nothing more than a factitious quality acquired by man . . . human beings . . . (may) be made savage or civilized, ignorant or enlightened', pp. 112–13).

Detrosier and 'Shepherd' Smith, while taking from Owen perhaps little more than an enthusiasm and a sense of identification with his overall aims, helped to spread a commitment to 'the same noble employment, the improvement of men's minds',[1] and the implications of the doctrine of circumstances.[2]

The momentum, in short, which carried Owenism beyond 1834 was the result not only of Owen's writing and activities (though these were to continue unabated until his death in 1858), but of the spread of ideas through organised groups of Owenites or individuals in other movements, through newspaper and pamphlet, the extended theoretical analysis and the lecture, the schoolroom and the congress debate. It was a momentum which kept Owen and Owenism alive in both the popular imagination,[3] and discussions of educational reform.[4] Owen himself in 1837 could still command an audience of, at Bronterre O'Brien's reckoning, at least fifteen hundred, to listen to him on the subject of the 'formation of character'.[5]

Owenism was, in fact, at the end of the 1830's, a 'great and spreading sect',[6] organising branches throughout the country, holding meetings, lectures and discussions, sending out missionaries and issuing cheap publications, organising Halls of Science,[7] and, through the very organisation of the movement itself, continuing and re-emphasising traditions of education in the widest sense. The Association of All Classes of All Nations (one of the many names adopted by the movement) adopted the Methodist 'class meeting' as its pivotal activity. The Salford Owenites, for example, in 1835 formed themselves into five

[1] The words are Detrosier's. See *Proceedings of the Second Co-operative Congress*, p. 6.

[2] For Detrosier see his Addresses in Manchester between 1829 and 1831 in GL. The address dated March 25, 1831, contains an account of his life. See also Holyoake, *Sixty years of an Agitators' Life*, 1902 edition, Vol. I, p. 188. For Smith, see Smith, *'Shepherd' Smith the Universalist*, particularly pp. 102 and 209; also Armytage, *Heavens Below*, pp. 134–6.

[3] For an example of working class support for Owen after the 1834 collapse, see report of a Trades Meeting reprinted from the Glasgow *New Liberator* in *N.M.W.*, Vol. III, No. 111, December 10, 1836 (thanking him for the 'boon you have conferred on mankind' by introducing infant schools, demonstrating that the character of man is formed for him, and pressing for rational education).

[4] See *N.M.W.*, Vol. III, No. 154, October 7, 1837, for report of a meeting in Salford, September 23, 1837.

[5] See *Bronterre's National Reformer*, No. 9, March 4, 1837, p. 67.

[6] *The Quarterly Review*, Vol. LXV, No. CXXIX, December 1839, p. 305.

[7] See A. Black, 'Education before Rochdale (2) The Owenites and the Halls of Science)', *The Co-operative Review*, Vol. XXIX, No. 2, February, 1955.

classes, each with a leader, and met 'once every week for social conversation and mutual instruction in the doctrine of the Social System'. They ran a school and had a lecture and discussion every Sunday evening.[1] In Huddersfield there was an 'organised system of meeting in classes . . . for their more effectual instruction in the principles, practice, morals, and economy of the rational system . . . the better cultivation of the faculties of their wives—female relations, and other female friends of the Social system . . .'[2] The educational organisation of the movement and of its Halls of Science, which offered a democratic alternative to the Mechanics' Institutes, provided, regardless of Owen's paternalism, a continued provocation to the consideration, and above all, the *experience*, of democracy.[3]

There has been, in this analysis of the continued momentum of Owenism and its impact on educational experience and ideals, one vital item largely omitted—the intimate concern with the organisation of community experiments. The attempts at community, indeed, made education a dominant feature of their plans. The 1821 Economical and Co-operative Society sought arrangements for the 'superintendence, training, and education of their children'.[4] The philosophy of the Orbiston community was that the children should be educated together 'upon the principles of undeviating kindness, without any artificial reward or punishment'.[5] At Ralahine, in Ireland, E. T. Craig and his wife, imported from the Manchester Owenian Co-operative Society, conducted, in the early 1830's, one of the most interesting of the community ventures, with an infant school, community payment of expenses on children's food, clothing, washing, lodging and accommodation 'from the time they are weaned until they arrive at the age of seventeen . . .'[6] The children were given vocational training, but the main accent was on keeping them 'gais, bien portants et heureux'.[7] It was this tradition of experiment through the 1830's, and the support for

---

[1] *N.M.W.*, Vol. I, No. 20, March 14, 1835, p. 157.

[2] *Ibid.*, Vol. IV, No. 181, April 14, 1838, p. 195.

[3] For a description of the Manchester Hall of Science see *Temple of Free Enquiry*.

[4] Quoted in Beer, *A History of British Socialism*, 1948 edition, Vol. I, p. 205.

[5] The Orbiston *Register*, No. 1, November 10, 1825.

[6] *The Lancashire and Yorkshire Co-operator*, New Series, No. 6, probably July 1832 (report of a lecture by E. T. Craig).

[7] Marie Moret, *Histoire de l'Association Agricole de Ralahine*, Saint-Quentin, 1882. See also *The Crisis*, Vol. II, No. 27, July 13, 1833, and *N.M.W.*, Vol. IV, Nos. 179–86, 190, 192–4, 201 and 205.

the community idea from a wide movement which included, for example Richard Oastler[1] and Feargus O'Connor,[2] that produced the wave of enthusiasm for Harmony Hall, Queenwood. Of this grandiose, but finally catastrophic scheme, the only successful element was, in fact, a boarding school for the children of members and others.

Owenite energy and vision had, however, helped to produce an alternative channel through which the impulse to educate for and in a better society was felt—Chartism. The London Working Men's Association, out of which Chartism grew, was dominated by men like Lovett and Hetherington, and accepted fully Owen's emphasis on the centrality of education in the transition to a new society. Its educational principles were expressed often in Owenite terms, and with considerable enthusiasm.[3] There was in addition considerable overlapping of effort and personnel locally, where Halls of Science were often meeting points for Owenites, Chartists and Owenite-Chartists. There was, of course, also friction between the Owenites and Chartists, but the point is the same as in relation to the National Union of the Working Classes; many Owenites had gone over to suffrage agitation, and though resentful of Owen's failure to support Chartism, put into the Chartist movement the vision they had learned from him. Owen, it has been said, acquired from the French Revolutionary period many of its doctrines, except those of 'revolt and the political gospel' which are to be found in Chartism, 'which Owen, without approving, powerfully affected'. Owen 'made many Chartists but did not himself believe in the slow process of democracy'.[4]

The lower orders, the working classes, had become the working class, and Owenism in the 1820's and early 1830's was the major factor in making the process explicit, and in making a claim to educational rights a part of the awareness of this identity. It was largely Chartism that continued this process. However suspicious the left wing of the movement might have been of educational plans (especially Lovett's in 1841) as milk-and-water substitutes for vigorous political action, the truth remains that for an immense number of rank and file Chartists the fight

---

[1] Oastler in 1837 supported an appeal by Owen for the government to advance money for the formation of communities (see M. Cole, *Robert Owen of New Lanark*, p. 212).

[2] He urged people to invest their savings 'in one of Owen's communistic colonies' (see Beer, *A History of British Socialism*, 1948 edition, Vol. II, p. 155).

[3] See an address on education in 1837, in *The Life and Struggles of William Lovett*, p. 135.

[4] Brown, *The French Revolution in English History*, pp. 199–200.

for the suffrage was inseparable from the fight for human dignity, of which education was a crucial element. The W.M.A. described education in 1837 as 'a universal instrument for advancing the dignity of man', and demanded it 'not as a charity, BUT AS A RIGHT, a right derivable from society itself'.[1] Never far away from Chartist agitation was action for rights of this kind. The 1851 Chartist programme proclaimed that 'as every man has a right to the means of physical life, so he has to the means of mental activity . . . Education should, therefore, be national, universal, gratuitous and, to a certain extent, compulsory . . .'[2] The Chartists discussed detailed proposals for educational administration, for democratic control, for teacher training and for the financing of schools. Working class commitment to education, not to education at random, but to well-defined concepts of democratic, popular education, was to be a factor, therefore, in the attainment of any kind of national educational provision, and the history of nineteenth century education that analyses the march to 1870 and after purely in terms of Commissions, Acts and parliamentary grants leaves out of the picture the role of those to be educated. The working class movement did not, of course, shape the 1870 Act, but without means of transmission of educational vision and activity throughout the century, the working class itself might have been something different, educational provision something less, and the pattern of educational control less adaptable to its modern social forms.[3]

Chartism, from the end of the 1830's, embodied, some of the most intensive a d far-seeing contributions to the tradition of working class collective self-help in the field of education yet made. The lives of Chartist leaders like Henry Vincent and Thomas Cooper show the passion with which they undertook their lecturing activities. The many Chartist publications set out to educate in a very precise sense, and on the first page of the first number of the *Northern Star*, for example, Feargus O'Connor wrote:

[1] *The Life and Struggles of William Lovett*, p. 138.
[2] Saville, *Ernest Jones: Chartist*, p. 260.
[3] Of the literature on Chartism, the most relevant to this discussion are: R. Alun Jones, 'Knowledge Chartism. A Study of the Influence of Chartism on Nineteenth Century Educational Development in Great Britain', Birmingham M.A. thesis, 1938; Slosson, *The Decline of the Chartist Movement*, and, particularly useful for the ideological kaleidoscope of Chartism, West, *A History of the Chartist Movement*. There is a valuable analysis in Brian Simon, *Studies in the History of Education 1780–1870*, Chapter V. See also *The Life and Struggles of William Lovett*, and Saville, *Ernest Jones: Chartist*.

'Reader, behold that little red spot in the corner of my newspaper. That is the stamp; the Whig *beauty* spot . . . there it is: it is my license to teach.'[1]

Chartism, like the Owenite organisations of the late thirties and early forties, helped to build up traditions concerned with the democratisation of education. The Chartist schools and halls, the discussions and debates, made men aware of the nature and weaknesses of such education as they might have received, that schooling was not necessarily an inefficient and inhuman process. In this context, Lovett's *Chartism* was important, with its stress on self-expression and the basing of educational discipline on 'that great precept of "love one another" '.[2] The first object to be achieved by Infant Schools 'is to render the school-room a little world of love, of lively and interesting enjoyments'. One of the duties of the people is that 'of rewarding and honouring the teachers of their children'.[3] Lovett's pamphlet, and his later activities in association with William Ellis, George Combe and the secular school movement, provide a bridge between Owen's philosophy of education and Chartist educational activities on the one hand, and less radical, more utilitarian educational thinking, concerned none the less with the need for more efficient and more democratic processes in education, on the other. George Combe, for example, was anxious to secure the teaching of really useful knowledge, and the provision of adequate leisure.[4] Combe, William Ellis and Professor W. B. Hodgson stressed the need to teach economics and government and a real knowledge of the workings of society (primarily to secure a smooth working of society and in particular prevent strikes).[5] Lovett, similarly, urged that the individual should be instructed 'in a knowledge of the science of human well-being . . . he should also have some knowledge of the government of his country'.[6] Ellis's Birkbeck Schools, and for example, the Williams Secular School

[1] Quoted in Holyoake, *Life of Joseph Rayner Stephens*, p. 17.
[2] *Chartism, A New Organization of the People*, p. 48.
[3] *Ibid.*, p. 85. A footnote states that 'Schools for infants were first established by Mr R. Owen of New Lanark'.
[4] Argued forcefully in *The Constitution of Man*, 1836 edition, Chapter V, Section III (ii).
[5] See, for example, Ellis, *An Address to Teachers on the Importance of Imparting a Knowledge of the Principles of Social Science to Children*, London, 1859, and Hodgson, *What is Capital?* (reprinted from the Transactions of the Devonshire Association for the Advancement of Science, Literature, and Art, 1868).
[6] *Social and Political Morality*, p. 139.

in Edinburgh carried these doctrines into practice,[1] and many people from the 1840's took up the theme (including, notably, the Rev. Thomas Spencer and Archbishop Whately, who became a phrenologist), urging that an education in social laws and structure and human behaviour was an essential part of the school curriculum.

Such educational thinkers and practitioners were not, of course, in any significant sense legatees of Owen, but they were, even within their education-as-insurance philosophy, extremely important collateral contributors, alongside Owenism and Chartism, to the process of democratising the schoolroom. Holding such views on the curriculum, they could not fail to see classroom method also in enlightened terms. Describing the Birkbeck schools, Ellis said, in 1851, that 'the children are questioned, and they are encouraged to question their teachers: they also question one another'.[2] (Robert Dale Owen, describing the education at New Lanark, said that the children were encouraged 'to express their opinions . . . freely, and to ask any explanation'.)[3] Throughout the middle of the century, therefore, alongside the strict, tyrannical and often sadistic practices that continued to prevail, a body of humane educational thought and practice was being built up. Owen and New Lanark had shown that it was possible to educate humanely; the Chartists and the secular school movement in their different ways helped to intensify this conviction among those who were involved in the struggle for the assertion of human dignity.

Finally, the most important educational function of the Chartist movement was probably not in asserting, as Lovett did, explicit educational aims, but in educating 'by collision',[4] in confronting the dispossessed with the realities of a society in which they held no political rights and were subject to little social justice, and in teaching them traditions of systematic action. In an Address to the Working Classes of Europe in 1838 the Working Men's Association stated that 'we regard the franchise as the best of schoolmasters'.[5] In the actual conditions of the 1840's, it might be said that the *fight* for the franchise and a free

---

[1] See *First Annual Report of the Williams Secular School*, Edinburgh, 1850 (George Combe was one of the promoters).

[2] *Education as a Means of Preventing Destitution with exemplifications from . . . the Birkbeck Schools*, London, 1851, p. 57.

[3] *An Outline*, p. 46.

[4] A. E. Dobbs took the phrase from the 1849 Committee on Public Libraries (*Education and Social Movements*, p. 207).

[5] *The Life and Struggles of William Lovett*, p. 158.

press was the best available schoolmaster. Listening to speeches and making speeches, writing handbills, public debate, the clash within the movement itself over concepts of democracy and rights and strategy—all these were part of the role of Chartism, and indirectly of Owenism, as teacher.

By the end of the 1830's, therefore, the image of a just, well-regulated society, in which men lived, worked and were educated as of right, was a mainspring of popular action. Perhaps no single sentence contributed more to the establishment of popular education as one of the targets of mass action than Owen's formulation that men's characters were formed for and not by them. That it was a too unsubtle interpretation of social processes,[1] that his rationalism led him into a mechanistic argument and trap, and that he did not have the same sensitive grasp of the dynamics of social change as more agile thinkers like Bronterre O'Brien, or earlier thinkers cast in a similar mould, such as Godwin and Mary Wollstonecraft—all these are true. But historically, Owen's dogged pursuit of his rationalist vision was an entirely relevant and socially liberating action, all the more so in that Owen had the opportunity to demonstrate, in terms of the early nineteenth century, its practicability. He never made a *complete* demonstration of what could be achieved by his system, because the complete demonstration was impossible to make. This was the limitation of his thesis: to implement it fully one had to step outside the 'old world' and begin the 'new moral world' from scratch. Owen, rationalist to the end, never learned that in social processes, one cannot step outside. But for those who were to continue, in one form or another, the pursuit of social and educational aims 'on higher ground', Owen had established something against relentless pressure from the early industrial revolution. A professor, visiting New Lanark, had been to see the infant school, 'and as the children were passing out, the kind-hearted Professor patted the head of a little girl, whose fair face and flowing hair had caught his eye. "Ah!" said Mr Owen to him, "you are like all the rest, it is the good-looking only that you notice; but it is those that are least favoured by nature that most need the touch of a kindly hand".'[2] The child had a right to kindness and the benefits of society. A man had

---

[1] For a criticism of it by the radical free-thought campaigner, Richard Carlile, see his *Creed*, published in *The Prompter*, No. 14, February 12, 1831, p. 235.

[2] See W. B. Hodgson, *Address to the Watt Institute and School of Arts*, Edinburgh, 1879, p. 4. The visitor was Professor Pillans, Hodgson's teacher and friend.

a right to work, and to leisure, and to protection by the community of which he was an integral part. For Owen there were no outcasts.

The reason for this preoccupation with the diverse impacts of Owen and Owenism lies, then, in the way in which his concept of educability and the influence of environment brought sharply into focus a generous approach to the role of education in preparing men for the fullest possible rights in and contribution to society. Eighteenth century 'popular' education practice aimed to produce a specific kind of man for a specific social role. The more enlightened continental educational thinkers aimed to liberate the human spirit, but it was a self-contained act of liberation, since the underlying assumption even of a Pestalozzi was that poverty was inevitable, or that it was, at least, no concern of the educator, except in that the liberation of intelligence and the transmission of certain skills would produce a more self-reliant, economically viable worker, capable of living diligently within the status quo. Any combination of general with industrial education in the view of a de Fellenberg had a strictly limited aim. De Fellenberg *endorsed* the status quo, but wished to teach skills that would improve the worker's chances in it; Pestalozzi *ignored* the status quo, to the same end.[1]

Owen went beyond these to place social responsibility for education in the context of opposition to the status quo. The result was the establishment of traditions bridging across from education to justice, collective action and responsibility, common decency, tolerance and humanity. It has been emphasised, rightly, that to see the real legacy of Owenism we must look deeper than 'merely institutional reforms . . . Owenism left the English people saturated with a faith in progress and a tradition of social perfectibility which are still fresh and vigorous . . . it made a profound and abiding impression not merely on English social institutions, but on the English character'.[2] When others outside the working class preached charity or the need for 'kinder language' and 'sympathy with their necessities, which fall though it oftentimes may on unimpressible hearts, never fails to find some that it comforts, and many that it softens',[3] Owenite energies made men aware of the alternative to such argument from charity. While spelling, reading, writing and arithmetic were being 'given in homoeopathic doses',[4] Owen was telling the

[1] See Green, *The Educational Ideas of Pestalozzi*, p. 129.
[2] Foxwell, Introduction to Menger, *The Right to the Whole Produce of Labour*, p. xciv.
[3] Shaftesbury, quoted in *A Memoir of the . . . Earl of Shaftesbury*, 1885, p. 36.
[4] Holyoake, *Sixty Years of an Agitator's Life*, 1902 edition, Vol. I, p. 128.

working man that he had a right 'learn what he is in relation to past ages, to the period in which he lives, to the circumstances in which he is placed, to the individuals around him, and to future events'. Men were learning by collision, but there were targets that made the clash meaningful and worthwhile. The range of attitudes to education and to the position of men in society had, by the 1830's, come to include one segment absent from that of the eighteenth century—the attitude which involved participation in social action.

APPENDIX A

From *Political Essays with Sketches of Public Characters*, London, 1819 by William Hazlitt (reviewing *A New View of Society* and *An Address to the Inhabitants of New Lanark*, review dated August 4, 1816).

'A NEW View of Society'—No, Mr Owen, that we deny. It may be true, but it is not new. It is not coeval, whatever the author and proprietor may think, with the New Lanark mills, but it is as old as the royal borough of Lanark, or as the county of Lanark itself. It is as old as the 'Political Justice' of Mr Godwin, as the 'Oceana' of Harrington, as the 'Utopia' of Sir Thomas More, as the 'Republic' of Plato; it is as old as society itself, and as the attempts to reform it by showing what it ought to be, or by teaching that the good of the whole is the good of the individual—an opinion by which fools and honest men have been sometimes deceived, but which has never yet taken in the knaves and knowing ones. The doctrine of Universal Benevolence, the belief in the Omnipotence of Truth, and in the Perfectibility of Human Nature, are not new, but 'Old, old,' . . . The chain in which they hung up the murdered corpse of human Liberty is all that remains of it, and my Lord Shallow keeps the key of it! If Mr Owen will get it out of his hands, with the aid of Mr Wilberforce and the recommendation of *The Courier*, we will 'applaud him to the very echo, which shall applaud again' . . . But as to this bald spectre of Liberty and Necessity conjured up by Mr Owen from the falls of the Clyde, with a primer in one hand, and a spinning-jenny in the other, coming down from the Highlands in a Scotch mist, and discoverable only by second-sight, we may fairly say to it—

> '*Thy bones are marrowless, thy blood is cold;*
> *Thou hast no speculation in those eyes,*
> *Which thou dost glare with.*'

Why does Mr Owen put the word 'New', in black-letter at the head of the advertisements of his plan of reform? . . . Does not Mr Owen know that the same scheme, the same principles, the same philosophy of motives and actions, of causes and consequences, of knowledge and virtue, of virtue and happiness, were rife in the year 1793, were noised abroad then, were spoken on the house-tops, were whispered in secret, were published in quarto and duodecimo, in political treatises, in plays, poems, songs, and romances—made their way to the bar, crept into the church, ascended the rostrum, thinned the classes of the universities, and robbed

222

'Durham's golden stalls' of their hoped-for ornaments, by sending our aspiring youth up to town to learn philosophy of the new teachers of philosophy; that these 'New Views of Society' got into the hearts of poets and the brains of metaphysicians, took possession of the fancies of boys and women, and turned the heads of almost the whole kingdom: but that there was one head which they never got possession of, that turned the heads of the whole kingdom round again, stopped the progress of philosophy and necessity by wondrous fortitude, and that 'thus repelled, philosophy fell into a sadness, then into a fast, thence to a watching, then into a weakness, thence to a lightness, and by this declension, to the lamentable state wherein it now lies,' hooted by the boys, laughed at by the women, spit at by fools, trod upon by knaves, damned by poet-laureates, whined over by maudlin metaphysicians, rhymed upon by mincing ballad-makers, ridiculed in romances, belied in histories and travels, pelted by the mob, sneered at by the court, driven from the country, kicked out of society, and forced to take refuge and to lie snug for twenty years in the New Lanark mills, with the connivance of the worthy proprietor; among the tow and spindles; from whence he lets us understand that it is coming up again to Whitehall-stairs, like a spring-tide with the full of the moon, and floating on the blood that has flowed for the restoration of the Bourbons, under the patronage of the nobility, the gentry, Mr Wilberforce, and the Prince Regent, and all those who are governed, like these great personages, by no other principle than truth, and no other wish than the good of mankind!...

Our author has discovered no new theory; he has advanced no new reasons. The former reasons were never answered, but the plan did not succeed. Why then does he think *his* must? All that he has done has been to leave out the reasons for his paradoxes, and to give his conclusions in capitals. This may take for a time with Mr Wilberforce and the Methodists, who like hieroglyphics, but it cannot last. Here is a plan, strange as it may seem, 'a new View of Society', published by two of our most loyal book-sellers, and what is still more extraordinary, puffed in *The Courier* as an extremely practical, practicable, solid useful, and good sort of work, which proposes no less than to govern the world without religion and without law, by the force of reason alone! This project is in one of its branches dedicated to the Prince Regent, by which (if carried into effect) he would be stuck up in his life-time as 'a useless piece of antiquity'; and in another part is dedicated to Mr Wilberforce, though it would by the same rule convert that little vital member of the community into 'a monkey preacher', crying in the wilderness with no one to hear him, and sneaking about between his character and his conscience, in a state of ludicrous perplexity, as indeed he always appears to be at present!

What is most remarkable is, that Mr Owen is the first philosopher we ever heard of, who recommended himself to the great by telling them disagreeable truths . . . he quietly walks into their houses with his credentials in his pocket, and reconciles them to the prospect of the innumerable Houses of Industry he is about to erect on the scite of their present sinecures, by assuring them of the certainty of his principles and the infallibility of his practice, in building up and pulling down. His predecessors were clumsy fellows; but he is an engineer, who will be sure to do their business for them. He is not the man to set the Thames on fire, but he will move the world, and New Lanark is the place he has fixed his lever upon for this purpose . . .

His schemes thus far are tolerated, because they are remote, visionary, inapplicable. Neither the great world nor the world in general care any thing about New Lanark, nor trouble themselves whether the workmen there go to bed drunk or sober, or whether the wenches are got with child before or after the marriage ceremony. Lanark is distant, Lanark is insignificant. Our statesmen are not afraid of the perfect system of reform he talks of, and, in the meantime, his cant against reform in parliament, and about Bonaparte, serves as a practical diversion in their favour. But let the good which Mr Owen says he has done in one poor village be in danger of becoming general—let his plan for governing men by reason, without the assistance of the dignitaries of the church and the dignitaries of the law, but once get wind and be likely to be put in practice, and his dreams of elevated patronage will vanish. Long before he has done as much to overturn bigotry and superstition in this country, as he says Bonaparte did on the continent, (though he thinks the restoration of what was thus overturned also a great blessing) Mr Wilberforce will have cut his connection. When we see Mr Owen brought up for judgment before Lord Ellenborough, or standing in the pillory, we shall begin to think there is something in this *New Lanark Scheme* of his. On the other hand, if he confines himself to general principles, steering clear of practice, the result will be the same, if ever his principles become sufficiently known and admired. Let his 'New View of Society' but make as many disciples as the 'Enquiry concerning Political Justice,' and we shall soon see how the tide will turn about. There will be a fine hue and cry raised by all *the good and wise*, by all 'those acute minds' who, Mr Owen tells us, have not been able to find a flaw in his reasonings, but who will soon discover a flaw in his reputation. Dr Parr will preach a Spital sermon against him; lectures will be delivered in Lincoln's Inn Hall, to prove that a perfect man is such another chimera as a golden mountain; Mr Malthus will set up his two checks of vice and misery as insuperable bars against him; Mr Southey will put him into the 'Quarterly Review'; his name will be up in the newspapers, *The Times*, *The Courier*, and *The Morning Post*; the three estates will set their faces against him; he will be marked as a Jacobin, a leveller, an incendiary, in all parts of the three kingdoms; he will be avoided by his friends, and become a byeword to his enemies; his brother magistrates of the county of Lanark will refuse to sit on the bench with him; the spindles of his spinning-jennies will no longer turn on their soft axles; he will have gone out for wool, and will go home shorn . . .

APPENDIX B

Correspondence addressed to Robert Owen, from the collection of MSS in the library of the Co-operative Union at Holyoake House, Manchester.

(i) CUL/31. From Rev. Dr Charles Mayo, Epsom, June 12, 1823

Sir,

When I had the pleasure of conversing with you the other day, I neglected to make the inquiry which Mr Brougham had just suggested. May I now request you to inform me what gentlemen you conceive to be most interested in those improvements in education which have been introduced at Hofwyl? May I also be permitted to ask if you consider the principles of Pestalozzi such an advance towards the truth as to induce you to become a subscriber to the plan I mentioned to you with a view to diffuse them? My address is Revd. Dr Mayo, Epsom.

I am, Sir,
Your obedt. Servt.
Charles Mayo.

(ii) CUL/522. From William Carson, Haigh, Near Wigan, March 1, 1832

Dear Sir,

The object I have in view will plead my apology for thus Troubling of you. I have to request your opinion on an Undertaking that is of importance to the cooperative system.—it is the wish of the cooperative Societies of the North of England (which are daily becoming more numerous and of grater importance) to establish a school for 500 Children from 4 years old to 14 years, but to take none older than 12 years at first; of Boys and Girls as I know your experience will enable you to give us some valuable information on this subject, and your generosity will not withhold it from us. We find the gratest difficulty to encounter in the formation and conducting of cooperative societies to be Egnorance, and we are determined if possible that our Children shall be so educated as to become not only better taught but to be the inlightened advocates of the system in the next Generation to do this. We propose to take an estate surficiently large, with Building calculated to Board and Lodge 500 Children with a surficient number of Instructors—the Means we propose to effect this are first; that every child from 4 to 7 years shall pay per Quarter £2— from 7 to 10 years £2.5—from 10 to 14 £2.10 each child to bring to the school—two compleat suits of clothing with 2 Sheats and 2 blankets and

1 Coverlid—and thus as 2 will sleep in a bed there will be always a change of Linen ready—Next that every child pay a Quarter per advance and not to be taken away without a quarter notice, thus £1125 will be advanced to commence with—We have considered that 12 persons properly quali-fyed 6 Men and 6 Women will be enough to to Teach and instruct the Children as well as to attend to the domestic and Agricultural departments the persons engaged to have every Necessary of Life found them, but with a very small Salary surficient to purchas clothing and other little articals —the Questions we wish to have your Opinion particularly upon, is weather the sums named (with due economy and producing most that is wanted on the Estate with what labour that can be made available from the children) will be surficient—, Next the quantity of Land, we think about 150 Acres: the Number of Cows we think 15—the Number of Horses we think two—and shall be happy to receive any opinions or instructions you think proper to give, we should likewise like to Know your opinion as to the system of education the Most fit—taking into consideration that the parents of the Children are composed of Persons of Different creeds—as Sir this is an undertaking that will have a consider-able influence on the Cooperative Wourld, and is taken up by the most Zelous Advocates of the system in this part of the Country. I hope you will give your opinion shortly as we wish to lay the whole of our plan before the Congress which will be held in London next April. I think it necessary to say that if it would take a much larger sum to accomplish our object than named for the children to pay I am much affraid it will not take place but if that will be surficient I have no doubt but 3 school can immediately be formed—of 500 each or as soon as proper Lands and Buildings can be taken as there are many Large House that are to be had (?) in different parts of the country. I have no doubt but one may be meet with which will suit our purpose—Any advice on the subject will be thankfully receved . . .

I am Dear Sir
Yours Resp. William Carson

(The latter part of this letter gives a description of producer-co-operative activity in the north).

(iii) *CUL/774. From Lloyd Jones, Manchester, February 14, 1836*

Respected Father

Strongly impressed with the truth of the doctrines propounded and advocated by you, and having an interest *in* and consequently a desire *for* their promulgation we have exerted ourselves to make them manifest to those by whom we are surrounded.

As a means of doing so we some time since established a school from which circumstances (no longer existing) precluded the admittance of any but those who had already been strongly imbued with the notions of the old World. Yet imperfect as were the materials upon which we had to work and strenuous as was the opposition of some who, professing an anxiety for our emancipation from the reign of ignorance really felt an interest in its continuance. The result we are happy to state has hitherto far surpassed our most sanguine expectations. Our success has created in us a desire to carry our experiment still farther by adding an Infant School to that already established for Adults. And to the completion of this desire we are strongly urged by the senior scholars who have rendered us their most vigorous assistance. We are to hold our next Quarterly meeting about the beginning of May and we think that your presence would tend to accelerate our project, and as the friends both in Manchester and Bolton anxiously expect your arrival, we wish to know if the time will meet your convenience in order that our arrangements may be made to suit the occasion. It must be a source of gratification to you to be informed that the principles of the social system so esssential to our happiness are rappidly spreading in this town by the means already mentioned as well as by our weekly meetings. But the most particular object of our solicitude is the implanting of these principles in the Infant mind, for this means we consider the best and most effectual for finally establishing them, and working out the end which you have in view and for the attainment of which you have so perseveringly labored, namely the emancipation of the Human race from its present state of misery and its establishment in a state of perfect and permanent felicity.

Lloyd Jones
Secretary to the Committee

Direct from Lloyd Jones at the Cooperative School White Cross Bank Salford

This letter was accompanied by the following address, dated February 1836, and also signed by Lloyd Jones:

FOR THE ERECTION OF A NEW CO-OPERATIVE INSTITUTION

ADDRESS

At the present period of advanced, and rapidly advancing intelligence, when the inestimable value of knowledge and the infinite importance of a proper education to the lasting happiness of mankind are so universally admitted, anything tending to promote such an object cannot fail to be deeply interesting to every philanthropic breast.

The Teachers, Scholars, and Friends, therefore of the Salford Co-operative Institution, respectfully solicit the attention of the Friends of Education, and of the Public in general, to the following object and detail.

About four years ago, a number of intelligent working men, seeing the misery and degradation in which society was placed for the want of education, opened a School, in Salford, in which they have gratuitously devoted the whole of their time after labor in the evening, and the whole of the day on Sunday, to the benevolent purpose of educating the children of the industrial classes. The principles upon which it is established, are essentially different from those of any other institution of the kind that has ever been formed; for, besides being wholly unconnected with any sect or party, the teachers have never used any coercion in imparting their knowledge to the pupils under their care; they have invited them to attend to their studies for the good that will accrue to themselves, and the pleasure they will derive from them during their lives. They are taught the usual routine of Reading, Writing and Arithmetic, besides Grammar, Logic, Composition, Geography, Geometry, Astronomy, &c. all of which are conveyed to the mind in the most simple and amusing manner. Much of their instruction is oral, which is deemed most effectual; conversations are held with the scholars upon all interesting subjects; lectures are given them once a week or oftener by the teachers or senior scholars, and the result has been pleasing to the teachers, valuable to the scholars, and beneficial to the public.

The attachment the scholars feel for the school, induces them to spend much of their time there, and recreation is provided for the elder pupils, to prevent them being enticed to places of public resort, where the innocent amusements of music, dancing and singing, are mixed up with the vicious habit of drinking intoxicating liquors, thereby seducing those who are betrayed by these allurements, to immoral practices, and finally to their destruction.

The senior scholars of the school have formed themselves into a class for their mutual instruction in the different branches of science and philosophy, and so far have they felt the beneficial effects of the instruction they have received, that they of themselves, have been induced thus publicly to set on foot a subscription for the erection of a new Institution, on a more extensive plan than their present one, in order that others may receive the same benefits as themselves. This laudable endeavor has been responded to by the teachers and friends of the institution, and a committee has been formed to carry forward the object of their warm and virtuous intentions, and it is sincerely hoped they will succeed.

The Public and Friends of Liberal Education are now respectfully solicited to render all the assistance possible to the promotion of this most excellent object. Shall the desire of these youthful minds be disappointed in the endeavor to benefit their species? Shall it be triumphantly reiterated by the enemies of mankind, that the people will not embrace the opportunity, when offered them, of laying the foundation of real and permanent liberty and happiness, and that consequently they are fit only to remain miserable and degraded slaves? No! The generous and exalted mind will feel the greatest delight in giving all possible assistance to this noble undertaking, and will not suffer the enterprising spirit of these youths to relax or be discouraged in the onset of their benevolent intentions. It is the cause of the industrious classes; it will benefit themselves, their generations, and the whole human family.

If the working people will now come forward to assist in general education (for it is their own cause) then will the emancipation of the human race be at hand. Ignorance, the parent of vice, crime and misery, shall depart; Knowledge, the friend of Truth and promoter of Happiness shall come and remain, and the blessings of Peace, Health, and Pleasure shall abide with mankind . . .

(iv) CUL/2293. From Henry Travis, October 21, 1854

(Travis was helping Owen to prepare his autobiography. See also an earlier letter, CUL/2289, dated October 18, 1854).

My dear Mr Owen,

I have received Vol 2 of W. Allen, and also your kind note of yesterday. I see the letter which is quoted in *our* Appendix—page V—is also quoted in W. A.'s life:— but it is curtailed in the latter of all that part which follows '*we must part*'—a circumstance which betrays the *seriousness* (?) with which you & Lanark have been treated by the compiler . . . The letters in Appendix A. will show . . . how fully on entering the partnership they acknowledged *you* to be the maker of New Lanark. All the rest in the life amounts to nothing more than that W.A. was constantly fretting himself and plaguing you because you did not act in accordance with his theological motives in your New Lanark proceedings. You must have been immensely annoyed with this continual interference. It is curious how these people who call themselves liberal confine their liberality to those who accept their theological dogmas in some form, and how they presume to pronounce those things essential, which in reality are only addenda to the rules of right . . .

APPENDIX B

(*v*) *CUL/2875. From William H. Ashurst, London, March 4, 1858*
My dear Mr Owen,

I am much obliged by the interesting publication you have sent me.—

I saw Herzen, the Russian patriot a day or two since, and he begged me to express his thanks to you for sending him the 1st. volume of your memoirs.—He says mankind will not recognise the wisdom and greatness of your principles, character, and career, until 50 years after you are in your grave; but that then you will be esteemed to be what you really are, one of the greatest men this Country ever produced . . .

I am dear Mr Owen
Yours affectionately
W. H. Ashurst

APPENDIX C

From *Philipp Emanuel von Fellenberg und Sein Erziehungsstaat*, Bern, 1953 by Kurt Guggisberg (Section on 'Owen und Fellenberg', Vol. II, pp. 481–6. Translated from the German).

. . . It is not without interest to look at Owen's ideas in the light of the letters in the Fellenberg Collection, and it is not difficult to trace common features shared by the two philanthropists. For both of them, their lives took second place completely to their mission, and their dedication to their purpose raised both of them from simple philanthropists to prophets. Both of them were organisers of great stature, conducted propaganda on a grand scale, and were fully convinced they were right. Both were attacked, among other reasons, for being destroyers of Christianity. But the differences between them should also not be ignored. Fellenberg, nowhere near so blindly confident as Owen, took a more positive stand in support of the Church, had a very different sociological aim and was much more deeply cultured than the visionary of New Lanark.

On his Swiss journey Owen saw more the chaos of Yverdon than the genius of Pestalozzi, whereas he was so enthusiastic about Hofwyl that he decided straight away that he would send his two elder sons there at once, and later the younger sons, to be educated by Fellenberg. He told Fellenberg of his decision on January 17, 1818. He had worked out a plan for the betterment of human society as long ago as 1799, and was trying to do the same as Fellenberg at Hofwyl. Only the methods and results of his efforts seemed to him to be the same: education via familiarity (Angewöhnung) and the development of potentialities, in which agricultural work was of great importance, because it was the sole source of true and permanent wealth. He also agreed with Fellenberg in saying that man must set aside as much as possible all inducements to crime. If all good innate qualities could be developed, it would be easier for men to live a moral life . . .

Fellenberg subsequently sent several of his pupils to New Lanark to see Owen's work with their own eyes. Hippolyte Chambrier, in his letters to Fellenberg, gives us some remarkable information about what he saw. In Owen's plans and institutions he found 'much that was attractive, instructive, and truly great and impressive. Mr Owen, of course, expresses his views and the theory behind them in such a manner as very easily to offend the views of the majority of people, whilst he is often expressing their own opinions in different words'. Owen did not comprehend human nature in its full profundity and many-sidedness—a judgment that was elaborated upon by another Hofwyl product, Hippolyte de Bercher, who felt that Owen embraced the whole of humanity, but stifled the individual. Chambrier told his Hofwyl foster father that Owen regarded agriculture as the only sure basis for human society, but he would combine it with industry. 'These communities should also be based exclusively on agriculture, but should contain the machinery needed to produce clothing and other primary needs, and in this way these mechanical powers would supply the needs, and not bring about the unhappiness, of mankind.' He mentions appreciatively that Owen intended to gamble his entire fortune on the establishment of a new Community three hours' ride from New Lanark. 'Everything is ready, and building is to start this very year; two thousand people are to live there together, and there have been some very respectable applications to join and live there; great attention is to be paid to the education of the children; and the necessary factories are to be built, so that these people will be independent of the outside world, of business and commerce. It is reckoned that it will not take many years for them to be in a position to pay off the initial loans contracted by the establishment.' New Lanark itself made a deep impression on Chambrier, although he could not fail to see the eccentric and exaggerated sides of Owen's optimism. Since Owen had been at work, there had not been a single punishable crime committed. The children were supervised and brought up in ways of friendship from their second year. Their games were gradually turned into instruction, which was given from the age of ten until sixteen or seventeen. It lasted two to three hours; the remainder of the time was spent in the factory. Owen himself said 'that factory work is the basis of everything, and is, in fact, the greatest possible evil, which can be mitigated but not abolished'; it could not be dispensed with. The overall judgment on the prophet of New Lanark was completely favourable: 'I have not yet found him once guilty of any inconsistency, and everything he does is in harmony with his principles; it would be difficult to be more disinterested and more liberal, for whatever his views on religion might be, every sect is tolerated and shown favour, and he acquiesces in all existing customs. He talks to everyone without reserve and acts on principle as often as possible. This is, however, much more possible in England than elsewhere.'

From J. J. Boucard, owner of a spinning mill in Gebweiler, and a former student at Hofwyl, also came news about New Lanark. He believed that Owen had, of course, a great deal of success to his credit, but his plans for world-betterment were going too far. His 'atheism' and his denial of free-will must be rejected. Fellenberg himself saw as important in Owen's work only the simple, practical way to satisfy social needs . . .

APPENDIX D

Bibliography

NOTE

THIS bibliography (with the exception of the section on material in Russian) has been confined to works acknowledged or quoted in the text, and a small number of other valuable sources considered to have been directly of use (in which case an indication of the useful content of the work is sometimes given).

The National Library of Wales *A Bibliography of Robert Owen, The Socialist 1771–1858* is the fullest available, though it is in need of revision, to remove inaccuracies, and to include material that has appeared since the second edition (1925), and omissions from the period before that date. *Robert Owen, 1771–1858. A New Bibliographical Study* by Shigeru Goto (mistakenly given as Roto in the London Bibliography), published in Japan in 1932, is a codification of works *by* Owen, but only the bibliographical references themselves are in English.

I. MSS SOURCES

Co-operative Union. A collection of letters from and to Owen in the possession of the Co-operative Union, Holyoake House, Manchester, containing some 3,000 items. CUL has a good index.

Meltham and Meltham Mills Co-operative Society. A collection of trading ledgers and other material.

Newcastle Central Reference Library. 2 vols. of papers read and other records of the Newcastle Literary and Philosophical Society, including a catalogue of books, 1798.

University of London, Goldsmiths' Library. A collection of MSS, newspaper cuttings and other material, collected by William Pare for a biography of Owen (from the library of the Family Welfare Association).

II. NINETEENTH CENTURY NEWSPAPERS AND PERIODICALS

A collection of newspaper cuttings relating to Owenite Co-operation from the library of William Pare (mostly 1820–30), including letters by Pare, Thompson and Owen (sources and dates are unfortunately not given). Goldsmiths' Library.

Single copies

The Annual Register . . . for the Year 1792.
Journal of the Royal Society of Arts, Supplement to Vol. II, No. 63, February 3, 1854.
The Prompter, No. 14, February 12, 1831.
The Working Bee and Herald of the Hodsonian Community Society, Vol. I, No. 34, March 7, 1840.

Files

The Birmingham Co-operative Herald.
The Birmingham Labour Exchange Gazette.
Blackwood's Edinburgh Magazine.
Bronterre's National Reformer, In Government, Law, Property, Religion and Morals.
The Co-operator.
The Crisis.
The Economist (1821–2).
The Edinburgh Review.
The Educational Circular and Communist Apostle.
The Fleet Papers.
Herald to the Trades' Advocate, and Co-operative Journal.
The Hull Advertiser (for 1832).
The Lancashire Co-operator (later *The Lancashire and Yorkshire Co-operator; or, Useful Classes' Advocate*).
The Mirror of Truth (only 2 issues appeared).
The New Moral World.
The North British Review.
The Philanthropist.
Politics for the People.
The Poor Man's Guardian.
The Quarterly Review.
The Register for the First Society of Adherents to Divine Revelation at Orbiston in Lanarkshire . . .
The Westminster Review.

III. WORKS BY ROBERT OWEN

A large percentage of the many addresses, manifestos and other material by Owen is quoted from the above MSS and newspaper sources, and the following:

The Life of Robert Owen, written by himself, with selections from his Writings and Correspondence, Vol. I, London, 1857. The edition of 1920, edited by M. Beer, omits the small number of appendices included in Vol. I.

A Supplementary Appendix to the first Volume of the Life of Robert Owen. Containing a Series of Reports, Addresses, Memorials, and other Documents, referred to in that Volume. 1803–1820. Vol. I.A., London, 1858 (containing some fifty items).

A New View of Society and other Writings by Robert Owen, with an Introduction by G. D. H. Cole, Everyman's Library, London, 1927, edition of 1949.

The most useful documents by Owen not in these last three include:

The Address of Robert Owen delivered at the great public meeting held at the National Equitable Labour Exchange . . . May 1, 1833 (reprinted in *The Crisis*, May 11, 1833).

Address to the Infant-school Societies, and to the Patrons of Infant-schools, in *Addresses of Robert Owen*, London, 1830.

Address to the Operative Builders, August 26, 1833 (reprinted in *The Crisis*, September 7, 1833).

Association for Removing the Causes of Ignorance and Poverty by Education and Employment, *Address to All Classes in the State from the Governor, Directors, and Committee of the Association*, January 14, 1832.

The Book of the New Moral World (published in parts between 1836 and 1844).

An Explanation of the Cause of the Distress which pervades the Civilized Parts of the World, in *The Economist*, August 11, 1821 (also in Bacon, *A Report of the Transactions at the Holkham Sheep-Shearing*, see below).

Institution of the Intelligent and Well-Disposed of the Industrious Classes, founded by the Association to Remove Ignorance and Poverty by Education and Employment, *Prospectus of the System of Education to be pursued in the Schools attached to the Institution*, London, 1833.

Letters on Education, as it is and as it ought to be, addressed to the teachers of the human race in all countries, London, 1851.

Letters on Government as it is and as it ought to be, London, 1851.

Manifesto of Robert Owen, the Discoverer and Founder of the Rational System of Society, and of the Rational Religion, London, 1840.

Outline of the Rational System of Society, London, 1830.

A Proclamation by Robert Owen, London, March 1, 1848 (in Pare MS 578).

The Signs of the Times; or, the Approach of the Millennium. Address to the Tories, Whigs, Radicals and Chartists; Churchmen, Catholics, Dissenters and Infidels, London, 1841.

Six Lectures delivered in Manchester previously to a discussion between Robert Owen and J. H. Roebuck, Manchester, 1837.

Two discourses on a new system of society; as delivered in the Hall of Representatives of the United States, Louisville, 1825 (also in *The New Moral World*, January 9, July 30 and August, 6, 1836).

IV. BOOKS, PAMPHLETS AND OTHER MATERIAL
PUBLISHED BEFORE 1858

Aiton, Rev. John, *Mr Owen's Objections to Christianity, and New View of Society and Education, Refuted, by a Plain Statement of Facts*, Edinburgh, 1824.

Allen, William, *Life of —, with Selections from his Correspondence*, London, 1846.

Bacon, Richard N., *A Report of the Transactions at the Holkham Sheep-Shearing, on . . . July 2, 3, 4 and 5, being the forty-third Anniversary of that Meeting*, Norwich, 1821 (containing Owen's reply to a toast, and a paper entitled *An Attempt to explain the Cause to a Commercial and other Difficulties . . .*, later published in *The Economist* as *An Explanation of the Cause of the Distress*, see above).

Baines, Edward (Jun.), *The Social, Educational, and Religious State of the Manufacturing Districts*, London, 1843. (The Voluntaryist case.)

Bamford, Samuel, *Passages in the Life of a Radical*, 1842–8, edited by Henry Dunckley, London, 1893.

Bell, Rev. Dr Andrew, *The Madras School, or Elements of Tuition*, London, 1808.

——*The Wrongs of Children: or a Practical Vindication of Children from the Injustice done them in early Nurture and Education*, London, 1819.

Bernard, Sir Thomas, *The Barrington School; being an illustration of the Principles, Practices, and Effects, of the New System of Instruction, in facilitating the Religious and Moral Instruction of the Poor*, London, 1812.

——*Of the Education of the Poor* (a digest of the Reports of the Society for Bettering the Condition of the Poor), London, 1809.

Biber, E., *Henry Pestalozzi, and his Plan of Education*, London, 1833.

Boswell, James, *The Life of Samuel Johnson*, 1791, O.U.P. edition of 1927.

Bray, John Francis, *Labour's Wrongs and Labour's Remedy or The Age of Might and the Age of Right*, 1839, reprinted 1931.

British and Foreign Philanthropic Society, *Proceedings of the First General Meeting of the — for the Permanent Relief of the Labouring Classes; held . . . on Saturday, the 1st of June, 1822*, London, 1822.

British and Foreign School Society, *Manual of the System of Primary Instruction pursued in the model schools of the —*, London, 1834.

Brougham, Henry, Lord, *Political Philosophy*, London, 1853.

——*Practical Observations upon the Education of the People, addressed to the working classes and their employers*, London, 1825.

Brown, John, *Remarks on the Plans and Publications of Robert Owen, Esq. of New Lanark*, Edinburgh, 1817.

Cappe, Catharine, *An Account of Two Charity Schools for the Education of Girls*, York, 1800.

Carlyle, Thomas, *Chartism*, 1839.

——*Sartor Resartus*, 1833-4.

Central Society of Education, second publication, London, 1838 (particularly 'Schools for the Industrious Classes', and Porter, Mrs G. R., 'On Infant Schools for the Upper and Middle Classes').

Chavannes, D. A., *Rapport sur l'Institut d'Education des Pauvres à Hofwyl*, Paris and Geneva, 1813.

'Christianus', *Mr Owen's Proposed Villages for the Poor shown to be Highly Favourable to Christianity*, London, 1819.

Combe, Abram, *The Life and Dying Testimony of — in favour of Robt. Owen's New Views of Man and Society* (largely written by George Combe, edited by Alex Campbell), London, 1844.

——*Metaphorical Sketches of the Old and New Systems, with Opinions on interesting subjects*, Edinburgh, 1823.

——*Observations on the Old and New Views, and their effects on the conduct of individuals, as manifested in the proceedings of the Edinburgh Christian Instructor and Mr Owen*, Edinburgh, 1823.

——*The Religious Creed of the New System, with an Explanatory Catechism, and Appeal in Favour of True Religion*, Edinburgh, 1824.

Combe, George, *The Constitution of Man considered in Relation to External Objects*, Edinburgh, 1828, edition of 1836.

——'Phrenological Analysis of Mr Owen's New Views of Society', *The Phrenological Journal and Miscellany*, Vol. I, December 1823-August 1824.

Concordium, *A Brief Account of the First —, or Harmonious Industrial College, A Home for the Affectionate, Skilful, and Industrious*, Ham Common, Surrey, n.d. (dated 1843-4 by GL).

Co-operative Congresses, Reports and Papers, 1831-2 (Proceedings of the first three congresses), GL.

Davis, William, *Hints to Philanthropists; or a Collective View of Practical Means of Improving the Condition of the Poor and Labouring Classes of Society*, Bath, 1821.

Detrosier, Rowland, *An Address delivered at the New Mechanics' Institution, Pool-Street, Manchester, on Wednesday Evening, December 30, 1829*, Manchester, n.d.

——*An Address, Delivered to the Members of the New Mechanics' Institution, Manchester, on Friday, March 25, 1831, on the Necessity of an Extension of Moral and Political Instruction Among the Working Classes*, Manchester n.d. (reprinted 1832 and 1834 with a *Memoir of the Late Rowland Detrosier*).

——*An Address on the Advantages of the Intended Mechanics' Hall of Science, delivered at the Manchester New Mechanics' Institution, on Saturday Evening, December 31, 1831, Manchester, n.d.*

Doherty, John, *A Letter to the Members of the National Association for the Protection of Labour*, Manchester, 1831 (possibly early 1832).

Dyer, George, *The Complaints of the Poor People of England*, 1793.

Dyer, J. C., *Remarks on Education*, Manchester, 1850.

Engels, F., *The Condition of the Working Class in England in 1844*, 1845, edition translated and edited by W. O. Henderson and W. H. Chaloner, Oxford, 1958.

Gauteron, F. L., *Coup d'Oeil sur l'Influence à espérer des Etablissemens d'Hofwyl*, Paris and Geneva, n.d. (Chavannes, see above, in 1813 describes it as published 'il y a quelques années'—probably 1809 or shortly after).

Glover, Robert Mortimer, *Remarks on the History of the Literary and Philosophical Society of Newcastle upon Tyne*, Newcastle, 1844.

Godwin, William, *The Enquirer*, London, 1797.

——*Enquiry concerning Political Justice and its Influence on Morals and Happiness*, London, 1793, facsimile edition edited by F. E. L. Priestley, Toronto, 1946.

——*'s Political Justice, A Reprint of the Essay on Property*, edited with a Prefatory Note by H. S. Salt, London, 1890, edition of 1949.

Hamilton, Richard Winter, *The Institutions of Popular Education. An Essay: to which the Manchester Prize was Adjudged*, Leeds and London, 1845.

Harrison, George, *Education respectfully proposed and recommended as the surest means within the power of government to diminish the frequency of crimes*, London, 1803.

Hazlitt, William, *Memoirs of the Late Thomas Holcroft*, 1816, *Complete Works of William Hazlitt*, London, 1932, Vol. 3.

——'On People with One Idea', *Table Talk*, 1821, Library of Classics edition, n.d.

——'On the Causes of Methodism', *The Round Table, Complete Works of William Hazlitt*, London, 1930.

——*Political Essays*, London, 1819.

——*The Spirit of the Age*, London, 1825.

Helvétius, C. A., *D l'Esprit*, 1758, London edition of 1776.

Hendley, W., *A Defence of the Charity-Schools*, London, 1725.

Hill, Frederic, *National Education*, London, 1836.

Hofwyl, *Extrait du second Cahier des Feuilles d'Economie rurale d'*—, Hofwyl, 1809.

Irvine, Andrew, *Reflections on the Education of the Poor*, London, 1815.

Jones, Margaret, E. M., *A Brief Account of the Home and Colonial Training Institution, and of the Pestalozzian System, as taught and practised in its Schools*, London, n.d.

King, William, *Gothic Hall Labour Bank*, London, n.d.

——*Owenite Leaflets* (a collection of 8, GL), 1831.

Lancaster, Joseph, *An Appeal for Justice in the Cause of Ten Thousand Poor Children*, 1806, third edition of 1807.

——*Improvements in Education as it respects the Industrious Classes of the Community*, London, 1806.

Library of Entertaining Knowledge, *The Pursuit of Knowledge under Difficulties*, London, 1830.

Locke, John, *Some Thoughts concerning Education*, London, 1690, edition of 1752.

Lovett, William, and Collins, John, *Chartism; A New Organization of the People*, London, 1841.

M'Gavin, William, *The Fundamental Principles of the New Lanark System, Exposed, in a Series of Letters to Robert Owen, Esq.*, Glasgow, 1824.

——*Letters on Mr Owen's New System*, Glasgow, 1823.

MacNab, Henry Gray, *The New Views of Mr Owen of Lanark Impartially Examined*, London, 1819.

Malthus, T. R., *An Essay on the Principle of Population*, London, 1798, Additions to the Fourth and Former Editions, 1817.

Manchester Board of Health, *Proceedings of the* —, Manchester, n.d.

Mandeville, Bernard de, *An Essay on Charity and Charity-Schools*, in *The Fable of the Bees*, second edition, London, 1723.

Martineau, Harriet, *The History of the Thirty Years' Peace, 1816–1846*, London, 1849–50, revised edition of 1858.

Mason, John, *Self-Knowledge. A Treatise, showing the Nature and Benefit of that Important Science, and the Way to attain it*, London, 1745, edition of 1778.

Mayo, Charles, *Observations on the Establishment and Direction of Infant Schools*, London, 1826.

——and Miss, *Practical Remarks on Infant Education*, London, 1837, edition of 1849, revised and enlarged.

More, Hannah, *Hints Towards Forming the Character of a Young Princess*, London, 1805.

——*The Poetical Works*, London, 1843 (particularly 'The Riot').

——*Remarks on the Speech of M. Dupont, made in the National Convention of France, on the Subjects of Religion and Public Education*, London, 1793.

——*Strictures on the Modern System of Female Education with a View of the Principles and Conduct Prevalent among Women of Rank and Fortune*, London, 1799.

Morgan, William, *Memoirs of the Life of the Rev. Richard Price*, London, 1815. (For the impact of the French Revolution in Britain.)

Newcastle upon Tyne, *A Brief Account of the Literary and Philosophical Society and of the New Institution of —*, by a Member of the Society, Newcastle, 1809.

The New Court, No. 1—The Records of the New Court, established by The First Society of, &c. for the Extinction of Disputes, 22d March 1825. (Relates to Orbiston, GL.)

Owen, *Mr —'s Proposed Arrangements for the Distressed Working Classes Shown to be Consistent with Sound Principles of Political Economy*, London, 1819. (Discusses Adam Smith and Robert Owen.)

——*R. — at New Lanark; with a Variety of Interesting Anecdotes: being a brief and authentic Narrative of the Character and Conduct of Mr Owen while Proprietor of New Lanark*, by one formerly a Teacher at New Lanark, Manchester, 1839.

Owen, Robert Dale, *An Outline of the System of Education at New Lanark*, Glasgow, 1824.

Paine, Thomas, *The Rights of Man*, 1791–2, *The Writings of Thomas Paine*, collected and edited by M. D. Conway, London, 1906.

Pare, William, *The Claims of Capital and Labour*, London, 1854.

Peacock, Thomas Love, *Crotchet Castle*, one volume edition of *The Novels of Thomas Love Peacock*, London, 1948.

Priestley, Joseph, *A Discourse: The Proper Object of Education in the Present State of the World*, April 27, 1791, *The Theological and Miscellaneous Works of Joseph Priestley*, edited by J. T. Rutt, London, 1831, Vol. XXV.

——*,An Essay on the First Principles of Government, and on the Nature of Political, Civil, and Religious Liberty*, London, 1771.

Percival, Thomas, *The Works, Literary, Moral, Philosophical, and Medical, of —*, M.D., London, 1807.

Pole, Thomas, *Observations relative to Infant Schools, designed to point*

out their usefulness to the Children of the Poor, to their Parents, and to
Society at large, Bristol, 1823.

Prentice, Archibald, Historical Sketches and Personal Recollections of
Manchester, intended to illustrate the progress of public opinion from 1792
to 1832, London, 1851.

Reeve, Clara, Plans of Education; with Remarks on the Systems of other
Writers, London, 1792.

Rengger, A., Rapport sur l'Institut d'Education des Pauvres à Hofwyl,
Paris and Geneva, 1815.

Rousseau, Jean-Jacques, Considérations sur le Gouvernement de Pologne,
1771, Collection Complète des Oeuvres, Geneva, 1782, Vol. II.

——Emile, 1762, ibid., Vol. IV.

Rules and Orders of the Mechanics' Institution, for Deptford and its Vicinity,
for the Promotion of Useful Knowledge among all Persons, but more
especially the Working Classes. Established Michaelmas 1825.

Rules and Regulations of the Mechanics' Institution, of Darlington and its
Vicinity. Established the 13th Day of May, 1825.

Rules for the Management of the Literary and Scientific Mechanics' Institute,
established in Hull, June 1, 1825.

Rules for the Observance of the London Co-operative Society, 1825.

Rules of the Farnley Tyas Reading Society for the Promotion of Useful
Knowledge.

Smith, Adam, The Wealth of Nations, London, 1776, The World's Classics
edition of 1904.

Society for the Diffusion of Useful Knowledge, Reports and Prospectus,
London, 1829.

——The Working Man's Companion. The Results of Machinery, namely,
cheap Production and Increased Employment, London, 1831.

Somerville, Alexander, The Autobiography of a Working Man, 1848,
edited with an Introduction by John Carswell, London, 1951.

Spencer, Rev. Thomas, The Pillars of the Church of England, pamphlet
No. 1, London, 1841.

——Remarks on National Education, pamphlet No. 5, London, 1843.

Stow, David, The Training System of Education, Glasgow, 1836, edition
of 1845.

Stowell, Rev. Hugh, A Second Letter to the Inhabitants of Manchester
on the Proposed System of National of Education, Manchester, 1837.

Sunday School Tracts (begun 1792). Particularly The History of Charles
Crawford (No. 1, January 1806) and The Plough-Boys' Lesson (No. 20,
n.d.).

Temple of Free Enquiry. A Report of the Proceedings consequent on laying
the Foundation Stone of the Manchester Hall of Science, with an Address

242

by Robert Owen, reprinted from No. 43, New Series, of *The New Moral World*, Leeds, 1839.

Thompson, William, *An Inquiry into the Principles of the Distribution of Wealth most conducive to Human Happiness*, London, 1824.

Trimmer, Sarah, *The Oeconomy of Charity; or, an Address to Ladies concerning Sunday Schools; the Establishment of Schools of Industry under Female Inspection; and the Distribution of Voluntary Benefactions. To which is added an Appendix containing an Account of the Sunday-Schools in Old Brentford*, London, 1787.

——*The Servants' Friend*, London, 1787.

Turner, William (Jr.), *Speculations on the Propriety of Attempting the Establishment of a Literary Society in Newcastle*, Newcastle, 1792.

The Unique: A Series of Portraits of Eminent Persons. With their Memoirs. No. 19, Robert Owen, Esq., London, n.d.

Watson, Robert Spence, *The History of the Literary and Philosophical Society of Newcastle-upon-Tyne (1793–1896)*, London, 1897.

Wesley, John, *A Thought on the Manner of Educating Children*, 1783, *Works*, Vol. XIII.

Wilson, William, *The System of Infants' Schools*, London, 1825.

Wollstonecraft, Mary, *A Vindication of the Rights of Woman*, London, 1792, Everyman's Library edition of 1955.

V. LATER NINETEENTH CENTURY SOURCES

Aveling, Edward and Eleanor M., *Shelley's Socialism*, 1888, for private circulation, reprinted Manchester, 1947.

Axon, William, E. A., *The Annals of Manchester*, London, 1886.

Bain, Alexander, *James Mill. A Biography*, London, 1882.

Balmforth, Owen, *Huddersfield Past and Present; in its Social, Industrial and Educational Aspects*, Huddersfield, 1894.

Bartley, George C. T., *The Schools for the People*, London, 1871.

Blyth, Edmund Kell, *Life of William Ellis (founder of the Birkbeck Schools)*, London, 1889.

Booth, A. J., *Robert Owen, the Founder of Socialism*, London, 1869.

Butler, Mrs Josephine E., *The Life of Jean Frédéric Oberlin, Pastor of the Ban de la Roche*, London, 1886.

Collet, C. D., *History of the Taxes on Knowledge. Their Origin and Repeal*, London, 1899, Thinker's Library Edition, 1936.

Colquhoun, John Campbell, *William Wilberforce: His Friends and his Times*, London, 1867.

Cooper, Thomas, *The Life of — written by himself*, London, 1879.

Craik, Henry, *The State in its Relation to Education*, London, 1884, extended edition of 1896.

Croft, W. R., *The History of the Factory Movement, or Oastler and his Times*, Huddersfield, 1888.

Davies, David P., *A Short Sketch of the Life and Labours of Ernest Jones, Chartist, Barrister, and Poet, to which is added several of his Poems*, Liverpool, 1897.

Dictionary of National Biography, entries on Robert Owen and George Combe by Leslie Stephen.

Dolléans, Edouard, *Le Chartisme (1831–1848)*, Paris, 1912–13, nouvelle édition refondue, 1949.

Dorling, William, *Henry Vincent: A Biographical Sketch*, London, 1879.

Ellis, William, *An Address to Teachers on the Importance of Imparting the Principles of Social Science to Children*, London, 1859.

——*An Address to Teachers on the Laws of Conduct in Industrial Life, and on the Method of Imparting Instruction therein in our Primary Schools*, London, 1870.

——*Education as a Means of Preventing Destitution; with Exemplifications from the Teaching the Conditions of Well-being and the Principles and Applications of Economical Science at the Birkbeck Schools*, London, 1851.

——*Where Must we Look for the further Prevention of Crime?*, London, 1857.

Engels, F., *Anti-Dühring*, 1878, English edition of 1934.

Espinasse, Francis, *Lancashire Worthies*, Second Series, London, 1877.

Fraser, William, *Memoir of the Life of David Stow: Founder of the Training System of Education*, London, 1868.

Frost, Thomas, *Forty Years' Recollections: Literary and Political*, London, 1880 (for Queenwood and Ham Common).

Hodgson, W. B., *Address to the Watt Institute and School of Arts, April 1879*, Edinburgh, 1879.

——*Exaggerated Estimates of Reading and Writing as Means of Education*, London, 1868, edition published in Reading, 1875.

——*What is Capital?*, reprinted from the Transactions of the Devonshire Association for the Advancement of Science, Literature and Art, 1868.

Holyoake, George Jacob, *Bygones Worth Remembering*, London, 1905.

——*History of Co-operation*, London, 1875–9, edition of 1908.

——*History of the Rochdale Pioneers 1844–1892*, London, 1893.

——*The Life and Character of Richard Carlile*, London, n.d.

——*Life and Last Days of Robert Owen, of New Lanark*, London, 1866.

——*Life of Joseph Rayner Stephens*, London, 1881.

——*Sixty Years of an Agitator's Life*, London, 1892, edition of 1902.

Home and Colonial School Society, *Pestalozzi and his Principles*, 1864.

Howitt, Mary, *An Autobiography*, edited by her daughter, Margaret Howitt, London, 1889.

Jolly, William (ed.), *Education. Its Principles and Practice as Developed by George Combe*, London, 1879.

Kaufman, Rev. M., *Utopias; or, Schemes of Social Improvement. From Sir Thomas More to Karl Marx*, London, 1879.

Kay-Shuttleworth, Sir James, *Thoughts and Suggestions on certain Social Problems, contained chiefly in addresses to meetings of workmen in Lancashire*, London, 1873.

Kirkup, Thomas, *A History of Socialism*, London, 1892, edition of 1920, revised and largely rewritten by Edward R. Pease.

Leitch, James, *Practical Educationists and their Systems of Teaching*, Glasgow, 1876.

Lovett, William, *The Life and Struggles of — in his Pursuit of Bread, Knowledge and Freedom*, London, 1876.

——*Social and Political Morality*, London, 1853.

Manchester Literary and Philosophical Society, *Memoirs and Proceedings of the —*, begun in 1785.

Marshall, Mrs Julian, *The Life and Letters of Mary Wollstonecraft Shelley*, London, 1889.

Martineau, Harriet, *Autobiography*, London, 1877.

——*Biographical Sketches 1852–1868*, London, 1870. (Including Brougham, Whately, George Combe, Owen and Lady Byron.)

Marx, K., *Capital*, 1867, English edition translation by Samuel Moore and Edward Aveling, and edited by Frederick Engels, 1887, reprinted Moscow, 1954 (Volume I).

——and Engels, F., *The Holy Family, or Critique of Critical Critique*, 1844, English translation published in Moscow, 1956.

Menger, Dr Anton, *Right of the Whole Produce of Labour*, 1886, with an Introduction by Prof. H. S. Foxwell, London, 1899.

Mill, John Stuart, *Autobiography*, London, 1873, The World's Classics edition, 1924, with six hitherto unpublished speeches.

Moret, Marie, *Histoire de l'Association Agricole de Ralahine. Résumé traduit des documents de M. E.-T. Craig, Secrétaire et Administrateur de l'Association*, Saint-Quentin, 1882.

Nodal, J. H., 'Coleridge in Manchester', *Notes and Queries*, 5th Series, Vol. VII, March 3, 1877. With subsequent correspondence from Hyde Clarke and John E. Bailey.

O'Brien, James Bronterre, *The Rise, Progress, and Phases of Human Slavery: How it came into the World, and How it shall be made to Go Out*. London, 1885. (A posthumous compilation from 1850 letters, useful on Chartism and social rights.)

——and Owen, Robert, *State Socialism*, London, 1885. (A posthumous compilation.)

Owen, Robert, *Report of the Proceedings of the Festival in Commemoration of the Centenary Birthday of* —, *the Philanthropist, held . . . London, May 16, 1871*, London, 1871.

Owen, Robert Dale, *Threading My Way, twenty-seven Years of Auto-biography*, London, 1874.

Packard, F. A., *Life of Robert Owen*. Philadelphia, 1866.

Peel, Frank, *The Risings of the Luddites, Chartists and Plugdrawers*, Brighouse, 1888.

Rogers, J. D., 'Robert Owen,' *Dictionary of Political Economy*, edited by R. H. I. Palgrave, London, 1899.

Roscoe, Sir Henry E., *John Dalton and the Rise of Modern Chemistry*, London, 1895.

Rose, J. Holland, 'The Unstamped Press, 1815–1836', *English Historical Review*, Vol. XII, No. XLVIII, October 1897.

Ruskin, John, *Time and Tide*, London, 1867. ('Of Public Education irrespective of Class Distinction'.)

Sargant, William Lucas, *Robert Owen and his Social Philosophy*, London, 1860.

Smiles, Samual, *Self-Help. With Illustrations of Conduct and Perseverance*, London, 1859, edition of 1908.

Smith, Edward, *The Story of the English Jacobins: being an Account of the Persons Implicated in the Charges of High Treason, 1794*, London, 1881.

Smith, W. Anderson, *'Shepherd' Smith the Universalist. The Story of a Mind. Being a Life of the Rev. James E. Smith, M.A.*, London, 1892.

Stanley, Arthur Penrhyn, *The Life and Correspondence of Thomas Arnold, D.D.*, London, 1844, edition of 1858.

Shaftesbury, *A Memoir of the Right Hon. the Earl of* —, *K.G.*, Compiled from Original Sources, under the Direction of the Editor of the 'Record', London, 1885.

Toynbee, Arnold *Lectures on the Industrial Revolution of the Eighteenth Century in England*, London, 1884, edition of 1916. (Particularly 'The Education of Co-operators'.)

Wallas, Graham, *The Life of Francis Place*, London, 1898, revised edition of 1918.

Whately, Richard, Archbishop of Dublin, *Miscellaneous Lectures and Reviews*, London, 1861. (Particularly 'On the Supposed Dangers of a Little Learning'.)

Wilberforce, William, *Private Papers of* —, collected and edited, with a Preface, by A. M. Wilberforce, London, 1897.

Williams Secular School, *First Annual Report of the* —, Edinburgh, 1850.

VI. TWENTIETH CENTURY SOURCES

Articles

Black, A., 'Education before Rochdale' (I. 'First Attempts Helped to Keep Movement Alive'. II. 'The Owenites and the Halls of Science'), *The Co-operative Reveiw*, Vol. XXVIII, No. 6, June 1954, and Vol. XXIX, No. 2, February 1955.

Cavenagh, F. A., 'Lord Brougham and the Society for the Diffusion of Useful Knowledge', *The Journal of Adult Education*, Vol. IV, No. 1, October 1929, p. 11.

Fraser, Miss E. M., 'Robert Owen in Manchester, 1787–1800', *Memoirs and Proceedings of the Manchester Literary & Philosophical Society*, Vol. LXXXII, 1937–8.

Mason, H. G., 'John Locke's Proposals on Work-house Schools', *The Durham Research Review*, Vol. VI, No. 13, September 1962, pp. 8–16.

Michaels, Peter, 'Robert Owen: Visionary of a New Society', *The UNESCO Courier*, October 1958.

Mill, John Stuart, 'Two Speeches on Population,' *The Journal of Adult Education*, Vol. IV, No. 1, October 1929 (from manuscripts in the possession of H. J. Laski).

Milliband, Ralph, 'The Politics of Robert Owen', *Journal of the History of Ideas*, Vol. XV, No. 2, April 1954.

Oliver, W. H., 'The Labour Exchange Phase of the Co-operative Movement,' *Oxford Economic Papers*, Vol. 10, No. 3, October 1958.

——'Robert Owen and the English Working-Class Movements,' *History Today*, November 1958.

Plummer, Alfred, 'The Place of Bronterre O'Brien in the Working Class Movement,' *Economic History Review*, Vol. II, No. 1, 1929.

Read, Donald, 'Robert Owen: From Manchester to Utopia,' *The Manchester Guardian*, November 17, 1958.

Sjölin, Walter, 'New Light on Robert Owen (Poetic Vein in the Reformer's Personality),' *The Co-operative Review*, Vol. XXIX, No. 2, February 1955.

Theses

Black, Archibald Muir, 'The Educational Work of Robert Owen,' Ph.D., St Andrews.

Gilbert Amy Margaret, 'The Work of Lord Brougham for Education in England', Ph.D., Pennsylvania (copy at Swansea).

Hope, Royden Birtley, 'Dr Thomas Percival, A Medical Pioneer and Social Reformer, 1740–1804,' M.A., Manchester.

Jones, R. Alun, 'Knowledge Chartism. A Study of the Influence of Chartism on Nineteenth Century Educational Development in Great Britain,' M.A., Birmingham.

Books and Pamphlets (a selected list)

Aldridge, Alfred Owen, *Man of Reason. The Life of Thomas Paine*, London, 1960.

Armytage, W. H. G., *Heavens Below: Utopian Experiments in England 1560–1960*, London, 1961.

Aspinall, Arthur, *Lord Brougham and the Whig Party*, Manchester, 1927.

Barker, Ambrose G., *Henry Hetherington 1792–1849. A Pioneer in the Freethought and Working Class Struggles of a Hundred Years Ago for the Freedom of the Press*, London, n.d.

Bastide, Ch., *John Locke. Ses Théories Politiques et leur Influence en Angleterre*, Paris, 1907.

Beales, H. L., *The Early English Socialists*, London, 1933.

Beer, Max, *A History of British Socialism*, London, 1919, edition of 1948.

Bennett, C. A., *History of Manual and Industrial Education up to 1870*, Illinois, 1926.

Bestor, Arthur Eugene, (Jr.), *Backwoods Utopias. The Sectarian and Owenite Phases of Communitarian Socialism in America, 1663–1829*, Philadelphia, 1950.

——(ed.), *Education and Reform at New Harmony (Correspondence of William Maclure and Marie Duclos Fretageot 1820–33)*, Indianapolis, 1948.

Binns, H. B., *A Century of Education. Being the Centenary History of the British and Foreign School Society, 1808–1908*, London, 1908.

Birchenough, Charles, *History of Elementary Education in England and Wales from 1800 to the Present Day*, London, 1938.

Bland, A. E., Brown, P. A., and Tawney, R. H., *English Economic History: Select Documents*, London, 1920.

Brailsford, H. N., *Shelley, Godwin and Their Circle*, London, 1914.

Bray, John Francis, *A Voyage from Utopia*, edited with an Introduction by M. F. Lloyd-Pritchard, London, 1957.

Briggs, Asa, *The Age of Improvement*, London, 1959.

——(ed.), *Chartist Studies*, London, 1959.

——*Robert Owen in Retrospect*, Co-operative College Papers No. 6, Loughborough, 1959.

Brinton, Crane, *The Political Ideas of the English Romanticists*, Oxford, 1926.

Brown, Ford K., *The Life of William Godwin*, London, 1926.

Brown, Philip Anthony, *The French Revolution in English History*, London, 1918.

Brown, W. Henry, *Brighton's Co-operative Advance, 1828–1938*, Manchester, n.d.

——*A Century of Liverpool Co-operation*, Liverpool, n.d.

Butler, J. R. M., *The Passing of the Great Reform Bill*, London, 1914.

Carpenter, S. C., *Church and People, 1789–1889*, London, 1933.

Cestre, Charles, *John Thelwall. A Pioneer of Democracy and Social Reform in England during the French Revolution*, London, 1906.

Chaloner, W. H., *Robert Owen, Peter Drinkwater and the Early Factory System in Manchester, 1788–1800*, Manchester, 1954.

Clayton, Joseph, *Robert Owen: Pioneer of Social Reforms*, London, 1908.

Clive, John, *Scotch Reviewers: The Edinburgh Review, 1802–1815*, London, 1957.

Cobban, Alfred, *In Search of Humanity. The Role of the Enlightenment in Modern History*, London, 1960.

Cobbett, William, *A History of the Last Hundred Days of English Freedom*, with an Introduction by J. L. Hammond, London, 1921 (reprinted from *The Weekly Political Register*).

——*The Opinions of —*, edited by G. D. H. and Margaret Cole, London, 1944.

Cole, G. D. H., *Attempts at General Union—A Study in British Trade Union History, 1818–1834*, London, 1953.

——*Chartist Portraits*, London, 1941.

——*The Life of Robert Owen*, London, 1925. (The edition of 1930 has a longer, modified Introduction assessing 'Owen's position in the Development of Socialist Thought'.)

——*Persons and Periods*, London, 1938, Pelican Books edition of 1945. (The Article on 'Robert Owen and Owenism' is an enlargement of the Introduction to Cole's edition of *A New View*.)

——*Socialist Thought: The Forerunners, 1789–1850*, London, 1953.

——and Postgate, Raymond, *The Common People, 1746–1946*, London, 1938, edition of 1949.

Cole, Margaret, *Robert Owen of New Lanark*, London, 1953.

Compayré, Gabriel, *Pestalozzi and Elementary Education*, 1904, English edition, London, 1908.

Connell, W. F., *The Educational Thought and Influence of Matthew Arnold*, London, 1950. (For Lovett, Ellis and the secularists.)

Cullen, Alexander, *Adventures in Socialism. New Lanark Establishment and Orbiston Community*, Glasgow, 1910.

Cumming, Ian, *Helvétius, His Life and Place in the History of Educational Thought*, London, 1955.

Daniels, George W., *The Early English Cotton Industry*, Manchester, 1920.

Dobbs, A. E., *Education and Social Movements, 1700–1850*, London, 1919.

Driver, Cecil, *Tory Radical, the Life of Richard Oastler*, New York, 1946.

Eliot, George, *The George Eliot Letters*, edited by Gordon S. Haight, Yale, 1954.

Fichter, Joseph H., S.J., *Roots of Change*, New York, 1939.

Fleisher, David, *William Godwin. A Study in Liberalism*, London, 1951.

Green, J. A., *The Educational Ideas of Pestalozzi*, London, 1905, edition of 1914.

Grylls, Rosalie Glynn, *William Godwin and his World*, London, 1953.

Guggisberg, Kurt, *Philipp Emanuel Von Fellenberg und Sein Erziehungs-staat*, Bern, 1953.

Hadow Report. *Report of the Consultative Committee on Infant and Nursery Schools*, London, 1933.

——*Report of the Consultative Committee on the Primary School*, London, 1931.

Halévy, Elie, *England in 1815*, 1913, English edition, London, 1924, revised 1949.

——*The Growth of Philosophic Radicalism*, London, 1928.

——*Thomas Hodgskin*, 1904, English edition edited with an Introduction by A. J. Taylor, London, 1956.

Hammond, J. L. and Barbara, *The Age of the Chartists, 1832–1854. A Study of Discontent*, London, 1930.

——*Lord Shaftesbury*, London, 1923.

——*The Town Labourer (1760–1832)*, London, 1917, Guild Books revised edition of 1949.

Harrison, J. F. C., *Learning and Living, 1790–1960. A Study in the History of the English Adult Education Movement*, London, 1961.

——*Social Reform in Victorian Leeds: the Work of James Hole, 1820–1895*, Leeds, 1954.

Harvey, Rowland Hill, *Robert Owen, Social Idealist*, California, 1949.

Hayward, F. H., *The Educational Ideas of Pestalozzi and Fröbel*, London, 1905.

Hearnshaw, F. J. C. (ed.), *The Social and Political Ideas of some Great French Thinkers of the Age of Reason*, London, 1930.

——(ed.), *The Social and Political Ideas of some representative Thinkers of the Age of Reaction and Reconstruction, 1815–65*, London, 1932.

Hertzler, Joyce Oramel, *The History of Utopian Thought*, London, 1922.

Holloway, Mark, *Heavens on Earth. Utopian Communities in America, 1680–1880*, London, 1951.

Holman, H., *Pestalozzi. An Account of his Life and Work*, London, 1908.

Hopkins, Mary Alden, *Hannah More and her Circle*, New York, 1947.

Hovell, Mark, *The Chartist Movement*, Manchester, 1918.

Hutchins, B. L., *Robert Owen, Social Reformer*, Fabian Tract No. 166, London, 1912. (For early period. Joad, see below, covers the later period.)

Joad, C. E. M., *Robert Owen, Idealist*, Fabian Tract No. 182, London, 1917.

Jones, M. G., *The Charity School Movement*, Cambridge, 1938.

——*Hannah More*, Cambridge, 1952.

Judges, A. V. (ed.), *Pioneers of English Education*, London, 1952. (Including 'Robert Owen,' by M. V. C. Jeffreys.)

Kelly, Thomas, *George Birkbeck: Pioneer of Adult Education*, Liverpool, 1957.

——*A History of Adult Education in Great Britain*, Liverpool, 1962.

Kendall, Guy, *Robert Raikes, A Critical Study*, London, 1939.

Knight, Frida, *The Strange Case of Thomas Walker. Ten Years in the Life of a Manchester Radical*, London, 1957.

Laski, Harold J., *The Rise of European Liberalism. An Essay in Interpretation*, London, 1936, edition of 1962.

Leopold, Richard William, *Robert Dale Owen, A Biography*, Harvard, 1940.

Lytton, the Earl of, *The Life of Edward Bulwer, First Lord Lytton*, London, 1913.

McCabe, Joseph, *Robert Owen*, London, 1920.

McCallister, W. J., *The Growth of Freedom in Education*, London, 1931.

MacDonald, J. Ramsay, *The Socialist Movement*, London, n.d.

McLachlan, H., *Records of a Family, 1800–1933. Pioneers in Education, Social Service and Liberal Religion*, Manchester, 1935.

Maltby, S. E., *Manchester and the Movement for National Elementary Education, 1800–1870*, Manchester, 1918.

Martin, Kingsley, *French Liberal Thought in the Eighteenth Century*, London, 1929, revised edition of 1962.

Mathews, H. F., *Methodism and the Education of the People, 1791–1851*, London, 1949.

Mayne, Ethel Colburn, *The Life and Letters of Anne Isabella, Lady Noel Byron*, London, 1929.

More, Hannah, *The Letters of —*, Selected with an Introduction by R. Brimley Johnson, London, 1925.

Morgan, Alexander, *Makers of Scottish Education*, 1929.

Morris, William Dale, *The Christian Origins of Social Revolt*, London, 1949.

Morton, A. L., *The English Utopia*, London, 1952.

——and Tate, George, *The British Labour Movement, 1770–1920*, London, 1956.

Pankhurst, R. K. P., *William Thompson (1775–1833) Britain's Pioneer Socialist, Feminist, and Co-operator*, London, 1954.

Plamenatz, John, *The English Utilitarians*, Oxford, 1949, revised edition of 1958.

Podmore, Frank, *Robert Owen, A Biography*, London, 1906, edition of 1923.

Pollard, Hugh M., *Pioneers of Popular Education, 1760–1850*, London, 1956.

Pollard, Sidney, *Dr William King of Ipswich: A Co-operative Pioneer*, Co-operative College Papers No. 6, Loughborough, 1959.

Pons, J., *Education en Angleterre entre 1750 et 1800*, Paris, 1919.

Postgate, R. W., *The Builders' History*, London, n.d.

Read, Donald, *Press and People, 1790–1850. Opinion in Three English Cities*, London, 1961.

Röhl, Adolph, *Die Beziehung zwischen Wirtschaft und Erziehung im Sozialismus Robert Owens*, Hamburg, 1930.

Rusk, R. R., *A History of Infant Education*, London, 1933.

Russell, Bertrand, *Freedom and Organization—1814–1914*, London, 1934.

Salmon, David and Hindshaw, W., *Infant Schools: their History and Theory*, London, 1904.

Saville, John (ed.), *Democracy and the Labour Movement*, London, 1954. (Particularly 'The London Corresponding Society', by Henry Collins.)

——*Ernest Jones: Chartist*, London, 1952.

Shapovalenko, S. G. (ed.), *Polytechnical Education in the U.S.S.R.*, UNESCO, Paris, 1963.

Simon, Brian, *Studies in the History of Education, 1780–1870*, London, 1960.

Simon, Helene, *Robert Owen. Sein Leben und Seine Bedeutung für die Gegenwart*, Jena, 1905.

Slosson, Preston William, *The Decline of the Chartist Movement*, New York, 1916.

Stephen, Leslie, *English Literature and Society in the 18th Century*, London, 1904.

Thomas, Maurice Walton, *The Early Factory Legislation*, London, 1948.

Thompson, E. P., *The Making of the English Working Class*, London, 1963.

Townshend, Mrs, *The Case for School Nurseries*, Fabian Tract No. 145, London, 1909.

Tylecote, Mabel, *The Mechanics' Institutes of Lancashire and Yorkshire before 1851*, Manchester, 1957.

Wagner, Richard Robert, *Robert Owen: Lebensroman eines Menschen-gläubigen*, Zurich, 1942. (A novel, glamorising Owen's life-story, but sticks quite close to main information known about him, particularly from Owen's *Life*.)

Warburton, W. H., *The History of Trade Union Organisation in the North Staffordshire Potteries*, with an Introduction by R. H. Tawney, London, 1931.

Webb, R. K., *The British Working Class Reader*, London, 1955. (Particularly on the theme of education as insurance.)

Webb, Sidney and Beatrice, *History of Trade Unionism*, London, 1894. (The 1902 edition has a considerable bibliography. The 1920 edition, reprinted 1950, contains valuable appendices.)

West, Julius, *A History of the Chartist Movement*, London, 1920.

Willey, Basil, *The Eighteenth Century Background*, London, 1940.

Wilson, Edmund, *To the Finland Station. A Study in the Writing and Acting of History*, London, 1942.

Woodcock, George, *William Godwin: a Biographical Study*, London, 1946.

Woodhead, Joseph, *The Education Question up to 1870. A Chapter of History*, Huddersfield, 1902.

Youngjohns, B. J., *Co-operation and the State, 1814–1914*, Co-operative College Papers No. 1, Loughborough, 1954.

VII. SOURCES IN RUSSIAN

Of direct relevance:

Анекштейн, А., *Педагогические идеи Роберта Оуена* (избранные отрывки из сочинений Р. Оуэна. Со вступительным очерком Проф. А. Анекштейна), Москва, 1940.

Anekshtein, A., *The Educational Ideas of Robert Owen* (selected extracts from the works of R. Owen. With an introductory essay by Prof. A. Anekshtein), Moscow, 1940.

In addition to a variety of extracts from Owen's works, there are extracts from MacNab, James Smith, John Griscom, Robert Dale Owen, the Leeds deputation, Engels, Marx, and others. This is a 'careful summary of Owen's thinking and practice, but is concerned almost entirely with New Lanark and Owen's community ideals, or communism. It criticises Podmore for attaching too little weight to economic circumstances, and G. D. H. Cole for underestimating the period after New Lanark, but itself fails to see the full impact of Owen on the labour movement. It is the only full treatment of Owen in relation to education in Russian.

Фейгина, С. А., *Роберт Оуэн. Избранные сочинения,* перевод с английского и комментарий С. А. Фейгиной. Вступительная статья В. П. Волгина, Москва-Ленинград, 1950.

Feigina, S. A., *Robert Owen. Selected Works,* translated from the English with notes by S. A. Feigina, with an introductory article by V. P. Volgin, Moscow–Leningrad, 1950.

Prof. Volgin's introduction is probably based largely on G. D. H. Cole's *Robert Owen.* The selections from Owen are divided into:

Vol. I: Reports and speeches, 1815–1820.
         Articles and reports from *The Crisis.*
       II: Works, 1836–1849.

The Bibliography refers to works in English by Beer, the Webbs, G. D. H. Cole, R. E. Davies, Holyoake, Lloyd Jones, McCabe, Podmore, Postgate and Sargant, and the *D.N.B.*

The following are some other sources in Russian:

Волгин, В. П., *История социалистических идей,* ч. 2, Москва, 1931.

Volgin, V. P., *The History of Socialist Ideas,* part 2, Moscow, 1931.

Герцен, А. И., *Былое и думы,* ч. УI, гл. IX (1852–67).

Herzen, A. I., *Past and Thoughts,* part VI, chapter IX (1852–67).

Добролюбов, Н. А., Роберт Оуэн и его попытки общественных реформ, *Полное собрание сочинений,* т. 4, Москва, 1937.

Dobroliubov, N. A., 'Robert Owen and his Attempts at Social Reform', *Complete Works,* Vol. 4, Moscow, 1937.

Каменский, А. В., *Роберт Оуэн. Его жизнь и общественная деятельность,* СПГ, 1892.

Kamenski, A. V., *Robert Owen. His Life and Social Activities,* St Petersburg, 1892. (A good summary, with an interest in ideas and men like Percival.)

Плеханов, Г. Б., 'Утопический социализм XIX века', *сочинения,* т. 18, Москва-Ленинград, 1925.

Plekhanov, G. B., 'Utopian Socialism in the 19th Century', *Works,* Vol. 18, Moscow–Leningrad, 1925.

Советская энциклопедия.

Soviet Encyclopaedia.

Цедербаум, С. О., *Роберт Оуэн*, Москва, 1925.
Tsederbaum, S. O., *Robert Owen*, Moscow, 1925.

For further bibliographical references of material in Russian, see in particular *Soviet Encylcopaedia* and Feigina, *Robert Owen. Selected Works*, Vol. II.

INDEX

N.B. Journals and authorities are listed where they are mentioned in the text